PERCEPTIONS OF STATE

Why, and to what extent, are states more or less likely to comply with international law? No overarching state compels compliance, and the international institutional context is thin, yet states seem largely to comply. How do we explain this behavior? Developed through interviews with eighty State Department senior officials from across five recent administrations, Philip Moremen provides a qualitatively and quantitatively rich study of the extent to which and under what conditions the United States and other countries comply with international law. US policymakers consider legal issues, national interest, and other factors together when making decisions – law is not always dispositive. Nevertheless, international law constrains states. In State Department policymaking, there is a strong culture of respect for international law, and lawyers play a highly influential role. In this context, the book concludes by investigating the effect of the Trump administration on the culture and processes of the State Department.

PHILIP MOREMEN is Chair and Associate Professor at Seton Hall University's School of Diplomacy and International Relations. He is also an Honorary Vice President of the American Branch of the International Law Association and has been published in US-based international law journals.

Perceptions of State

THE US STATE DEPARTMENT AND INTERNATIONAL LAW

PHILIP MOREMEN
Seton Hall University, New Jersey

CAMBRIDGE
UNIVERSITY PRESS

CAMBRIDGE
UNIVERSITY PRESS

Shaftesbury Road, Cambridge CB2 8EA, United Kingdom

One Liberty Plaza, 20th Floor, New York, NY 10006, USA

477 Williamstown Road, Port Melbourne, VIC 3207, Australia

314–321, 3rd Floor, Plot 3, Splendor Forum, Jasola District Centre, New Delhi – 110025, India

103 Penang Road, #05-06/07, Visioncrest Commercial, Singapore 238467

Cambridge University Press is part of Cambridge University Press & Assessment, a department of the University of Cambridge.

We share the University's mission to contribute to society through the pursuit of education, learning and research at the highest international levels of excellence.

www.cambridge.org
Information on this title: www.cambridge.org/9781108835152

DOI: 10.1017/9781108891783

First published 2024

A catalogue record for this publication is available from the British Library

Library of Congress Cataloging-in-Publication Data
NAMES: Moremen, Philip, author.
TITLE: Perceptions of state : the US State Department and international law / Philip Moremen.
DESCRIPTION: Cambridge, United Kingdom ; New York, NY : Cambridge University Press, 2024. | Includes index.
IDENTIFIERS: LCCN 2023053956 (print) | LCCN 2023053957 (ebook) | ISBN 9781108835152 (hardback) | ISBN 9781108799751 (paperback) | ISBN 9781108891783 (ebook)
SUBJECTS: LCSH: International law–United States. | International law–Political aspects–United States. | United States–Foreign relations–Law and legislation. | International law. | State, The. | International relations. | United States. Department of State.
CLASSIFICATION: LCC KF4581 .M67 2024 (print) | LCC KF4581 (ebook) | DDC 341.0973–dc23/eng/20231128
LC record available at https://lccn.loc.gov/2023053956
LC ebook record available at https://lccn.loc.gov/2023053957

ISBN 978-1-108-83515-2 Hardback

Contents

Tables

Preface and Acknowledgments

This project has taken shape over more than ten years. My original plan was to interview a significant number of former high-level State Department officials from different areas across administrations to examine their views about compliance with international law. The purpose was simply to get a sense, from the experience of these former officials, about the extent of compliance and about the reasons states comply or do not comply. By taking a relatively large and extensive sample, my hope was to distill a representative cross section of views.

Over time, the scope of the project changed in a number of ways. First, it became clear that the subject of the project was not just the views of policy-making elites about compliance but also the role of State Department structure, procedures, and culture in decision-making. Helpful comments by anonymous reviewers confirmed that direction and suggested relevant additional literature to help frame it. Second, as the project extended, it became possible to interview former officials of the Obama and the Trump administrations to add their perspectives. Including the Trump officials was particularly significant since the attitudes of Trump political appointees were different, at least in degree, from the mainstream of views from the other administrations. This allowed an opportunity to analyze the nature and extent of those differences and what they portended for the State Department in both the short and the long term.

Over the course of the project, many have helped in ways large and small. Most importantly, I would like to thank all the former State Department officials who participated in interviews for this project. Many extended their interview time, some participated in follow-up telephone conversations, a couple treated me to lunch, and all were unfailingly gracious and helpful. Meeting and interviewing this accomplished group of foreign policymakers was a fascinating and enriching experience.

Next, I would like to thank my Deans at the School of Diplomacy at Seton Hall University for their support and encouragement. Dean Andrea Bartoli arranged for an especially helpful seminar with other faculty preceding my sabbatical in the 2017–2018 academic year. My current Dean, Courtney Smith, participated in the pre-sabbatical seminar, reviewed portions of the book proposal and the manuscript, and provided unfailing encouragement.

My faculty colleagues at the School of Diplomacy provided additional help and support. In particular, Martin Edwards reviewed portions of the manuscript in various stages and provided significant advice on methodological issues. Assefaw Bariagaber and Margarita Balmaceda provided helpful suggestions and encouragement along the way. Ann Marie Murphy and I periodically shared research and writing goals to help keep us both on track with our respective projects. Other supportive Seton Hall faculty friends included David Beneteau, Judith Lothian, Jack Shannon, Jonathan Farina, and Marianne Lloyd. I cannot thank my colleagues enough for their advice and friendship.

I would also like to thank Seton Hall University and interim Provost Dr. Karen Boroff for granting me a sabbatical in 2017–2018. An earlier sabbatical allowed me to prepare the ground for the project – thanks to then Provost and later President, Dr. Gabriel Esteban.

I have had the benefit of help over the years from a number of research assistants including Roger Alfani, Akhror Khatamov, Cristian Ramos Miranda, and Samuel Roods. My thanks to all of them.

As indicated before, three anonymous Cambridge University Press reviewers provided positive and helpful comments, especially reviewer two. The editorial and production team at Cambridge were first-rate throughout. I owe particular thanks to my commissioning editors, Marianne Nield and Tom Randall. Thanks also to Biju Shah. And thanks to John Berger, former senior editor, who provided some helpful advice before I submitted my book proposal.

In addition, I would like to thank my dear friends Alan Untereiner and Dr. Karen Donfried: Alan provided feedback at key early moments in the project, and Karen facilitated introductions to a number of former officials. In addition, they hosted me at their home in Washington, DC, during many trips there to conduct interviews.

I would also like to mention several past mentors and advisors, who, while not directly contributing to this project, helped equip me to take it on and to see it through. They are Joel Trachtman, John Noyes, Alfred Rubin, Phillip Trimble, Charles Siegal, and Patrick Breen.

Last, but not least, I would like to thank my wife and daughters not only for supporting my efforts and tolerating my time away from them but also for their concrete contributions to the project. My wife, Mitra, served as sounding board, occasional editor, and reviewer of emails to potential interview subjects and others. My daughters, Charlotte and Geneva, were old enough by the end of the project to serve as summer research assistants. Among other things, Charlotte developed drafts of the tables in Chapter 1 and the Appendix. This book is for them.

Of course, any and all errors in the final manuscript are mine.

1

Introduction

Why, to what extent, and under what conditions are states more or less likely to comply with international law? No overarching state compels compliance. Compared to domestic law, the international institutional context is thin; courts and tribunals are limited in their jurisdiction and relatively uncoordinated. International law, moreover, is plagued by ambiguity. Treaties may be the most certain source of international law rules because they are in writing, but the language of treaties is not always clear and can be purposefully vague, giving states discretion in applying them. Non-treaty norms are even more subject to ambiguity. Why, indeed, should states ever comply?[1] Yet they seem to, much of the time. How do we explain this behavior?

Through interviews with eighty former State Department senior officials, this book explores when, why, and how states in general and the United States in particular comply with international law. Those former officials were drawn from five administrations, from George H. W. Bush to Donald Trump. Their interviews were coded qualitatively and quantitatively. The State Department was selected because, of any US government agency, its personnel are the most likely to deal frequently with international law matters and, on the whole, are most likely to be familiar with international law.

The focus of the project is three-fold. First, former officials were asked about the compliance of states generally with international law. More specifically, they were asked whether they believed international law constrained state behavior and how regularly states tended to comply. Former officials were also asked about the factors that favored or disfavored compliance. The

[1] Robert Keohane stated the perennial question in the following way: "[t]he puzzle of compliance is why governments, seeking to promote their own interests, ever comply with rules that are not in their immediate self-interest." Robert O. Keohane, After Hegemony: Cooperation and Discord in the World Political Economy 99 (1984).

perceptions of former officials not only provide insight into the behavior and motivations of states in response to international law, they also reveal attitudes that are likely to shape their own behavior and decision-making.

Second, former officials were asked in depth about the United States' compliance with international law and about State Department decision-making concerning compliance. Accordingly, former officials were asked why, to what extent, and under what conditions the United States complies with international law. As part of this second focus, former officials were also asked about the decision-making process in the State Department and about the role of international law in those decisions. They were asked about the role of lawyers in the decision-making process and the weight policymakers gave to their counsel.

Finally, the project examines the effect of the Trump administration on the culture and processes in the State Department and the potential for change if a new Trump administration, or a similar administration, takes power in 2024. A number of former Trump administration officials were interviewed, and other former officials were consulted about their perceptions of the Trump State Department. The efforts of the Trump administration to control the State Department were also examined.

Regarding the project's first focus, the extent of state compliance with international law, the overwhelming majority of former officials believed that international law constrains state behavior and that states comply with international law to a significant extent. To the extent that this result reveals actual state practice, it supports the proposition that international law plays a significant role in international affairs.

The most important factors constraining state behavior are the power of reputation costs and the fear of reciprocal retaliation, these former officials said. Two other factors played notable roles in constraining state behavior. First, ethical factors played a significant role, giving a boost to normative theories about compliance. Second, former officials revealed that systemic interests provided a significant impetus to complying with international law. That is, the interest in maintaining a stable legal and institutional system served the interests of all states, and particularly the interests of the United States. Essentially, the perceptions of most former officials from both parties supported a multilateral, institutional, and rule-based view of the international system.

The second focus of this project is on the United States, examining attitudes of former policymakers regarding US compliance with international law. In general, policymakers perceived a high degree of compliance by the United States with international law. When asked about the reasons that the

United States complies or does not comply with international law, responses of former officials tracked many of the factors they listed for states in general. While the overall predilection of policymakers was to comply with international law, international law was not always dispositive, they said. Legal issues were considered as one among a variety of factors, essentially involving a cost–benefit analysis.

The project explores the tension between two basic elements in this cost–benefit analysis, national interest or policy considerations and international legal requirements. Qualitative analysis of the interviews revealed a range of views regarding this tension. Policymakers roughly fell into three categories. A small group of former officials indicated that they and the United States complied with international law as a matter of course, almost all of the time. In the second category – the largest group – formal officials suggested that national interest sometimes took priority, even though the United States followed international law much of the time. The third category consisted of some former officials who asserted that international law was subservient to policy concerns and the national interest.

The project also explores the dynamics of the interaction between policymakers and lawyers in the Legal Adviser's Office. The role of lawyers in the State Department reflects the significant role of international law in Department decision-making generally. Former officials clearly regarded the views of the Legal Adviser's Office as highly influential. Former officials' perceptions tracked and reinforced the rough, tripartite division of views regarding the role of international law in decision-making more generally. The majority viewed the positions of the Legal Adviser's Office as significant and indicated that the development of policy was a collaborative process, in which lawyers' advice was taken seriously, but was not always determinative.

Regarding the project's third focus, it is safe to say that the Trump administration displayed a skeptical or narrow view of international law, institutions, and agreements, as evidenced by its words and its actions. More significantly, the Trump administration took extreme steps to repress dissent within the State Department and to impose its views of foreign policy. Former officials expressed a range of perceptions regarding the Trump administration's effect on the State Department. Some believed that the administration's views and actions significantly affected attitudes and practices within the Department regarding international law and institutions. Others believed that effects were more likely to be felt at the policy decision level, rather than at the lower, policy development level. Similarly, they believed political appointees were more likely to apply the administration's views compared to career Foreign Service Officers, who had less incentive to do so. Nonetheless, most former officials believed that the depth of change and the potential of previous attitudes to "bounce back" turned on the outcome of the 2020 election.

1.1 BRIEF OVERVIEW OF RELEVANT LITERATURE

Chapter 2 describes the relevant literature in greater depth, but this section sketches out the main points in order to orient the reader. Two related bodies of literature correspond to the first two prongs of this study.[2] Both bodies of literature are generally associated with the primary schools of international relations theory and related legal approaches. They overlap to a large extent but can be divided for ease of analysis. The first body of literature essentially explores the question of *why* states in general might comply with international law, largely from a theoretical perspective. The second body of literature is a subset of the first but examines more closely *how* states comply, theorizing about factors affecting domestic compliance with international law and, in particular, focusing on domestic policymaking within the US government. These two bodies of literature overlap in another way. The literature addressing why states comply may help to explain individual and institutional motivations to comply in the domestic context.

On the first question, various theories attempt to explain whether, why, and under what conditions states comply with international law. In general, they can be divided further into two categories: a rational choice or instrumentalist approach and a normative approach.[3] The former assumes that states make a rational assessment of costs and benefits in deciding whether to comply with international law; international law is simply an instrument of state interests, not a driver of them. The latter assumes that norms or rules, in and of themselves, have independent force in guiding state behavior and

[2] For detailed, recent summaries of the compliance literature in both international relations and international law see, e.g., Courtney Hillebrecht, *Compliance: Actors, Context and Causal Processes, in* RESEARCH HANDBOOK ON THE POLITICS OF INTERNATIONAL LAW 27 (Wayne Sandholtz & Christopher A. Whytock, eds., 2017); Carmela Lutmar & Cristiane L. Carneiro, *Compliance in International Relations, in* OXFORD RESEARCH ENCYCLOPEDIA OF POLITICS (June 25, 2018) https://oxfordre.com/politics/display/10.1093/acrefore/9780190228637.001.0001/acrefore-9780190228637-e-576; Jana von Stein, *The Engines of Compliance, in* INTERDISCIPLINARY PERSPECTIVES ON INTERNATIONAL LAW AND INTERNATIONAL RELATIONS: THE STATE OF THE ART 477 (Jeffrey L. Dunoff & Mark A. Pollack, eds., 2012). Portions of this section are drawn from Philip M. Moremen, Private Rights of Action to Enforce Rules of International Regimes, 115–132 (2005) (unpublished Ph. D. dissertation).

[3] *See* Robert O. Keohane, Jr., *International Relations and International Law: Two Optics*, 38 HARV. INT'L L. J. 487 (1997); George W. Downs et al., *Is the Good News about Compliance Good News about Cooperation?* 50 INT. ORG. 379 (1996).

compliance. This division into two categories applies to the international relations literature, but also applies to much of the international law scholarship on compliance. The primary instrumentalist theories are realism and neorealism, neoliberal institutionalism, and liberalism. The primary normative theories are constructivism, as well as various legal theories, including international legal process theories, managerialism, and theories of legitimacy.

The review of compliance theories is relevant to the study for several reasons. First, the study may confirm or illustrate the applicability of these theories to state compliance, although that is not necessary for the study to be valuable in illuminating the motivations that affect policymakers and states. The study takes a rather eclectic view of the application of compliance theories. As one political scientist asserts, the problem with the main theoretical perspectives – realism, liberalism, and constructivism – is that "they are all right, at least for some stages of the governance process, in some systems of governance, some of the time."[4] This observation is supported by the responses received from participants in this study. Second, the relevant theories provide a context for the current study and a conceptual set of tools for understanding. So, for example, the literature informed some of the questions for interview subjects, as well as the coding of their responses.

The second part of this study focuses on the *how* question by examining attitudes and processes in the US State Department related to compliance with international law. Especially in the last twenty years or so, scholars from both law and international relations have turned to mechanisms and forces in the domestic context that press for compliance with international law.[5] Some of these scholars are instrumentalist in orientation, while others take a more constructivist approach. Instrumentalists, primarily neoliberal institutionalists, have focused on ways in which domestic politics and domestic institutions influence domestic actors' decisions to comply with international law.[6] Constructivists have investigated the ways international legal norms become embedded in domestic law and politics, shaping state behavior from within.[7]

4 *See* Rebecca Sanders, Plausible Legality: Legal Culture and Political Imperative in the Global War on Terror 25–26 (2018).

5 *See*, Hillebrecht, *supra* note 2, at 34 (noting a turn to "the nexus of domestic politics and international law," and focusing on literature that is mostly empirical and mostly neoliberal institutionalist).

6 *See, e.g.*, Beth Simmons, Mobilizing for Human Rights: International Law in Domestic Politics (2010) (international law is used by domestic actors to pressure governments to comply). *See* also Hillebrecht, *supra* note 2, at 34, sources cited at note 18.

7 *See generally, e.g.*, Harold H. Koh, *Why Do Nations Obey International Law?*, 106 Yale L. J. 2599 (1997); Derek Jinks & Ryan Goodman, Socializing States: Promoting Human Rights through International Law (2013); Derek Jinks & Ryan Goodman,

The present study concentrates on two normative, process-oriented approaches, one from international law and the other from international relations. The international law theory is the international legal process approach. From international relations theory, Wayne Sandholtz and Christopher Whytock, along with like-minded scholars, have developed a framework emphasizing process, structure, institutional culture, and the constraining and channeling power of legal rules. Both of these frameworks are particularly helpful in understanding this study's findings regarding the operation and effect of international law within the State Department and the US government.

Both the international legal process schools and the Sandholtz and Whytock framework emphasize the role of internalized norms in decision-making by individuals and government organizations. Both recognize the importance of process and organizational structure in guiding political decision-making and the potential effect of individuals inhabiting that structure and their preferences. Both recognize the challenge that ambiguity poses for the application of international law. Yet neither approach claims that law or institutions control the exercise of state power, and both admit that power and power differences are often influential and even decisive.

The majority and collective view of former officials in this study corresponds reasonably to the range of views presented by these approaches. That is, law, process, and institutions may constrain or channel the policy of the United States, but not always and to varying degrees. As one former senior official stated, policymakers always want to do the right thing and their predilection is to comply with international law, but their job is to pursue the interest of the United States.[8]

1.2 OVERVIEW OF MAIN FINDINGS

In the course of the project, seventy-six interviews were conducted of former State Department officials at the level of Assistant Secretary and above, from the George H. W. Bush administration through the Trump administration. This group included a rough balance between Republicans and Democrats,

How to Influence States: Socialization and Human Rights Law, 54 DUKE L.J. 261 (2004). Jinks and Goodman examine processes of acculturation and socialization that drive states' compliance with international law.

8 *See* Interview 7, Former Senior State Department Official. The official went on to say that they [policymakers] wanted to understand it all: what did the law mean? What was its intent? How much flexibility is there? They wanted to find a way to comply, but when they chose not to do so, they wanted to make an informed choice.

and a mix of seniority levels and different areas within the State Department (see Table 1.1). In addition, three former, high-level attorneys from the Office of the Legal Adviser were also interviewed for context. The interviews were coded for qualitative and simple quantitative analyses involving frequency counts and cross-tabulations.

1.2.1 *Compliance with International Law*

The first focus of this project is whether, why, and to what extent states comply with international law. A large majority of former officials interviewed for this project believed that states comply with international law to a significant extent and that international law affects state behavior. For example, 96 percent agreed that international law constrained state behavior at least some of the time. This result, to the extent that it reveals actual state practice, provides support for the proposition that international law plays an operative role in international affairs. Nevertheless, this conclusion comes with caveats and qualifications. The former officials expressed nuanced – and varied – views about the role of international law in state decision-making.

The conclusion that international law plays a significant role in international affairs runs contrary to realist predictions that law is irrelevant and comports better with theories that recognize the role of international law in state behavior, from rationalist theories such as liberalism or neoliberal institutionalism to normative theories such as constructivism. That does not mean, however, that law *controls* state power: Law, institutions, and process may only *constrain* state power sometimes and to some extent.

The former officials were asked about the factors that they believed favored compliance with international law. The most positive factors determined by frequency counts were, in order, as follows:

- Reciprocity, or the prospect for retaliation
- State interest in a stable legal and institutional system
- Reputation
- Ethical considerations, including ethical values underlying international law rules and respect for the rule of law
- Idiosyncratic factors, including the political culture of states and their adherence to the rule of law
- Benefits flowing from participation in international regimes.

Among the factors militating against compliance by states, it will come as no surprise that state interest was by far the dominant factor. Rounding out the top six negative factors were as follows:

- the ambiguity of international law
- the notion that some states (i.e., rogue states) just do not care about international law or have no interest in it
- the perception that compliance by some states is shallow
- the role of domestic politics
- sovereignty concerns.

Two aspects of these results are particularly noteworthy. The prominent role for ethical factors gives a boost for normative theories about compliance. The normative factors mentioned included not only the ethical values underlying legal rules – for example, human rights – but also respect for the rule of law. A number of officials, moreover, stated that countries with a history or culture of adhering to the rule of law domestically were likely to apply rule of law norms to the international realm as well. Again, the presence of this factor indicates the power of normative and cultural factors in compliance.

A large proportion of former officials, moreover, also explicitly stressed the importance of the international legal system more generally, including not only international law rules, but international organizations. A significant reason former officials gave for complying with international law rules is the maintenance of the system as a whole. International institutions are worthwhile because they provide collective goods from which states benefit. The interest in maintaining a stable international system serves the interests of all states, particularly the interest of powerful states.

Many former officials explicitly suggested that decisions about compliance with international law involved a cost–benefit calculation, a calculation that involved a balance of many considerations along with legal considerations. Legal considerations might not always prevail in that calculation, they indicated, though legal factors were influential. Such an approach might suggest that states follow an instrumentalist approach to decision-making, but, if they do, the costs and benefits considered often include ethical factors, not just hard costs and benefits.

Former officials' perceptions differed regarding the factors that other states take into consideration and the reasons that the United States takes into consideration when making decisions about compliance. As for other states, former officials perceived many states to be more concerned with hard benefits and costs, including carrots and sticks offered by the international community, as opposed to systemic or altruistic concerns. They perceived the United States as being motivated in part by these systemic and altruistic concerns, in contrast. The perception that other countries engage in relatively self-interested behavior is consistent with realist notions regarding the effect of direct incentives offered by powerful states to encourage others to comply. Perhaps that perception reflects reality: Smaller countries may be more susceptible to pressure than big powers. But one wonders whether government officials from these other countries might take a more charitable view toward their own motivations.

The project also assessed demographic information about the study participants. Notably, differences in political affiliation clearly affected how former officials viewed the effects of international law on state behavior. Officials appointed by Democratic presidents were more likely than officials appointed by Republican presidents to believe that international law substantially constrains states. Nevertheless, almost all Republican appointees believed that international law played some role in constraining the behavior of states. The results demonstrate a general consensus in the views of former officials regarding the effects of international law.

1.2.2 *US Compliance and State Department Decision-Making*

Former officials were also asked a series of questions about the United States' compliance with international law. They were asked generally about the factors US policymakers take into account when thinking about compliance. They were encouraged to discuss their own experiences in this regard. This assessment of attitudes contributes to a picture of the cultural and normative context to help understand policymaking outcomes within the State Department. Former officials were also asked about policymaking processes in the State Department. More specifically, they were asked about the role of State Department lawyers in making recommendations regarding compliance compared to the role of policymakers.

Former officials indicated that the United States exhibited a high degree of compliance with international law. Of those who responded to the relevant question, 18 percent of former officials said that the United States always followed international law, 72 percent said the United States followed international law most of the time, and 10 percent said the United States followed international law some of the time. Their perception of compliance may not match reality in an objective sense. A number of former officials pointed out that states tend to define compliance based on their own subjective interpretation of international law.

The United States was motivated by considerations similar to those of other states, with some differences. First, the role of ethics was the most frequently cited factor favoring compliance, which may come as a surprise. Ethical considerations are also reflected in two other factors in the top ten or so factors on the list: the notion of US exceptionalism, in the sense of moral responsibility leadership, and the significance of treaty obligations and the importance of adhering to them. Perhaps American policymakers are more likely to ascribe ethical behavior to the United States, as opposed to other countries.

Second, the United States has an interest in maintaining the international order, including existing international law. Third, the views of allies can support US compliance, but can also sometimes aid the United States in taking action when international law is murky or even in opposition. Fourth, the United States is concerned about setting desirable precedent and avoiding a negative precedent that can affect other states' decisions involving international law. Finally, the United States' commitment to treaties can encourage the United States to comply.

The factors that former officials cited that militate against compliance by the United States included national interest, ambiguity of legal obligations, sovereignty concerns, domestic law complications in the application of international law, bureaucratic or budgeting difficulties in complying with international law, and domestic politics. Another factor in decision-making was the State Department's policymaking process generally and the role of international law and of Department lawyers in that process. That process is summarized and discussed separately below.

1.2.3 *Tensions between International Law and National Interests*

The project assessed tensions in US decision-making between the requirements of international law, on the one hand, and policy concerns or national interest, on the other. The predilection of former officials was to follow international law, but as indicated earlier, legal issues were considered as one factor among a variety of factors, essentially involving a cost–benefit analysis. The most significant factors appeared to be the nature of the national interest or policy at stake, the nature and importance of the international legal rule involved, the ethical considerations involved, the views of allies, the ambiguity or precision of the legal obligation, the weight of domestic political and bureaucratic concerns, and the effect of the policymaking process.

Qualitative examination of former officials' interviews revealed a range of views regarding the tension between international law and national interest, falling into three loose categories. The first category (31 percent) consisted of former officials who indicated that they and the United States complied with international law almost all of the time, or that international law controls except in cases of high national interest. In the second category – the largest at 41 percent – former officials suggested that while the United States followed international law much of the time, there were occasions when significant national interests took priority, and the application of international law could be flexible. In the third category (27 percent), former officials argued that international law generally was subordinate to policy and national interest considerations. A few former officials indicated that the primacy of policy goals held especially for issues of national security and that, conversely, international law took on more weight when the policy issues were not as significant. Others were less emphatic about the primacy of policy or national interest but, nonetheless, indicated that legal concerns often took a backseat to significant policy interests. Policymakers, they said, would push the envelope to meet policy objectives.

1.2.4 *Examples of Weak and Strong Compliance by the United States*

In response to specific questions, or volunteered of their own accord, former officials provided examples of instances where the United States may have violated or bent international law and examples where the United States acted scrupulously in complying with international law. These examples are anecdotal and impressionistic; they do not provide a comprehensive catalog. Nevertheless, the examples provide some insight into US behavior and apply insights gleaned from previous analysis.

They also extend and complement a separate assessment of the legal areas in which all states were more or less likely to comply, a slightly different but similar question that yielded similar results. The least likely area for state compliance was national security. The most likely areas for compliance were trade and economic law, environmental law, humanitarian law, arms control, law enforcement, and cooperative arrangements such as aviation agreements and postal unions.

Examples of potential US overreach included various military interventions of the past sixty years, the NATO bombing of Kosovo in 1999, and enhanced interrogation or torture after 9-11. Areas of the law in which the United States has tended to be more scrupulous include arms control, humanitarian law, diplomatic relations, and trade (until recently). Specific examples of the United States' scrupulous compliance include the application of the Convention on International Trade in Endangered Species (CITES) and at least one incident involving interception of a ship on the high seas.

These responses tended to support an instrumentalist take on compliance: Compliance was less likely in areas of high politics and more likely in areas of low politics; reciprocity bolstered compliance in several cases. Former policymakers also stated that compliance by states generally was more evident in coordination situations, such as postal unions, as predicted by instrumentalists. Some of the examples, however, and other results from this study highlight the role of ethical and normative considerations in compliance decisions. Another striking feature is that most of these areas involve extensive, specific treaty obligations. That result suggests the importance for compliance of precision in international obligations, which increases the difficulty for states to wiggle out of their obligations. This is usually a feature of normative theories.

One general point about these examples is the level of skepticism and realism about the dubious legality of some US actions expressed by some former officials. This demonstrates the diversity of views among policymakers and governmental organizations: Neither the State Department nor the US government is monolithic. A related point is the necessity expressed by former officials for a legal justification to support US action, even when US action stretches the boundaries of international law. The legal justification can play a central role in the political justification provided by the US government to its citizens and the rest of the world for its actions.

1.2.5 *Process in the State Department*

The project explored the role of international law in State Department decision-making. Bureaucratic structure, procedural requirements, and cultural norms within the Department ensure that international law considerations play a role in decision-making, both formally and informally. Nevertheless, that role is not always determinative. These results are consistent with the approaches discussed earlier developed by the international legal process school and Sandholtz and Whytock.

The role of lawyers in the State Department reflects the significant role of international law in Department decision-making generally. The Legal Adviser's Office, informally known by its acronym "L," consists of some 200 lawyers and has significant clout. It plays a formal role in decision-making, signing off on relevant policy recommendations and staffing every functional and regional bureau in the Department. The Legal Adviser is politically appointed, holds a rank equivalent to Assistant Secretary of State, and reports directly to the Secretary. Moreover, State Department lawyers may constitute an "epistemic community," able to leverage their expertise and legitimacy to influence policymaking.

Policymakers generally have authority to make decisions on the issues presented to them, taking legal advice into consideration. The extent of their authority depends on the seniority of the policymaker and the nature of the issue. Significant matters would be decided at upper levels, and really significant matters would be decided above the State Department.

Although policymakers may ultimately have final decision-making authority, the views of the lawyers in the Legal Adviser's Office are treated with a great deal of deference because of their official role in the decision-making process and because of the State Department's culture of respect for international law. Policymakers differed about the ultimate extent of that deference, yet almost 90 percent of former officials said that the advice of the Legal Adviser's Office was determinative (21 percent) or significant (68 percent) regarding US compliance with international law. The specific comments of former officials reflect more nuanced attitudes toward the role of advice from the Legal Adviser's Office. In these comments, by far the majority of respondents said that legal advice was influential, though not necessarily determinative. There seemed to be wide agreement that when the lawyers said no, that some course of action was definitely illegal, that was the final word, at least within the State Department. One or two respondents said that this happened rarely, however. Otherwise, the weight of L's advice varied depending on the circumstances and the weight of other interests, according to policymakers, though it was always influential.

Policymakers could sometimes change the lawyers' minds or could override legal advice. The Legal Adviser's Office, however, has formal and informal mechanisms for pressing its positions, particularly against Assistant Secretaries and certainly against lower-ranking officials. Significant matters, including those subject to the formal approval process, would be decided ultimately at higher levels than Assistant Secretary. As issues went up the decision-making chain within the State Department and above, policy concerns could sometimes overcome legal objections, though this may not have been normal operating procedure and may have caused superiors to think hard about the legal issues involved.

Some contestation was evident in the relationship between lawyers and policymakers and between policymakers themselves. While many former officials indicated that the development of policy was a collaborative and constructive process, a significant number of former officials indicated that they pushed back against the lawyers regarding the interpretation or application of the law, or other issues, in favor of policy concerns. For this group, the interaction between policymakers and lawyers resembled more of a negotiation. In addition, decisions on issues involving international law were subject to the influence of powerful individuals and to bureaucratic politics throughout the State Department and the entire government. Within the State Department, turf battles might be especially keen among the regional and functional bureaus of the Department.

Issues were not presented as a stark choice between law and policy, however. Rather, a situation would be presented in the following manner: these are the circumstances, these are the options, and these are the legal implications. There might be a range of options available to policymakers, and compliance may represent a choice among shades of gray. Good lawyers might present those options, identify ambiguities, and discuss the relative risks of the options.

Many former officials emphasized the ambiguity of much international law and the resulting opportunity for interpretation, which could provide a broad umbrella to justify a variety of actions. As a result, several former officials indicated that the United States rarely was unable to pursue its policy goals, though it might have to take different, legal means to achieve them. There was some dispute about the extent to which policymakers could push the lawyers to change an interpretation once it had been made, however. Some policymakers insisted that they could direct the lawyers toward a more convivial interpretation, some indicated they could sometimes convince the lawyers to change their minds, but others indicated that the lawyers would strenuously resist altering an interpretation once they had given it. Perhaps there was more flexibility in developing legal advice initially as a result of ambiguity.

When international law really did conflict with significant policy or national interests, there were several mechanisms that were sometimes employed to overcome those conflicts. Former officials indicated that three strategies were employed, in a descending order of preference. First, they or the lawyers might identify alternative, legal approaches to achieve the same result. The lawyers were often willing to explore these alternatives. Second, policymakers and lawyers might sometimes consider alternative interpretations of international law. Finally, on rare occasions, if the national interest was strong enough and probably after review at higher levels, policymakers might decide to proceed with a course of action that pushed against the limits of international law.

Thus, at least in the face of significant national interests, the application of international law can be flexible, and policymakers and lawyers have developed strategies and processes to accommodate tensions between law and policy. Nevertheless, international law has a key role in formulating policy in the State Department. The predilection of most former officials was to follow international law, and they generally supported the multilateral, rule-based, collaborative world order and the United States' place in that order. The views of the Legal Adviser's Office regarding legality were taken seriously, and L's status and its role in the decision-making process ensured that international law had a voice in that process. These findings fall within the spectrum of the relationship between law and state interest sketched by the international legal process school, Sandholtz and Whytock, and Sanders.

1.2.6 *Attitudes toward International Law in the Trump Administration*

As we have seen, the culture of norms in the State Department, as well as structure and process, provides a role for international law in policymaking. What would it take to modify that normative culture, to revise it wholesale in a relatively short amount of time, beyond the normal accretion of change? The Trump administration essentially tried to do just that, by installing political appointees who strongly adhered to the administration's views, by discouraging dissent, and in other ways described further in the following text. The Trump administration also pursued views at odds with the dominant norms within the Department, a narrow view of international law and unilateralist views and policies. In a sense, the Trump administration experience provides a natural experiment in cultural change within a bureaucratic organization.

One narrative that frames discussion of international relations, US foreign policy, and international law is the idea that the United States established and led a rule-based, liberal, multilateral international order following World War II. While the existence and nature of the liberal international order are contested, it is hard to deny the existence of the multilateral institutions that the United States created after World War II and its leadership role in maintaining and propagating those institutions for more than half a century. Many of the interview subjects in this study alluded to maintenance of the liberal international order as a reason for the United States to comply with international law.

Certainly, whatever we call it, the Trump administration demonstrated an antipathy to the ostensible international order. Instead of a multilateral approach, the Trump administration pursued a transactional, bilateral, case-by-case approach to relations with other states. That transactional approach focused on zero-sum wins and losses in the context of each bilateral relationship, disavowing and disparaging multilateral organizations and systemic costs and benefits. Maintaining multilateral institutions, in this view, was not worth the cost. Trump non career political appointees described the administration's views in similar, if more favorable fashion.

Various actions and statements by President Trump and his administration demonstrated antipathy to international institutions and international law generally. Former officials critical of President Trump cited, among other things, withdrawal from the Paris Climate Agreement, withdrawal from the Iran Nuclear Deal (JCPOA), and withdrawal from the U.N. Human Rights

Council. The Trump assault on multilateralism included, at best, a narrow application of international law and, at worst, potential violations of international law. As actions that ventured into illegality, they cited the bombings in Syria, the treatment of asylum seekers, the travel bans on citizens of Muslim countries, and pushing the boundaries of trade law. The President and the administration, moreover, regularly issued statements hostile to international institutions and international law.

Some commentators take the view that the Trump administration significantly undermined international law and institutions in unprecedented ways. Others have taken a more sanguine view, arguing that the Trump onslaught on international law has had a more limited effect, for various reasons. These include the broad scope of international law and limited bandwidth of any administration, as well as the limited time available to an administration in one term, and the inevitable swing away from many of the Trump administration's policies by the Biden administration.

A fair assessment of the Trump administration's effect reveals some damage to international institutions and to the international legal order. Most importantly, the Trump administration's unilateralist rhetoric and its and isolationist policies damaged the standing and influence of the United States. President Trump's attacks on international institutions also undermined those institutions and their legitimacy, and his disparagement of international law and the rule of law in general may have encouraged and provided cover for foreign leaders to take a similar stance.

In order to pursue its policies, the administration sought to bend the foreign policy machinery of the United States government to its bidding.[9] Indeed, the undermining of the State Department was part and parcel of President Trump's effort to bend the government and the civil service – the "Deep State" – to his will, to root out opposition to him and his policies throughout the government.[10] President Trump sought to make political appointments primarily on the basis of loyalty to him. In order to hobble the bureaucracy further, he left numerous positions vacant, or appointed "acting" officials who did not require Senate approval and could be more directly under the administration's thumb. In the State Department specifically, appointments to the

[9] *See generally*, Democratic Staff, United States Senate Committee on Foreign Relations, *Diplomacy in Crisis: The Trump Administration's Decimation of the State Department* (July 28, 2020).

[10] *See generally*, George Packer, *The President Is Winning His War on American Institutions: How Trump Is Destroying the Civil Service and Bending the Government to His Will*, The Atlantic (Apr. 2020), *available at* https://www.theatlantic.com/magazine/archive/2020/04/how-to-destroy-a-government/606793/.

senior leadership were heavily skewed toward non career appointees, as opposed to career officials. The Trump administration also made notably more political appointments to ambassadorships than previous administrations.

The President's appointed officials, in turn, sometimes sought to enforce the administration's will and stifle debate and opposition within the government to administration policies. Trump appointees purged a number of State Department officials deemed insufficiently loyal, as documented in reports by the State Department Inspector General.[11] Not surprisingly, the atmosphere within the State Department became toxic. It was clear from interviews that there was no love lost between at least some Trump political appointees and at least some of the career officers in the State Department.

Several former officials, moreover, noted a breakdown of the decision-making process in general. Decision-making was chaotic from the beginning, said one high-level former official. In particular, the interagency process broke down under John Bolton's tenure as National Security Advisor depriving the State Department of an opportunity to provide broad input into government-wide decision-making. One former ambassador asserted that the process breakdown extended outside of Washington to operations of ambassadors.

During the Trump administration, former officials differed regarding the extent to which the administration's position would affect attitudes within the State Department. Some expressed the view that the changes could be significant, but the majority believed that while some particular policies and practices might change, underlying attitudes among the rank and file would not change substantially. The consensus view appeared to make a distinction between those at the policy decision level – high-level political appointees, with the potential exception of career officials and other technocrats appointed to those positions – and those at the policy development level – Foreign Service and Civil Service Officers.

At the policy decision level, most political appointees adhered to administration policies and beliefs and, according to the aforementioned reports, attempted to impose their preferences on the Department as a whole. At the policy development level, the established culture prevailed, favoring multilateralism and respecting international law. Permanent change at the policy development level would have been more difficult because that would have entailed changing an established culture among a comparatively large number of career officials. One former official pointed out that the State Department could not bring in a whole cadre of new people willing to ignore

[11] *See* U.S. Department of State, Office of Inspector General, *Review of Allegations of Politicized and Other Improper Personnel Practices Involving the Office of the Secretary* (Nov. 2019).

international law and institutions.[12] As a result, several former officials suggested that the overall culture and even the overall approach of the State Department likely did not shift very much during the Trump administration.

That is not to say, however, that attitudes from the top did not constrain action or shift attitudes at all. Over time, there was an exodus of senior officials from the State Department who might have been more likely to resist pressure. Pressure was certainly applied. In addition, officials may have tried to use legal analysis that opposed a particular view but, when stymied, faced frustration and were less willing to go out on a limb or present a disfavored view later on.

When asked whether views about international law and international institutions might snapback or change after the Trump administration, respondents said that the outcome depended largely on the presidential election in 2020. As one former official pointed out, the views of the State Department are likely to hew to the position of the President. If Mr. Trump had been re-elected, then the views of his administration were likely to become more entrenched, making an eventual snapback less likely.

Following the 2020 election, the State Department and its culture seemingly did revert toward the norm. President Biden and his foreign policy team made it clear in statements and actions that they intended to maintain traditional US support for the multilateral international order, while recognizing challenges from a rising China and a more multipolar world. There still may be a question of how much of a snapback there has been, however.

If Mr. Trump, or someone else adhering to his views and tactics, is elected in 2024, we could see a return to further erosion of the traditional norms in the State Department, especially if that President served two full terms in office. In that event, cultural and policy change at the State Department is likely to escalate. A Trump administration or similar likely would implement the same approach employed in the last Trump administration. Such an administration could even implement plans to revamp the civil service, which would seem to apply to the Foreign Service, to undermine civil service protections in order to subject it to political pressure. News stories in the summer of 2022 reported that such a proposal has become a part of the plan for a Trump second term and has support among other Republican presidential hopefuls.[13] So, contrary to the seemingly far-fetched hypothetical of one

[12] *But see* discussion *infra* note 13 and accompanying text.

[13] *See* Loren DeJonge Schulman, *Schedule F: An Unwelcome Resurgence*, LAWFARE (Aug. 12, 2022), https://www.lawfareblog.com/schedule-f-unwelcome-resurgence. *See also*, Jonathan Rauch, *Trump's Second Term Would Look Like This*, THE ATLANTIC (Aug. 29, 2022), *available at* https://www.theatlantic.com/ideas/archive/2022/08/trump-2024-reelection-viktor-orban-hungary/671264/.

former official mentioned earlier, a new administration could conceivably bring in an entirely new cadre of lower-level officials. In that case, we could see a change in the culture of the State Department, which, with some variation from party to party, has been consistent for decades. This book, then, would constitute not a description of a living culture and a living process, but a historical record of a vanished culture.

1.3 PROJECT DESIGN

In the course of the project, seventy-seven interviews were conducted with former officials in the State Department at the level of Assistant Secretary and above from the administrations of George H. W. Bush through Donald Trump. The State Department was selected because, of any US government agency, its personnel are likely to deal most frequently and regularly with international law matters and are likely to be the most familiar with international law. They have wide experience in both foreign affairs and international law, have thought about these issues, and have participated in US decision-making. Indeed, the State Department and its Legal Adviser's Office have long been considered the preeminent voices in the government regarding foreign affairs and international law.

The attitudes of policymakers within the State Department do not necessarily represent the attitudes of policymakers in the government as a whole. The prominence of the State Department in international affairs and international law has eroded somewhat in modern times as the roles of other entities, such as the White House, the National Security Council, the Defense Department, and the intelligence agencies have increased. The interagency process and the White House decision-making process are addressed briefly in Chapter 5, but detailed study is beyond the scope of this project. Still, to a large extent, the views of State Department officials represent the attitudes and perspectives of a large and important segment of government elites who work on international affairs and may indicate the contours of attitudes throughout the US government.

To be sure, interview subjects' perceptions do not necessarily reflect, or always reflect, reality. Cultural, political, or other biases may interfere with subjects' perceptions, or subjects may have reason to shade their narrative. Nevertheless, these particular subjects were experienced observers, and assessing the perceptions of a large number of subjects may help to correct for biases.

The mix of interview subjects provided a rough balance between Republicans and Democrats, although more Republicans were represented

TABLE 1.1 *Distribution of Assistant Secretaries*

Assistant Secretaries	Total
European and Eurasian Affairs (EUR)	4
East Asian and Pacific Affairs (EAP)	3
South and Central Asian Affairs (SCA)	3
Western Hemisphere Affairs (WHA)	5
International Organizations (IO)	4
Oceans and International Environmental and Scientific Affairs (OES)	1
International Security and Nonproliferation (ISN)	2
Political-Military Affairs (PM)	5
Diplomatic Security (DS)	1
Democracy, Human Rights, and Labor (DRL)	5
Population, Refugees and Migration (PRM)	4
Intelligence and Research (INR)	3
African Affairs (AF)	2
Arms Control Verification and Compliance	1
Public Diplomacy and Public Affairs/Global Public Affairs	0
International Narcotics and Law Enforcement (INL)	3
Total	46

(thirty-three Democrats/forty-four Republicans). While almost twice as many assistant secretaries were Republicans, twice as many under secretaries were Democrats. The mix also provided a selection of interview subjects across administrations. Eight interview subjects were from the George H. W. Bush administration, twenty-three from the Clinton administration, thirty-one from the George W. Bush administration, ten from the Obama administration, and five from the Trump administration. The George W. Bush and Clinton administrations were more highly represented because they were available during the main interviewing stage of the project and also, perhaps, were more willing to participate because they were farther away from their service.

Interview subjects came from a variety of areas within the State Department (see Tables 1.1 and 1.2).[14] Forty-six Assistant Secretaries and twenty Under

[14] Some bureaus have been reconfigured or changed names over the years: bureaus are listed by their designation in 2020. Bureaus with no representation include Near Eastern Affairs, Energy Resources, Consular Affairs, and Global Public Affairs, as well as some administrative bureaus and various offices. Richard Boucher served as Assistant Secretary for Public Affairs in the Clinton administration, but was counted as Assistant Secretary of South and Central Asian Affairs, a position in which he also served.

TABLE 1.2 *Distribution of Under Secretaries*

Under Secretaries	Total
Under Secretary for Political Affairs (P)	4
Under Secretary for Economic Growth, Energy, and Environment (E)	4
Under Secretary for Arms Control and International Security Affairs (T)	2
Under Secretary for Public Diplomacy and Public Affairs (R)	4
Under Secretary for Management (M)	3
Under Secretary for Civilian Security, Democracy and Human Rights (J)	3
Total	20

Secretaries were interviewed, including four Under Secretaries of Political Affairs, the number three position in the State Department. Three former Deputy Secretaries were interviewed, and a brief email response was received from former Secretary of State Colin Powell. A former State Department Counselor, Philip Zelikow, was also interviewed. These numbers do not include seven other former officials who were interviewed off the record, three of whom were former Under Secretaries. Almost all of the former officials were Senate-confirmed appointees, with the exception of a handful of acting appointments. In addition, three former, high-level attorneys from the Office of the Legal Adviser were consulted about their experiences to compare with those of policymakers and to provide context, although their responses were not coded, and they were not included in the count of former officials interviewed.

The project required identifying and locating former high-level officials, arranging interviews, and conducting them. Most subjects were interviewed in-person, or, where necessary, by telephone, especially during the pandemic. Detailed notes were taken, and the interviews were not recorded, to encourage these high-level former officials to speak more frankly.

Former officials were asked a series of questions from a common protocol, consisting of open-ended and close-ended questions, starting with questions about the extent to which states comply with international law. They were also asked to identify the various factors states may take into account and the mechanism or process through which they operate. They were asked explicitly about the extent to which they think that moral or normative considerations play a role in compliance. In addition, subjects were asked whether foreign states have different reasons for complying or not complying than the United States.

Former officials were then asked a series of questions about the United States' compliance with international law. They were asked generally about the factors US officials take into account when thinking about why, or whether, or the extent to which, the United States should comply. The list of factors for coding was developed in the following way. An initial list of potential factors favoring or disfavoring compliance was developed by consulting the political science and international law literature regarding compliance. That list was supplemented and modified during the course of coding by adding new or more specific factors mentioned by the subjects.

Former officials were asked about examples of situations when the United States violated international law, or at least pushed the boundaries of compliance, and about situations when the United States complied assiduously or even over-complied with international law. They were encouraged to discuss their own experiences in this regard. Former officials were also asked in detail about the decision-making process within the State Department. As part of this discussion, they were asked explicitly about the role and relative influence of State Department lawyers in making recommendations regarding compliance, compared to the role of policymakers.

To analyze the results, the project employed a mixed methods approach appropriate for analyzing interviews involving open-ended questions. The project employed a qualitative and mixed-method coding software called MAXQDA, which performs some quantitative analyses and allows for organized and rigorous qualitative comparison and analysis of the subjects' views. The project primarily employed qualitative analysis, but included appropriate quantitative analysis as well, including frequency counts and cross-tabulations. The qualitative analysis allowed the identification of common themes and relevant quotes in the interviews. In keeping with a primarily qualitative approach overall, the project also developed a rich, detailed understanding of subjects and their perceptions and views about compliance. For example, with the help of crosstabs, the project was able to explore whether and how political ideology or presidential administration affects how policymakers view compliance with international law.

1.4 CHAPTER SUMMARY

Chapter 2 will briefly summarize the compliance literature in international relations and international law, addressing theoretical and empirical work. Readers interested more in the book's empirical findings and analysis can skip to Chapter 3. The first body of literature examined explores why states comply with international law. The study may confirm or illustrate the applicability of one or more theories of compliance, although that is not necessary for it to be valuable in illuminating the motivations that affect policymakers and states.

The second body of literature examines more closely *how* states comply at the domestic level and focuses on domestic policymaking within the United States government.

Chapter 3 explores the views of former officials regarding compliance by states with international law. The chapter first explores the views of former officials concerning compliance by states with international law in general. The chapter next examines the factors that former officials believe positively and negatively affect compliance. The chapter concludes by considering the former officials' perceptions about the reasons that states outside of the United States take into consideration regarding compliance with international law.

Chapter 4 focuses on the United States' compliance with international law. The chapter begins by examining the range of former officials' perceptions regarding the extent to which the United States complies. The chapter next highlights the factors that former officials believe affect compliance and compares and contrasts those to the factors that affect compliance by states generally. The chapter explores the overall interplay between law and policy, exploring how policymakers balance these competing concerns. It then examines factors that may affect policymaker perceptions, including party affiliation.

Chapter 5 examines the role of international law in State Department policymaking from the perspective of the former officials, focusing on the role of the Legal Adviser's Office. It describes the formal and informal processes within the State Department and then briefly examines the interagency process and the role of the White House in decision-making. The chapter then examines closely the weight given by policymakers to legal advice and the nature of the interaction between policymakers and lawyers.

Chapter 6 takes a look at the role of international law in the Trump administration State Department. Policymakers' attitudes in the previous four administrations serve as the basis for comparison. Former policymakers give their opinion on the extent of the effect of the Trump administration on State Department policymaking as a whole and discuss potential long-term effects. Chapter 7 summarizes the study's conclusions.

2

Background Literature

This chapter provides an overview of two related bodies of literature, corresponding to the first two prongs of this study. The first prong examines the attitudes of former officials toward compliance with international law by states in general and by the United States in particular, and the second prong addresses the role of international law in decision-making within the State Department. The literature that applies to both prongs overlaps to some extent but can be divided for ease of analysis.

The first body of literature addresses state compliance with international law, essentially exploring the question of *why* states in general might comply with international law from a theoretical perspective. The second body of literature is a subset of the first but examines more closely *how* states comply, theorizing about factors affecting domestic compliance with international law and, in particular, focusing on domestic policymaking within the US government. As such, this second body of literature is particularly relevant to an examination of the role of international law in State Department decision-making. These two bodies of literature overlap in that the compliance literature may help to explain individual and domestic institutional motivations to comply and, in particular, help to explain cultural norms within domestic institutions.

On the first, broader question of why states comply with international law, various theories attempt to explain whether, why, and under what conditions states comply with international law. These theories are generally associated with the primary schools of international relations theory. In general, they can be divided into two categories: a rational choice or instrumentalist approach and a normative approach.[1]

[1] *See* Robert O. Keohane, Jr., *International Relations and International Law: Two Optics*, 38 HARV. INT'L L. J. 487 (1997); George W. Downs et al., *Is the Good News about Compliance Good News about Cooperation?* 50 INT. ORG. 379 (1996).

The former assumes that states make a rational choice of costs and benefits in making the decisions about compliance with international law; international law is simply an instrument of state interests, not a driver of them. The latter assumes that norms or rules, in and of themselves, have independent force in guiding state behavior and compliance. This division into two categories applies to the international relations literature but also applies to much of the international law scholarship on compliance. The primary instrumentalist theories are realism and neorealism, neoliberal institutionalism, and liberalism. The primary normative theories are constructivism, as well as various legal theories, including international legal process theories, managerialism, and theories of legitimacy.

The review of compliance theories is relevant to the study for several reasons. It provides a context for the current study. Relevant to that context, the literature informed some of the questions for interview subjects, as well as the development of codes for their responses. Most importantly, this study may confirm or illustrate the applicability of these theories to state compliance, although that is not necessary for the study to be valuable in illuminating the motivations that affect policymakers and states. Thus, the study takes a rather eclectic view of the application of compliance theories. As one political scientist asserts, the problem with the main theoretical perspectives – realism, liberalism, and constructivism – is that "they are all right, at least for some stages of the governance process, in some systems of governance, some of the time."[2] This observation is supported by the responses received from participants in this study. The purpose of the first part of the study is not necessarily to test contending theories, but rather to provide context for the project and to provide conceptual tools for understanding.

Several theoretical perspectives could help understand domestic policymaking involving compliance with international law in general and the role of international law and lawyers in State Department policymaking in particular. A realist approach would predict that law, policymakers, and institutions serve the interests of the state. A constructivist or liberal approach would predict that law, institutions, and process could channel or constrain the exercise of raw state interest through the operation of norms and processes, or through rationalist means.[3] Do international law, institutions, and processes

[2] Wayne Sandholtz & Christopher Whytock, *The Politics of International Law*, *in* The Research Handbook on the Politics of International Law 1–2 (Wayne Sandholtz & Christopher A. Whytock, eds., 2017).

[3] *See* Rebecca Sanders, Plausible Legality: Legal Culture and Political Imperative in the Global War on Terror 3 (2018).

serve only to further the interests of the United States, or do they serve to constrain the state and the exercise of power?

While surveying the major theories and scholars, this chapter concentrates on two normative, process-oriented approaches, one from international law and one from international relations. The international law theory is the international legal process approach consisting of two related strands, the transnational legal process and the international legal process schools. In international relations, Wayne Sandholtz and Christopher Whytock, along with other like-minded scholars, have developed a framework emphasizing process, structure, institutional culture, and the constraining and channeling power of legal rules.

Both of these approaches are particularly helpful in understanding this study's findings regarding the operation and effect of international law within the State Department and the US government. That is, both the international legal process schools and the Sandholtz and Whytock framework emphasize the role of internalized norms in decision-making by individuals and government organizations. Both recognize the importance of process and organizational structure in guiding political decision-making. Both recognize the challenge that ambiguity poses for the application of international law. Neither claims that law or institutions control the exercise of state power, and both admit that power and power differences are influential and even decisive.

Rebecca Sanders is more skeptical still about the limits of these mechanisms to control state power. She finds both realism, on the one hand, and liberalism or constructivism, on the other, inadequate to explain the relationship between power and law. Realists emphasize the supremacy of state power over law, or law as permit, whereas liberals and constructivists emphasize the normative and procedural constraints on the exercise of power, or law as constraint.[4] Instead, law is both permissive, to the extent that ambiguities can be manipulated to justify a range of behavior, and constraining because law is still a measure of appropriate conduct.[5] Sanders' approach is adjacent to those of the international legal process school and Sandholtz and Whytock on a spectrum regarding accommodation between law and power.

With these theoretical approaches in mind and based on the empirical results described in this study, it may be possible to engage in modest, inductive theory-building about how US policymakers think about international law and about law's role in US policymaking, focusing on the State

4 *Id.*

5 SANDERS, *supra* note 3, at 16.

Department. Some might call this approach midrange theorizing, building theory from empirical study in a limited fashion.[6]

In brief, the collective views of former officials in this study correspond reasonably to the theoretical perspectives of the international legal process school, Sandholtz and Whytock, and Sanders. Legal norms, institutional structure, and processes may constrain or channel the policy of the United States, but not always and to varying degrees. International law and lawyers have a key role in formulating policy in the State Department. Policymakers generally support the multilateral, rule-based, collaborative world order, and the US' place in that order. As one former senior official stated, policymakers always want to do the right thing and their predilection is to comply, but their job is to pursue the interest of the United States.[7] In terms of process, international law considerations are influential but are not always determinative and sometimes can be overcome by considerations of national interest.

2.1 THEORIES OF STATE COMPLIANCE WITH INTERNATIONAL LAW

An extensive theoretical literature addresses state compliance with international law, seeking to explain whether, why, and under what conditions states comply. Because other scholars have conducted excellent, recent surveys of this literature, a lengthy review will not be necessary here.[8] Rather, this section will provide a general overview of this literature.

6 *See* Gregory Shaffer & Tom Ginsburg, *The Empirical Turn in International Legal Scholarship*, 106 AM. J. INT'L L. 1, 1 (2012); Sandholtz & Whytock, *supra* note 2, at 2, 19. A general theory of the relationship between law and power in all situations may be unworkable, because it would struggle to explain the relationship between politics and law in diverse circumstances. The relationship between politics and law varies depending on the site of interaction between the two and the task is to demarcate these sites and explain the relationship between law and politics there. *See* Sandholtz & Whytock, *supra* note 2, at 2, 19.

7 *See* Interview 8, Former Senior State Department Official. The official went on to say that they [policymakers] wanted to understand it all: what did the law mean? What was its intent? How much flexibility is there? They wanted to find a way to comply, but when they chose not to do so, they wanted to make an informed choice.

8 For detailed, recent summaries of the compliance literature in both international relations and international law see, e.g., Courtney Hillebrecht, *Compliance: Actors, Context and Causal Processes*, *in* RESEARCH HANDBOOK ON THE POLITICS OF INTERNATIONAL LAW 27 (Wayne Sandholtz & Christopher A. Whytock, eds., 2017); Carmela Lutmar & Cristiane L. Carneiro, *Compliance in International Relations*, *in* OXFORD RESEARCH ENCYCLOPEDIA OF POLITICS (2016; online publication date June 2018), DOI: 10.1093/acrefore/9780190228637.013.576, https://edisciplinas.usp.br/pluginfile.php/4424948/mod_resource/content/1/Lutmar%20and%20Carneiro%202018.pdf; Jana von Stein, *The Engines of Compliance*, *in* INTERDISCIPLINARY PERSPECTIVES ON INTERNATIONAL LAW AND INTERNATIONAL RELATIONS: THE STATE OF THE ART 477 (Jeffrey L. Dunoff & Mark A.

Political scientists and legal scholars have investigated compliance with international law, with international relations scholars increasingly focused on the question in the last twenty years or so.[9] The central puzzle facing scholars has been "why governments, seeking to promote their own interests, ever comply with rules that are not in their immediate self-interest."[10] Yet, states do comply with international law to a large extent. This main question raises subsidiary questions that the literature attempts to address. When do states comply? Are states more likely to comply in some situations, rather than others? When states do comply, are they motivated by rational choice considerations of short- or long-term self-interest, or by some normative force that generates compliance?

In this study, compliance will be defined as behavior in accordance with the particular rules of an international institution or regime.[11] Extensive debate has surrounded the very definition of compliance and how to measure it. Normatively oriented scholars may be more interested in attitudinal change that shapes identities and social identities.[12] Other scholars draw a distinction between compliance with rules and implementation (actual incorporation of rules into domestic governance), or effectiveness (the extent to which international rules affect an underlying problem), suggesting that the latter two are more meaningful measures of states' change in behavior.[13] Nonetheless, compliance with rules arguably provides a good enough proxy for assessing the effect of international law on behavior[14] and may be easier to measure and evaluate.[15]

Pollack, eds., 2012); Barbara Delcourt, *Theory of Compliance*, *in* MAX PLANCK ENCYCLOPEDIA OF PUBLIC INTERNATIONAL LAW (Rudiger Wolfrum, ed., last updated 2013), https://opil.ouplaw.com/display/10.1093/law:epil/9780199231690/law-9780199231690-e1043. Portions of this section are drawn from Philip M. Moremen, Private Rights of Action to Enforce Rules of International Regimes, 115–132 (2005) (unpublished Ph.D. dissertation) [hereinafter Moremen, Private Rights]. *See also* Philip M. Moremen, *Private Rights of Action to Enforce Rules of International Regimes*, 79 TEMPLE L. REV. 1127 (2007); Philip M. Moremen, *International Private Rights of Action: A Cost–Benefit Framework*, 8 SAN DIEGO INT'L L. J. 5 (2006).

9 von Stein, *supra* note 8, at 477.

10 Robert O. Keohane, AFTER HEGEMONY 99 (1984).

11 *See* von Stein, *supra* note 8, at 478, citing ORAN R. YOUNG, COMPLIANCE AND PUBLIC AUTHORITY: A THEORY WITH INTERNATIONAL APPLICATIONS 104 (1979) (compliance is "the degree to which state behavior conforms to what an agreement prescribes or proscribes").

12 *See* von Stein, *supra* note 8, at 493.

13 *See id.*

14 *See id.*; Tim Meyer, *IL/IR Symposium: Comment on von Stein*, OPINIO JURIS (Sept. 9, 2013), http://opiniojuris.org/2013/09/19/ilir-symposium-comment-von-stein/; Moremen, Private Rights, *supra* note 8, at 142.

15 *See* von Stein, *supra* note 8, at 494.

Noncompliance is probably better thought of as a spectrum, rather than as a dichotomy, at least in conceptual terms.[16] While treating compliance or noncompliance as a dichotomy may make measurement easier for empirical studies, the reality is messier. It may not be realistic to expect exact compliance from states, and doing so may privilege the perfect at the expense of the good. More to the point, given the indeterminacy of much international law, even treaties, it may not always be possible to identify the exact nature of an obligation or compliance with it.

In general, theories of compliance can be divided into two categories: a rational choice or instrumentalist approach and a normative approach.[17] The former assumes that states make a rational choice of costs and benefits in making the decisions about compliance with international law; international law is simply an instrument of state interests, not a driver of them. The latter assumes that norms or rules, in and of themselves, have independent force in guiding state behavior and compliance.

2.1.1 *The Instrumentalist Lens*

The instrumentalist camp includes the realist and neorealist approaches, which argue that states pursue a narrow self-interest, only complying with international law when it is in their interest to do so.[18] International law has no independent effect on state behavior: It is epiphenomenal.[19] Some legal scholars, such as Goldsmith and Posner, can also be placed in the realist camp.[20] Like neorealist political scientists, they argue that international law does not affect state behavior, but instead is endogenous to states' interests and the international institutions they create to further that interest. International law is a tool that states use to further their interests, particularly powerful states.[21]

Hegemonic stability theory is an offshoot of realism that seeks to explain how a system of cooperation involving norms and institutions can emerge and

[16] *See id.* at 478, Meyer, *supra* note 14.

[17] *See* Keohane, *supra* note 1.

[18] *See* Hillebrecht, *supra* note 8, at 478, citing HANS MORGENTHAU, POLITICS AMONG NATIONS: THE STRUGGLE FOR POWER AND PEACE (1948); John J. Mearsheimer, *The False Promise of International Institutions*, 19 INT'L SECURITY 5 (Winter 1994–1995).

[19] Hillebrecht, *supra* note 8, citing James Fearon, *Bargaining, Enforcement and International Cooperation*, 52 INT'L ORG. 296 (1998); Downs et al., *supra* note 1.

[20] JACK GOLDSMITH & ERIC POSNER, THE LIMITS OF INTERNATIONAL LAW (2005) (legal scholars examining compliance from a realist perspective).

[21] *See* von Stein, *supra* note 8, at 31 (characterizing Goldsmith and Posner).

exist within the anarchical state system posited by instrumentalists.[22] That system can only sustain itself as long as it corresponds to, or is supported by, the underlying distribution of power. The current global order, in effect since World War II, has been sustained primarily by the United States and its allies. To the extent that US power declines, or that other powerful states emerge to challenge it, that global order is likely to diminish or shift, according to this theory.

In a related vein for realists and other instrumentalists, states may apply straightforward material inducements, either positive or negative, to encourage others to comply. That is, they may dangle carrots to other states or brandish sticks to keep them in line. Compliance may be important enough to some states that, individually or collectively, they are willing to provide these inducements.[23] Positive inducements (carrots) might include increased aid, increased trade, or generalized cooperation. Punishments (sticks) might include sanctions, reduction in aid or trade, diplomatic pressure, or even military pressure.[24] For example, Western states may seek to compel other states to improve their human rights records by tying them to preferential trade agreements,[25] or by applying other inducements. Self-evidently, these tools are the province of stronger states against weaker states. The flip side of this analysis is that inducements or reprisals are less effective against stronger states, so that self-help remedies against them for international law violations may be unavailing.[26]

Also in the instrumentalist camp are neoliberal institutionalists, who argue that states have a longer-term interest in cooperating with each other than realism would suggest. Through international regimes or institutions,[27] states

[22] *See* William C. Wohlforth, *Realism, in* THE OXFORD HANDBOOK OF INTERNATIONAL RELATIONS 130, 142 (Christian Reus-Smit & Duncan Snidal, eds., 2008).

[23] *See* von Stein, *supra* note 8, at 479–480.

[24] *See id. See also*, Lutmar & Carneiro, *supra* note 8, at 8.

[25] *See id.*, citing Emilie M. Hafner-Burton, *Trading Human Rights: How Preferential Trading Agreements Influence Government Repression*, 59 INT'L ORG. 593 (2005); EMILIE M. HAFNER-BURTON, FORCED TO BE GOOD: WHY TRADE AGREEMENTS BOOST HUMAN RIGHTS (2009).

[26] *See* von Stein, *supra* note 8, at 479.

[27] In the early years of neo liberal institutionalism, from the 1970s to the 1990s, scholars studying international governance focused on what they called "regimes," to the extent that they were sometimes labeled regime theorists. They defined regimes as rules, norms, principles, and procedures that focus expectations regarding international behavior. Lisa Martin & Beth Simmons, *International Organizations and Institutions, in* HANDBOOK OF INTERNATIONAL RELATIONS 326, 328 (Walter Carlsnaes et al., eds., 2d ed., 2012) (citing STEPHEN D. KRASNER, INTERNATIONAL REGIMES (1983)). Because that definition generated some confusion, according to Martin and Simmons, by 2012 the word institution had largely replaced regime in the international relations literature. *Id.* at 328. Institutions may be defined

may achieve goals that otherwise would be thwarted by the difficulties of cooperation: uncertainty, collective action problems, and transaction costs. Institutions, and their compliance mechanisms, may serve to overcome these difficulties in a number of ways. Institution may reduce uncertainty (reduce fears of cheating) by increasing the transparency of actors' behaviors. They may also reduce transaction costs by making it easier to negotiate with each other over time in the same issue area. For the purposes of this book, the terms regime, institution, and international legal system will be used interchangeably and will, for simplicity's sake, include international organizations as well as rules and norms, except as otherwise specified.

One tool neoliberal institutionalists focus on is the use of reciprocity by states in the form of tit-for-tat behavior. States promise to comply if others comply and threaten to retaliate or sanction others if they violate obligations, thereby inducing long-term cooperation.[28] Regimes facilitate reciprocity by clarifying ambiguous rules, providing transparency and monitoring, and providing information about other states' intentions.[29] Regimes may also facilitate the application of reciprocity through agreed-upon penalties and processes.

Neoliberal institutionalists also focus on the effects of reputation, arguing that states have an interest in maintaining a reputation for compliance.[30] That is, a reputation for compliance may make it easier for states to gain cooperation from other states in the future. By the same token, a reputation for noncompliance may discourage other states from cooperating with them.[31] Regimes enhance the application of reputation costs through many of the same mechanisms, such as increased monitoring leading to transparency of behavior. Thus, because of the fear of retaliation and the value of reputation, states may follow the rules of international regimes even when short-term self-interest would suggest that they defect.

In liberal international relations theory,[32] individuals and associations of individuals are the primary unit of analysis, not states. Accordingly, state

as sets of rules meant to govern international behavior. *Id.* There is still some difference of opinion regarding whether "institutions" includes international organizations. *See, e.g., id.* at 329; John Duffield, *What Are International Institutions?* 9 INT'L STUDIES REV. 1 (2007).

[28] *See generally, e.g.*, ROBERT M. AXELROD, THE EVOLUTION OF COOPERATION (1984); Robert O. Keohane, *Reciprocity in International Relations*, 40 INT'L ORG. 1 (1986); Robert Axelrod & Robert O. Keohane, *Achieving Cooperation under Anarchy: Strategies and Institutions*, *in* COOPERATION UNDER ANARCHY 226 (Kenneth Oye, ed., 1986).

[29] *See* von Stein, *supra* note 8, at 480; Hillebrecht, *supra* note 8, at 31.

[30] *See generally, e.g.*, ANDREW GUZMAN, HOW INTERNATIONAL LAW WORKS (2008).

[31] *See* von Stein, *supra* note 8, at 481.

[32] *See, e.g.*, Ann-Marie Slaughter, *A Liberal Theory of International Law*, 94 AM. SOC. INT'L L. PROC. 240 (2000), reprinted *in* FOUNDATIONS OF INTERNATIONAL LAW AND POLITICS 95,

behavior is determined by the politics and domestic processes of each individual state, with specific state interests deriving from individual and group preferences within that state. "The distinctive contribution of Liberal IR theory is its emphasis on interaction between individuals operating in society and the 'state,' meaning an aggregation of government institutions, and the way in which that interaction shapes state behavior at the international level."[33]As applied to international and domestic law, this results in a dynamic account of law-making, implementation, and enforcement. The role of individuals and domestic institutions and their interaction with international law is heightened in a liberal conception.

In addition, liberal international relations and legal theorists have argued that the primary factor that determines whether nations will obey international law is whether they belong to the community of "liberal" states.[34] These theorists extrapolate from the Kantian concept of the liberal peace – liberal states do not fight with one another – and postulate that liberal states are more likely to rely on legal rules and adjudication to resolve disputes because that process mirrors their domestic institutions.

2.1.2 *The Normative Lens*

The normative lens, in contrast, eschews the rationalist focus on costs and benefits. Political scientists and legal scholars with a normative or constructivist bent assert that norms and identities shape state interests and, therefore, state behavior and compliance.[35] In brief, normative scholars argue that the identities and interests of states are not simply a given, as rationalist approaches assert. Rather, identities and interests are constituted through state interaction, which constructs norms that then affect state behavior.[36]

96 (Oona A. Hathaway & Harold H. Koh, eds., 2005) [hereinafter Slaughter, *Liberal Theory*]; ANN-MARIE SLAUGHTER, A NEW WORLD ORDER (2004); Andrew Moravcsik, *Liberal Theories of International Law*, *in* INTERDISCIPLINARY PERSPECTIVES ON INTERNATIONAL LAW AND INTERNATIONAL RELATIONS: THE STATE OF THE ART 83 (Jeffrey L. Dunoff & Mark A. Pollack, eds., 2013).

33 Slaughter, *Liberal Theory*, *supra* note 32, at 96.

34 *See* Harold H. Koh, *Why Do Nations Obey International Law?*, 106 YALE L. J. 2599 (1997) at 2633 [hereinafter, Koh, *Obey*].

35 *See* Hillebrecht, *supra* note 8, at 489.

36 *See* Ann Marie Slaughter et al., *International Law and International Relations Theory: A New Generation of Interdisciplinary Scholarship*, 92 AM. J. INT'L L. 367, 373 (1998); John G. Ruggie, *What Makes the World Hang Together? Neo-Utilitarianism and the Social Constructivist Challenge*, 52 INT'L ORG. 855, at 862–864 (1992).

Norms and identities affect state behavior because they become internalized by individuals, and the domestic and international institutions that they comprise. Indeed, the internalization of norms by individuals and domestic institutions is a key mechanism in normative or constructivist theories, though the exact mechanisms of internalization vary by approach.[37] "Central to these approaches is the role of domestic institutions, as channels of norm diffusion and enablers of policy change."[38] Constructivist approaches tend to blur the distinctions between national and international governance, viewing them as parts of one overarching system, so that domestic enforcement of internalized international norms constitute an enforcement mechanism for the system as a whole.

Constructivist international relations scholars and legal scholars have identified various mechanisms of internalization.[39] In the former camp, Finnemore and Sikkink offer a model primarily describing the operation of norms at the international level and their acceptance by states.[40] Risse and Sikkink, and others, offer models more oriented toward the role of domestic actors and their influence on their states.[41] They argue that diffusion of international norms, at least in the human rights area, depends on the development of networks among domestic and transnational actors. These advocacy networks empower and legitimate claims of domestic groups against norm-violating governments and create a transnational structure that pressures those governments from above and below. This begins a process of socialization, in which governments may ultimately begin accepting the validity and significance of norms. Gradually, states may institutionalize these norms, to the extent that they become internalized and become standard operating procedures.[42]

37 *See* von Stein, *supra* note 8, at 488.

38 Lutmar & Carneiro, *supra* note 8, at 5.

39 *See* von Stein, *supra* note 8, at 487.

40 *See generally* Martha Finnemore & Kathryn Sikkink, *International Norm Dynamics and Political Change*, 52 INT'L ORG. 887 (1998). *See also* KATHRYN SIKKINK, THE JUSTICE CASCADE: HOW HUMAN RIGHTS PROSECUTIONS ARE CHANGING WORLD POLITICS (2011).

41 *See generally* Thomas Risse & Kathryn Sikkink, *The Socialization of International Human Rights Norms into Domestic Practices: Introduction*, *in* THE POWER OF HUMAN RIGHTS: INTERNATIONAL NORMS AND DOMESTIC CHANGE (Thomas Risse et al., eds., 1999).

42 Ryan Goodman and Derek Jinks, two legal scholars, have emphasized the importance of acculturation, a similar notion to social influence. *See* Ryan Goodman & Derek Jinks, *How to Influence States: Socialization and International Human Rights Law*, 54 DUKE L.J. 621 (2004) [hereinafter Goodman & Jinks, *Influence States*]; Ryan Goodman & Derek Jinks, SOCIALIZING STATES: PROMOTING HUMAN RIGHTS THROUGH INTERNATIONAL LAW (2013) [hereinafter, GOODMAN & JINKS, SOCIALIZING STATES]. Acculturation means "the

Another constructivist strand, particularly influential among international law scholars, is the transnational legal process approach primarily associated with the work of Harold Koh, a prominent legal scholar and former Legal Adviser to the State Department.[43] This strand focuses on transnational law, law that regulates actions or events that transcend national frontiers, including both public and private law.[44] Transnational legal process examines how public and private actors – states, international organizations, multinational corporations, and private individuals – interact in various public and private, domestic, and international fora to make, interpret, internalize, and enforce rules of transnational law.

In his approach to transnational legal process, Koh emphasizes three stages as determinants of why nations obey: interaction within the transnational legal process, interpretation of international norms, and domestic internalization of those norms.[45] From the interaction of transnational actors arises patterns of behavior that become institutions, regimes, and transnational networks. The repeated interaction of transnational actors, both governmental and nongovernmental, generates and interprets international norms and seeks to internalize those norms domestically.

As norms become internalized domestically, they help to determine why nations obey international law.[46] Norms become internalized into domestic legal and political structures through executive action, legislation, and judicial decisions.[47] These legal norms become engrained in the attitudes of domestic decision-makers, who then perceive their actions as lawful or unlawful.

general process by which actors adopt the beliefs and behavioral patterns of the surrounding culture." Goodman & Jinks, *Influence States*, *id.* at 627. In this process, pressures to assimilate, some imposed by others and some self-imposed, result in behavioral changes of individuals and, through them, of organizations and states. That is, individual behavior and behavioral regularities in communities are partly a function of social structure, the relation between individuals and a reference group or groups. Acculturation operates to change behavior by changing an individuals' incentive structure or mind and by changing their social environment.

[43] *See* Koh, *Obey*, *supra* note 34, at 2650–2651. *See also*, Harold H. Koh, *Transnational Legal Process*, 75 NEB. L. REV. 181 (1996); Harold H. Koh, *Transnational Public Law Litigation*, 100 YALE L. J. 2347 (1991).

[44] Koh, *Obey*, *supra* note 34,at 2599, citing Philip Jessup's definition of transnational law. PHILIP JESSUP, TRANSNATIONAL LAW 2 (1956).

[45] Koh, *Obey*, *supra* note 34, at 2634, 2649.

[46] *See id.* at 2646, 2651.

[47] *See id.* at 2656–2657. Koh distinguishes between social, political, and legal internalization. Social internalization occurs when a norm acquires such a degree of public legitimacy that people generally obey it. Political internalization occurs when political elites accept an international norm and adopt it as a matter of government policy. Legal internationalization occurs when an international norm is incorporated into the domestic legal system through

Thus, domestic decision-making becomes "enmeshed" with international legal norms. Domestic institutions then adopt procedures and internal mechanisms that result in habitual compliance with the internalized norms, evolving into path-dependent patterns of behavior.[48] As a descriptive matter, Koh asserts that states follow transnational norms primarily because of internalization, not through coerced compliance, although coerced compliance may play a role. Indeed, Koh asserts that the key to better compliance is more internalized compliance, or as he calls it "obedience," as opposed to coerced compliance.

2.1.3 *International Legal Process*

Harold Koh states that his transnational legal process school developed from the earlier international legal process school.[49] The two approaches might be considered two branches of a broader, international legal process tradition.[50] The international legal process branch is noteworthy for its insights not only into legal process at the international level, but perhaps even more importantly, for its close examination of domestic legal process related to international law and to the operation of international law within the US government and within the State Department.

Abram Chayes, Thomas Ehrlich, and Andreas Lowenfeld launched the international legal process branch with their text, *International Legal Process*,[51] drawing on their experiences within the State Department. Their book addressed the international legal process, rather than simply the content

executive action, judicial application or interpretation, legislative action, or a combination of the three.

48 *See id.* at 2654–2655.

49 *See id.* at 2626–2627, 2634.

50 *See* Mary Ellen O'Connell, *The New International Legal Process*, 93 Am. J. Int'l L. 334 (1999). Other scholars that could be said to fall in the international legal process tradition include Louis Henkin. *See* Koh, *Obey*, *supra* note 34, at 2621. The New Haven School also represented the legal process tradition, according to Koh, although it grew from different roots in the American theory of legal realism.

> In its modern incarnation as the "World Public Order" school, New Haven School leaders Myres McDougal and W. Michael Reisman argued that international law is itself a "world constitutive process of authoritative decision," not merely a set of rules, whose goal is a world public order of human dignity, designed to serve particular ends and values by establishing regimes of effective control. (*Id.* at 2618.)

That is, the school's emphasis is on the process of interaction through which rules and decisions are made in the international legal system.

51 Abram Chayes et al., International Legal Process: Materials for an Introductory Course xi (1968). *See* Koh, *Obey*, *supra* note 34, at 2619. Their approach explicitly drew from the American legal process school, which claimed that legal doctrine

of legal rules. They asked how and how far do law, lawyers, and legal institutions operate to affect international affairs.[52]

More specifically, Chayes, Ehrlich, and Lowenfeld were interested in the interaction of institutions and processes as they related to four questions: the allocation of decision-making competence between national and international decision-makers, the reasons behind the adoption of regulatory arrangements for particular subjects, the ways in which institutions and the system develop to restrain and organize national and individual behavior, and the elements of the political, economic, and cultural setting that influence that development.[53] Law may not be determinative of every issue, but law is relevant and the role of lawyers is important.

Because international law is institutionally thin in comparison with domestic law, most disputes in international law are resolved not by courts, but by the parties, through mixed political and legal channels. Yet, the differences between international law and domestic law are more of degree than of kind. Most domestic legal controversies are also resolved without adjudication. Perhaps courts are not so central to the idea of law; assent, as opposed to command, plays a significant role.[54]

Accordingly, Chayes, Ehrlich, and Lowenfeld were interested in how law and lawyers affected political decision-making and resolution of international disputes. They focused on formal and informal institutions and processes, including the way the foreign offices incorporated international law in decision-making.[55] Chayes, in a later work on the Cuban Missile Crisis, discussed later in more depth, addresses directly the role of law and domestic decision-making in international affairs, examining the role of international law and international lawyers in US government decision-making. [56]

2.1.3.1 The Managerial Approach

Chayes went on later to develop the Managerial School of compliance theory, along with his wife, Antonia Chayes. Their work has clear international legal process roots. They assert that states have a propensity to comply with

develops from the interaction of institutions and procedures, as applied in particular cases before both public and private decision-makers. *See id.* at 2019–2621.

52 *See* Chayes et al., International Legal Process, *supra* note 51, at xi.

53 *See id.* at xii.

54 *See id.* at xiv.

55 *See* O'Connell, *supra* note 50.

56 *See* Abram Chayes, The Cuban Missile Crisis: International Crises and the Role of Law (1974).

international law, partly because of a sense of normative obligation to obey the law or other commitments.[57] Only rarely is noncompliance a premeditated and deliberate violation of a treaty obligation. Rather, the reasons that states violate treaty norms include the ambiguity and indeterminacy of treaty language, various limitations in capacity, and the fact that adaptation to new legal regimes takes time for adjustment.

Accordingly, managerialists advocate a "managerial" approach to compliance rather than an "enforcement" approach. Under the managerial approach, for example, lack of capacity should be addressed through financial and technological assistance and staged implementation. Thus, the managerial compliance strategy builds on the parties' general sense of obligation to comply and adds a cooperative approach to addressing violations.

The managerial approach also relies on ratcheting up the pressure on persistent noncompliance, employing an interactive process of justification, discourse, and persuasion.[58] Justification of violations requires states to justify departures from treaty norms in various forums, inevitably involving them in a discourse about compliance. In this discursive process, international organizations and other states engage in "jawboning": an effort to persuade the miscreant to change its ways. The emphasis on persuasion here recalls an element of the constructivist approaches discussed previously. But the managerial approach also incorporates an instrumental, rationalist logic. When more cooperative measures are unavailing, compliance efforts can involve the threat of exposure, shaming, loss of reputation, and reciprocal penalties. Always, the possibility of stronger pressure is present in the background: Bargaining and persuasion take place in the shadow of the law.

2.1.3.2 Legitimacy

Another normative legal school, focused on the norm of legitimacy, asserts that states are more likely to comply with rules that are developed by bodies and processes that are perceived to be legitimate.[59] Legitimacy means "a property of a rule or rulemaking institution which itself exerts a pull toward

[57] *See* Abram Chayes & Antonia Handler Chayes, The New Sovereignty (1995).

[58] *See id.*

[59] *See* Thomas M. Franck, The Power of Legitimacy among Nations (1990) [hereinafter Franck, Legitimacy]; Thomas M. Franck, Fairness in International Law and Institutions (1995) [hereinafter Franck, Fairness]; Thomas M. Franck, *Legitimacy in the International System*, 82 Am. J. Int'l L. 705 (1988).

compliance on those addressed normatively because those addressed believe that the rule or institution has come into being and operates in accordance with generally accepted principles of right process."[60] Thus, legitimacy exerts a "compliance pull." There are four indicators of a norm's legitimacy: its clarity or "determinacy"; its "symbolic validation," or compliance with ritual or other formalities; its "coherence" in treating like cases alike and in relating in a principled fashion to other rules of the same system; and its adherence to the community's rules of right process.[61]

2.1.4 *Instrumentalist Critiques*

One instrumentalist critique of the managerial approach specifically and normative theories more generally involves the claim that states follow international law most of the time, which may suggest that sanctions are not necessary, that norms may serve to corral state behavior, and that managerial methods such as persuasion may suffice for compliance.[62] But, according to this critique, the observation that states follow international law most of the time does not indicate that norms or law cause compliance.[63] Instead, these critics argue it is likely that states only commit to agreements that do not require deep cooperation and that only require minor departures from what they would do already. Strong enforcement is necessary for deeper cooperation. Thus, observing only compliance with existing treaties reflects a selection bias, leaving out of consideration many situations that would require strong enforcement to achieve compliance.

Keohane – open-minded, if skeptical, about normative perspectives – poses an interesting thought experiment.[64] Perhaps existing compliance can be explained through the following factors that do not involve the operation of norms: Agents are good at assessing their interests and anticipating the actions of others; a few powerful states make most of the rules and try to enforce them;

[60] Franck, Legitimacy, *supra* note 59, at 25.

[61] Franck, Fairness, *supra* note 59, at 30–41. Franck's conception of legitimacy attracted criticism from many quarters. *See* Koh, *Obey*, *supra* note 34, at 2629–2630. Most notably, Keohane asserted that Franck's link between legitimacy and compliance was essentially circular. "'[L]egitimacy' is difficult to measure independently of the compliance that it is supposed to explain.... Franck describes a rule's compliance 'pull power' as 'its index of legitimacy.' Yet legitimacy is said to explain 'compliance pull,' making the argument circular." Keohane, *supra* note 1, at 493.

[62] *See, e.g.*, Keohane, *supra* note 1; Downs et al., *supra* note 1; von Stein, *supra* note 8, at 487, 491–493 (describing the critique).

[63] *See* Keohane, *supra* note 1.

[64] *See id.*, at 493–494.

and coordination and assurance situations are common. Coordination and assurance situations are those in which all parties have an interest in following the rules as long as others do, too, so that compliance with the rules is in the parties' interest. Examples of a coordination situation include postal agreements and airline agreements. The task is to agree upon a focal point, a common process or standard of international behavior, which is comparatively straightforward.

Reflecting a similar critique, neoliberal institutionalism suggests that legal rules and norms matter most in areas of low politics – economic law, or environmental law, for example – and less in areas of high politics related to use of force and similar contexts.[65] In the area of high politics, legal rules and norms cannot compete with basic underlying political and economic interests, which could suggest the limited purchase of normative mechanisms more broadly. To be sure, the instrumentalist critique has generated responses and questions in turn.[66] Normative scholars, for example, might wonder whether neoliberal institutionalism fully captures the effects and importance of norms and rules beyond an instrumentalist effect.[67]

2.2 TURN TO DOMESTIC EFFECTS

In the last twenty years or so, some international relations scholars have turned to "the nexus of domestic politics and international law" to examine compliance with international law.[68] Some of these scholars are instrumentalist or empirical in orientation, while others take a constructivist approach. These international relations scholars are catching up with international legal scholars, who have focused longer on domestic compliance efforts.[69] International legal scholars, such as Harold Koh, have also brought to bear the insights and tools of international relations scholarship, especially through a constructivist lens.

65 *See* Anthony Clark Arend, *Do Legal Rules Matter? International Law and International Politics*, 38 V. J. INT'L L. 107, 122–125 (1998).

66 *See* von Stein, *supra* note 8, at 491–493 (summarizing these responses). For example, why are treaties necessary if they reflect what states were already going to do anyway? Even if that were true, treaties would still perform important functions, defining non compliance, for example. Treaties can also screen states willing to uphold particular rules from those that are not.
In addition, even if endogeneity is a problem, states may still find themselves complying with a treaty when it diverges from their interests.

67 *See* Arend, *supra* note 65.

68 *See* Hillebrecht, *supra* note 8, at 34 and sources cited therein.

69 *See* Lutmar & Carneiro, *supra* note 8, at 5 (focusing on the domestic courts and other domestic legal mechanisms).

It is not surprising that international legal scholars have focused longer on domestic aspects of compliance, since legal scholars have always been aware of the importance of domestic legal processes for translating and implementing international law into domestic law and, in many ways, giving effect to international law. Many international legal regimes are essentially enforced or facilitated through domestic law that incorporates international law rules.[70] In this respect, international law scholars bring something to the table: One critique of some international relations scholarship on domestic compliance issues is that it does not take fully into account legal concepts and processes, such as the specific procedures for setting and interpreting the content of international treaties.[71]

Some of the international relations and international law literature that addresses domestic adaptation of international law norms was discussed in the last section because that scholarship also plays a major role in the international relations and international law literature on compliance. That discussion focused on the ways that international legal norms become embedded in domestic law and politics. The scholarship described in this section focuses on the domestic side of the equation.

Accordingly, the following section describes scholarship focusing on the domestic components of compliance systems. It briefly discusses instrumentalist and empirical scholarship for context, even though that will not be the focus of analysis. The section then concentrates on two normative, process-oriented approaches, one from international law and one from international relations. On the international law side, these are the related international legal process and transnational legal process approaches discussed earlier, represented by the work of Abram Chayes and others, and by Harold Koh, respectively. On the international relations side, Wayne Sandholtz and Christopher Whytock, along with other like-minded scholars, have applied a constructivist framework emphasizing the role of norms, along with an appreciation for process, structure, and the constraining and channeling power of legal rules.

70 Indeed, a separate branch of international law, or perhaps even a related discipline, consists of foreign relations law, which deals in large part with the incorporation of international law into domestic law and the broader relationship between the two. *See* Curtis A. Bradley, *What Is Foreign Relations Law? in* The Oxford Handbook of Comparative Foreign Relations Law 1–6 (Curtis A. Bradley, ed., 2019), *available at* https://scholarship.law.duke.edu/faculty_scholarship/3743. The study of foreign relations law as a discrete subject has been particularly robust in the United States.

71 Arturo Jimenez-Bacardi, Speaking Law to War: International Law, Legal Advisers, and Bureaucratic Contestation in U.S. Defense Policy 15 (2015) (unpublished, Ph.D. dissertation, UCI), quoting E. M. Hafner-Burton et al., *Political Science Research on International Law: The State of the Field*, 106 Am. J. Int'l L. 47 (2012).

Both of these frameworks are particularly helpful in understanding this study's findings regarding the operation and effect of international law within the State Department and the US government.

The international legal process school and the Sandholtz and Whytock school assert, in opposition to realists, that legal norms may constrain state power. Realist scholars tend to view law as subject to state interests and generally reject the notion that law can restrict state behavior. Constructivist and liberal scholars, on the other hand, believe that legal norms may constrain state violence because of norms, institutions, process, or other means.[72] Even the international legal process school and Sandholtz and Whtytock, however, are often sanguine about the limits of these mechanisms, as discussed below.

Rebecca Sanders is slightly more skeptical about the limits of these mechanisms to control state power. She finds both realism, on the one hand, and liberalism or constructivism, on the other, inadequate to explain the relationship between power and law.[73] Instead, she argues, law is both permissive, to the extent that ambiguities can be manipulated to justify a range of behavior, and constraining because law is still a measure of appropriate conduct.[74]

The section will conclude by exploring other related literatures that influenced the international legal process tradition and the Sandholtz and Whytock approach. The section will first examine recent studies regarding US domestic enforcement of international law, some inspired by Sandholtz and Whytock. It will then examine the literatures regarding organizational theory, bureaucratic politics, foreign policy, epistemic communities, and ambiguity in international law.

2.2.1 *Instrumentalist and Empirical Approaches*

Instrumentalists have focused on ways in which domestic politics and domestic institutions influence domestic actors' decisions to comply with international law, suggesting that domestic institutions fill enforcement gaps in international law.[75] For example, Beth Simmons has argued that formal human rights treaties can affect domestic politics and, ultimately, government treatment of its citizens.[76] The making of an explicit, public, and law-like credible commitment by authorities to respect human rights raises

[72] *See* SANDERS, *supra* note 3, at 15.
[73] *See id.*
[74] *See id.* at 16.
[75] *See* Hillebrecht, *supra* note 8, at 32, 34 and sources cited therein.
[76] *See* BETH SIMMONS, MOBILIZING FOR HUMAN RIGHTS: INTERNATIONAL LAW IN DOMESTIC POLITICS (2010).

expectations of political actors, which can be enforced in three ways. Governing elites can initiate compliance, litigation can enforce treaties in some domestic situations, and most importantly for Simmons, treaties can generate popular mobilization to demand compliance by providing political, legal, and social resources to groups and individuals. These individuals and groups use the commitment strategically to improve their rights.

As an empirical matter, scholars have focused on the particular roles of domestic institutions in fostering compliance with international law.[77] Scholars have focused on the role of domestic courts,[78] the ability of elections to hold leaders accountable,[79] and legislatures.[80] As Hillebrecht points out, the executive is a key actor in the compliance process. "Executives and the civil servants they employ are at the front line of compliance."[81] Executives are involved in the creation, operations, and decisions of international institutions and are responsible to a great extent for state's implementation and enforcement of international law domestically.[82]

Several recent studies have focused on the role of lawyers in the US executive branch and their effect on incorporation of international law norms into policymaking. They include studies addressing the role of government lawyers in moderating the US program of enhanced interrogation in the war on terror,[83] discussed in greater detail

[77] *See* von Stein, *supra* note 8, at 483, and sources cited therein.

[78] *See id.*, citing Anne-Marie Slaughter, *International Law in a World of Liberal States*, 6 EUR. J. INT'L L. 503 (1995). *See also* generally Melissa A. Waters, *Mediating Norms and Identity: The Role of Transnational Judicial Dialogue in Creating and Enforcing International Law*, 93 GEO. L.J. 487 (2005) (considering the ways in which domestic court decisions become a part of transnational judicial dialogue); SLAUGHTER, *supra* note 32, at 65–103 (arguing that the world operates as a complex network of government officials, including judges, who perform functions of global governance); Anne-Marie Slaughter, *A Global Community of Courts*, 44 HARV. INT'L L.J. 191 (2003) (describing how a growing community of national and international courts act in concert despite national boundaries). *But see* Philip M. Moremen, *National Court Decisions as State Practice: A Transnational Judicial Dialogue*, 32 N.C.J. INT'L L. & COM. REG. 259 (2006) (describing the role of domestic court decisions as state practice, but cautioning about their use as evidence of a transnational judicial dialogue because of logistical and practical hurdles in referring to foreign court decisions).

[79] *See* von Stein, *supra* note 8, at 483, citing, *inter alia*, Joel P. Trachtman, *International Law and Domestic Political Coalitions: The Grand Theory of Compliance with International Law*, 11 CHI. J. INT'L L. 127 (2010).

[80] *Id.*

[81] Hillebrecht, *supra* note 8, at 36.

[82] *See id.*

[83] Other studies include: Jimenez-Bacardi, *supra* note 71 (exploring the effect of the role and influence of legal advisers on institutionalizing international law in US agencies); Fernando G. Nunez-Mietz, *Lawyering Compliance with International Law: Legal Advisers in the "War on Terror"*, 1 EUR. J. INT'L SECURITY 25 (2016) (exploring the effect of the presence of legal

here.[84] One or two studies have focused on the State Department in particular. Scharf and Williams interviewed former state Department Legal Advisers to examine, among other things, the role of international law in US government decision-making and US compliance with international law.[85] The Scharf and Williams study focuses on the views of a numerically small, but influential, group of ten former Legal Advisers. They conclude, through examples of compliance in the face of countervailing pressures, that international law sometimes has a restraining effect on US policy.[86] This project seeks to add to these studies about the effects of law and lawyers on decision-making, but focusing on the perspective of policymakers.

2.2.1.1 Normative and Process-Oriented Approaches

Two distinct but similar approaches that address domestic compliance with international law focus on the effect of norms, process, and institutions. The first is the transnational legal process and international legal process schools represented by the work of Harold Koh and Abram Chayes, collectively referred to as the international legal process school from now on. The second consists of recent scholarship represented by the work of Wayne Sandholz and Christopher Whytock, as well as like-minded constructivist scholars. These approaches overlap to a remarkable degree. To some extent, the overlap between these two theories is not surprising – they both incorporate

advisers in government decision-making in the war on terror); Arturo Jiminez-Bacardi, *The Power and Limits of International Law: Challenging the Bush Administration's Extra-Legal Detention System*, *in* THE POLITICS OF THE GLOBALIZATION OF LAW: GETTING FROM RIGHTS TO JUSTICE 127 (Alison Brysk, ed., 2013) (examining the effect of normative contestation among bureaucratic actors in the US government on interrogation and detention policies during the Bush administration); Laura T. Dickinson, *Military Lawyers on the Battlefield: An Empirical Account of International Law Compliance* 10 A. J. INT'L L. 1 (2010) (examining the ways military lawyers have internalized and seek to operationalize international law values).

[84] *See* discussion *infra* Section 2.2.5.1.

[85] MICHAEL P. SCHARF & PAUL R. WILLIAMS, SHAPING FOREIGN POLICY IN TIMES OF CRISIS: THE ROLE OF INTERNATIONAL LAW AND THE STATE DEPARTMENT LEGAL ADVISER (2010).

[86] Another study, a Ph.D. thesis from 1971, examined the influence of law and lawyers in State Department decision-making at that time, in part by interviewing both policymakers and lawyers. That study focused on the background of State Department lawyers, the roles of Department lawyers, the organizational and decision-making structure of the Department, and conceptions of international law held by decision-makers. It addressed issues of compliance to a limited extent. John Warner Outland, Law and the Lawyer in the State Department's Administration of Foreign Policy (1971) (unpublished Ph.D. dissertation, Syracuse University).

constructivist logics – but to some extent the similarities are unexpected, since one comes from the international law tradition and the other comes primarily from international relations theory. Sandholtz and Whytock developed their approach later and cite Koh, but they do not elaborate explicitly on the parallels between their approach and the international legal process approach.

Both the international legal process approach and the Sandholtz and Whytock framework emphasize the role of internalized norms in decision-making about international law, and both recognize the importance of process and bureaucratic organizations in structuring political decision-making.[87] They insist that it is not so helpful to distinguish between domestic and international governance systems, emphasizing that they can be seen as components of a single system, so that understanding domestic enforcement is key to a larger enterprise. In addition, both literatures are primarily concerned with decision-making in the executive branch and both literatures refer, to a greater or lesser extent, to relevant domestic literatures regarding policymaking, such as literature on bureaucratic politics, organizational behavior, and foreign policy decision-making. Several works in both camps have addressed the role of legal advisors in national government agencies in nudging decision-making toward international law.

2.2.2 *International Legal Process/Transnational Legal Process*

Both the transnational legal process school and the original international legal process school were introduced earlier when discussing theories of compliance, primarily at the international level. The following discussion focuses on their application to domestic policymaking. Recall that Koh asserted that interaction among public and private actors at the international level generated legal norms, which are interpreted and further defined, and then internalized into domestic legal and political structures. These norms become engrained in the attitudes of domestic decision-makers and enmeshed in domestic institutions and procedures. Law has become transnational, with

87 *Cf.* Harlan Grant Cohen, *Are We (Americans) All International Legal Realists Now?*, University of Georgia School of Law Legal Studies Research Paper No. 2017–23 (2017), at 10–11, https://papers.ssrn.com/sol3/papers.cfm?abstract_id=3025616#, *later printed* in WHITHER THE WEST? CONCEPTS ON INTERNATIONAL LAW IN EUROPE AND THE UNITED STATES 33 (Chiara Giorgetti & Guglielmo Verdirame, eds., 2017). Cohen identifies a focus on process rather than doctrine in international legal realism. This is reflected not only in the international legal process and transnational legal process literature, but also in rationalist and rational design literatures, liberal international theory, and constructivist literature that focuses on the communities who practice within international law and the norms they develop that guide their discussions and debates.

various actors operating at both levels. In addition, Koh asserts that transnational law is also normative and constitutive.

The international legal process school also emphasized the normative element of international law in its role in domestic policymaking, as well as the role of process, organizational structure, and bureaucratic politics. In Chayes' later work, a case study of the Cuban Missile Crisis, he addressed directly the role of international law and lawyers in US government domestic decision-making.[88] Chayes was the State Department Legal Adviser in the Kennedy administration and participated directly as a member of the White House decision-making group resolving the crisis. His emphasis on process, bureaucratic politics, and the role of law in policy decisions finds echoes in the perceptions of the interview subjects in this project.

Chayes proposed that international and domestic law affect political action by operating "[f]irst, as a constraint on action; second, as the basis of justification or legitimation for action; and third, as providing organizational structures, procedures, and forums" for political decision-making.[89] In terms of constraint, Chayes suggests that the law narrowed the choice of action or excluded certain courses of action. Chayes identifies, first, a number of complicating factors in assessing constraint, or compliance with law.[90] It is not clear how law operates to channel individual behavior, let alone collective behavior in a state's government. Compliance by an individual may be driven by internalized, socialized norms, not just external inducements and penalties. Also, even if conduct violates a rule, it still may have been affected by a rule: For example, the speed of a car violating a 60 mile per hour speed limit and going 65 miles per hour has seemingly still been limited. In most cases, moreover, the law is not as clear as the speed limit because of law's indeterminacy and possible contingencies in its application.

It becomes more difficult to understand conduct when government action is involved. Bureaucratic routine or momentum, political bargaining, the effect of personality, and training can all play a role, as can the different positions, responsibilities, and individual stakes of the participants. In policymaking, where you stand depends on where you sit.[91] In addition, legal considerations are only one factor in the final decision – military, diplomatic, or political considerations also play a role – and they all operate mediately, filtered through the different perspectives and positions of the

[88] *See* CHAYES, *supra* note 56.

[89] *Id.* at 7.

[90] *See id.* at 26–28.

[91] *Id.* at 30, citing GRAHAM ALLISON, ESSENCE OF DECISION: EXPLAINING THE CUBAN MISSILE CRISIS 176 (1971).

players. That is, the players are likely to have a differential response to legal considerations. And those whose position is otherwise bolstered by legal considerations will make sure to bring them to bear. Given all these variables, the best that legal advice can accomplish is to provide an assessment of risks and probabilities, "with the client, by and large, making the choice of which he will bear."[92] Whatever the client's choice, Chayes suggests, law has affected their conduct.

Law's role as a "mere" justification for policy decisions can be misunderstood, moreover, as simple rationalization for a decision taken on other grounds. But, just as the requirement of a published opinion imposes on a court the discipline and check of formulating its decision in terms of legal rules and procedures, so does an explicit legal rationale serve the same purpose of showing that a decision is reconcilable with a generally accepted set of norms. Another function of providing a legal rationale for a foreign policy decision is to assist in legitimating the action to the public at home and abroad. Publication of the legal rationale subjects it to critique regarding whether it justifies the policy decision. Failure to provide a justification, or an adequate justification, warrants and legitimizes disapproval and negative responses from other governments in the horizontal international system. The problem of justification influences not only the execution of a policy but also the choice of that policy to begin with, depending on the strength of the particular justification.

2.2.3 *Sandholtz and Whytock*

Sandholtz and Whytock approach the relationship between politics and international law in both the international and domestic contexts along constructivist lines.[93] Their overall approach has been followed by a number of scholars exploring, in particular, the domestic aspects of compliance with international law.[94] The emphasis of this school is clearly on process, on *how* states comply, rather than *why* they comply.[95] Part of their approach involves, both at the domestic and international levels, focusing on *who* is involved in the compliance process, *how* compliance operates in different stages of

[92] *Id.* at 27.

[93] Sandholtz & Whytock, *supra* note 2.

[94] *See, e.g.*, ELIZABETH GRIMM ARSENAULT, HOW THE GLOVES CAME OFF: LAWYERS, POLICY MAKERS, AND NORMS IN THE DEBATE ON TORTURE (2017) [Hereinafter ARSENAULT, GLOVES]; Jimenez-Bacardi, *supra* note 71.

[95] *See* Hillebrecht, *supra* note 8, at 35–46. "[E]xecutives and the civil servants they employ are at the front line of compliance." *Id.* at 36.

governance, and *which* political contexts and governance structures facilitate compliance.[96]

More specifically, Sandholtz and Whytock assert that there are diverse sites of interaction between law and politics and that the nature, causes, and effects of interactions between them vary across those different sites. They focus on two units of analysis, stages of governance and governance systems. The stages of governance are rulemaking, interpretation, decision-making, implementation, and rule change. Governance systems are social mechanisms for constructing rules and for applying them to concrete situations. Governance systems may be defined by their subject matter (peace and security, civil aviation), their geographical scope (international, regional, national), or both.

Each stage of governance is characterized by contestation among the actors involved. Accordingly, it is important to identify those actors, their interests and values, and their power and resources, a point also made by Chayes and by the literature on bureaucratic politics. Of the five stages, the most relevant for our purposes are interpretation, decision-making, and, to a lesser extent, rule change.

Interpretation is crucial because of the ambiguous nature of most rules, at least in terms of degree, leading to contestation at that stage. The decision-making stage involves decision-making by the subjects of the rules, such as decisions on whether or how to comply with international law. Norms, rules, procedures, and institutions affect compliance decisions, once again in a way reminiscent of the international legal process approach. Although they do not tame power or nullify power differences, law and legal institutions mediate power and channel behavior. Rules "configure the political institutions through which further rules and policies are defined and carried out and disputes resolved."[97] Law tempers power by requiring that it be exercised through institutions and by rule-defined processes.[98]

Informal norms also shape behavior through organizational culture, an insight gleaned from the literature on organizations and organizational behavior.[99] Furthermore, even powerful actors need to frame proposed legal norms

96 *See also* Sandholtz & Whytock, *supra* note 2 (arguing that interactions between law and politics vary across different stages of governance within particular governance systems and across different governance systems).

97 *Id.* at 17.

98 *See id.* at 7–9, 17–20.

99 *See id.* at 7. That is, actors may follow a logic of appropriateness, generated by the informal norms that exist in organizations or that may result from an individual's identity. *See id.*, citing James G. March & Johan P. Olsen, *The Institutional Dynamics of International Political Orders*, 52 INT'L ORG. 943 (1998). *See also*, ARSENAULT, GLOVES, *supra* note 94; Elizabeth

not as serving narrow interests but as general rules that address common interests.[100] This notion is similar to Chayes' view of justification.

The governance stage of legal change addresses the application of norms to conduct and the process of normative change. Sandholtz's basic premise, described more extensively in an earlier article, is that social rules guide the conduct of actors, but that actors also constantly reshape the rules. "The inescapable tension between general norms and specific actions ceaselessly casts up disputes, which in turn generate arguments, which then reshape both rules and conduct."[101] He describes a cycle of norm change, beginning with the set of existing norms, which provides a structure within which actors operate. Their actions trigger disputes: Rules cannot cover every contingency and are, by their very nature, more or less ambiguous, so that actors argue about the application and meaning of norms. The outcomes of disputes and arguments modify the norms under dispute in one way or another, strengthening or weakening them, making their application broader or narrower. Other scholars have elaborated on this theory of norm change in the domestic context.[102]

In the Sandholtz conception, the direction of normative change within government structures is not predetermined. It depends on the outcome of contestation, affected by power relationships and resources, cabined by processes and institutional structures. Norm change does not necessarily always move in a progressive, teleological way toward the good, however defined, whether that be improved protections of human rights, or economic well-being. Some constructivist authors seem to assume or imply an ineluctable progress as international norms are internalized into domestic systems, though most are careful to provide caveats. Sandholtz makes clear that the results of contestation may be varied.[103]

Grimm Arsenault & Catherine Chiang, *The U.S. Department of Defense and Its Torture Program* 46 (2) ARMED FORCES & SOC'Y. 191 (2019).

[100] *See* Sandholtz & Whytock, *supra* note 2, at 9.

[101] Wayne Sandholtz, *Dynamics of International Norm Change: Rules against Wartime Plunder*, 14(1) EUR. J. INT'L REL. 101 (2008) (in this article, Sandholtz explains his theory of norm change, later incorporated into his work with Whytock).

[102] *See* Hillebrecht, *supra* note 8; ARSENAULT, GLOVES, *supra* note 94, at 6–21; Arsenault & Chiang, *supra* note 99; Jimenez-Bacardi, *supra* note 71; Jiminez-Bacardi, *supra* note 83 (examining the effect of normative contestation among bureaucratic actors in the US government on interrogation and detention policies during the Bush administration).

[103] *See* SANDERS, *supra* note 3, at 19 (critiquing constructivist research that focuses on successful cases of norm diffusion and not addressing violations: "There is nothing inherently progressive about legal culture.").

The Sandholtz and Whytock approach attempts to transcend the hard distinction between the role of law in domestic and international politics in favor of a continuum that depicts a range of variation in law and legal systems. The international legal process approach also makes this point; for example, Koh argues that law has become transnational, with various actors operating at both levels. The Sandholtz/Whytock approach calls for examining sites of interaction between law and politics that cross the divide between the national and international. Recall their point that legal institutions can temper the exercise of power and channel behavior through the operation of rules that govern political institutions and define further rules, policies, and procedures for action and for resolving disputes. "The meaningful distinction ... is not between domestic and international but rather between a greater or lesser role of law in mediating and channeling the exercise of power."[104] Accordingly, it is necessary to open the black box of the state to examine the effect of domestic decision-making on compliance with international law.[105]

2.2.4 *Commonalities between International Legal Process and Sandholtz and Whytock*

As noted earlier, the international legal process approach and the Sandholtz and Whytock approach share a number of common characteristics. Both emphasize the role of internalized norms in decision-making about international law. Both recognize the importance of process, organizational structure, rules, and procedures in guiding political decision-making. Both approaches, in turn, often have incorporated insights from the organizational theory, bureaucratic politics, and foreign policy literatures that also focus on some of the same factors to explain decision-making.

In addition, both approaches argue that the distinction between the international and the domestic is overdrawn. One does not need to adopt a completely monist view of international law to appreciate that the international and domestic realms interact and interrelate extensively, both in the formulation of international law and in its application. It makes sense to examine governance systems and policymaking at the domestic level as part of the structure of international law compliance, writ large.

In addition, both the international legal process tradition and the Sandholtz and Whytock approach emphasize the indeterminacy of law. Indeed, law's indeterminacy contributes inevitably to contestation over the application of

[104] Sandholtz & Whytock, *supra* note 2, at 18.
[105] *See* Jimenez-Bacardi, *supra* note 71, at 16.

the rules. Normative and political contestation leads to the application and development of law.[106]

Most importantly, both approaches also share a similar view about the specific role of international law rules in constraining state behavior in domestic policymaking. For both approaches, as in constructivism generally, organization structure, rules, and procedures constrain power and national interest. The international legal process tradition and Sandholtz and Whytock are sanguine about the prospect of curbing power, however. Even powerful actors need to legitimate their actions in terms of existing legal norms. Actors must frame proposed legal norms not as serving narrow interests but as general rules that apply to common interests or projects. While this does not mean that law tames power, it means that law tempers power by requiring that it be exercised through institutions and by rule-defined processes.

Rebecca Sanders is more skeptical still. She finds both realism and constructivism or liberalism inadequate to describe US government approaches during the War on Terror. Realists "emphasize the supremacy of sovereign power over law, or *law as permit*," while "liberals and constructivists identify the rationalist and normative pathways through which law shapes state practice, or *law as constraint*."[107] She argues, instead, for a model of permissive constraint, that "law is best characterized as a permissive constraint on state practice – permissive insofar as ambiguities and loopholes in the law can be manipulated to justify ... [legal] abuses through plausible legality, but constraining in that law following remains an influential standard of appropriate conduct."[108] Self-serving interpretations of legal requirements blunt criticism

[106] Tim Meyer critiques the normative emphasis in these and other process-oriented theories. *See* Meyer, *supra* note 14. He argues that a process-based theory need not be normative and need not involve a process of acculturation or adaptation of social identities. Nor, he asserts, need it be linked to an assumption that states have an independent preference for complying with international law. From a rationalist, law and economics perspective, he argues that a better conception of legal process would reflect the transactional nature of state interaction. That is, treaties are "incomplete contracts that states are constantly negotiating and renegotiating, contesting the meaning of legal rules .... In most cases, state expectations as to what constitutes compliance form and shift on the basis of this contestation, rather than on the basis of the text of a treaty." Treaties can be seen as a form of relational contracting between parties in long-term relationships, and the process of contestation over meaning is a rational one, to elaborate on particular rules. Meyers makes the useful point that normativity and process are not necessarily linked analytically and can be assessed separately. This study accepts, to an extent, the normative framework of the international legal process and Sandholtz/Whytock approaches, but emphasizes the process and organizational aspects. Meyers' analogy of treaties to incomplete contracts is also useful in thinking about the role of ambiguity and interpretation in the application of international law, discussed below.

[107] *Id.*

[108] SANDERS, *supra* note 3, at 16.

because they provide the veneer of legality, even when those interpretations are criticized. But the very use of law as justification accepts the legitimacy of the law as a standard of evaluation and provides a basis for others to criticize that behavior.[109] Other mechanisms also support the constraint of law, she argues, including reputational costs, the potential threat of legal sanctions, social sanctions, and legitimacy.[110] Sanders' perspective provides a pragmatic, nuanced gloss on the international legal process and Sandholtz/Whytock approaches regarding the relationship between state interest and legality.

2.2.5 *Complementary Literatures: US Enforcement, Organizational Theory, Bureaucratic Politics, Epistemic Communities, Ambiguity, and Interpretation*

The international legal process tradition and the Sandholtz and Whytock approach, in turn, have incorporated insights from other literatures that make the same or similar points. This section will explore these literatures briefly, teasing out some of their implications and highlighting the significance of the relevant issues. Accordingly, the section will examine literatures that address organizational theory, bureaucratic politics, foreign policy, ambiguity, and other topics that address some of the same factors to explain domestic decision-making, or make similar points. The section will begin by exploring recent studies regarding US domestic enforcement of international law, some influenced by Sandholtz and Whytock. Many of these studies focus on the effect of the presence of lawyers in the decision-making process. The section will then proceed to examine literatures that influenced both Sanders and Whytock and the international legal process tradition.

2.2.5.1 Recent Studies of US Domestic Enforcement of International Law

Several recent studies have examined domestic enforcement of international law in connection with changing rules and norms regarding the use of enhanced interrogation techniques or torture following the 9-11 attacks, focusing on the role of government lawyers. Elizabeth Arsenault and Arturo Jimenez-Bacardi explicitly follow the Sandholtz and Whytock approach and illustrate how it might be applied specifically to domestic compliance mechanisms.[111] Laura Dickinson and Fernando Nunez-Mietz explore the role of

[109] *See id.*
[110] *See id.* at 24–25.
[111] In addition to Jimenez-Bacardi, Elizabeth Arsenault examines the development of norms regarding enhanced interrogation as an example of normative change, asserting that norms evolve through a process of contestation by actors with the access and influence to interpret

government lawyers in affecting compliance with international law using different theoretical lenses, though in many respects, they complement the Sandholtz and Whytock approach.[112] All four scholars borrow from other domestic literatures, including literature on organizations and bureaucratic politics. Most importantly, all emphasize the significance of the role of lawyers and legal advisers in decision-making and shaping compliance with international law norms.

For example, essentially following Sandholtz and Whytock, Jimenez-Bacardi advances a theory of "legalized bureaucratic politics," which examines decision-making in the executive branch to explain how and under what conditions international law constrains state behavior.[113] In general, he argues that the more international law is institutionalized into a state's decision-making process, the more likely it is that the state will comply with international law. Legal institutionalization involves the incorporation by bureaucracies of international law as part of their formal and informal rules and procedures. The mechanisms that influence the institutionalization of law within a bureaucracy are approval and review procedures, training, a significant role for legal advisers, and inculcating a law-abiding ethos. The level of institutionalization, in turn, will affect the outcome of the bureaucratic decision-making process, and the compliance of that outcome with international law. The outcome of the decision-making process is hardly a

and adapt their meaning. *See* ARSENAULT, GLOVES, *supra* note 94. In examining contestation over these norms, Arsenault explored the actions and attitudes of government policymakers, lawyers, and interrogators. Push back within and without the government reinforced the norm against torture, leading to a new, if not entirely secure, *status quo*.

112 Laura Dickinson explores international law compliance through interviews with US military lawyers, exploring the ways these lawyers "have internalized and seek to operationalize the core values inscribed in international law," human rights and limits on the use of force. Dickinson, *supra* note 83. She investigates the application of organizational theory regarding norms to this behavior. Fernando Nunez-Mietz explores the effect on compliance of institutional rules and the incorporation of legal advisers in the policymaking of various states. Nunez-Mietz, *supra* note 83. He argues that these domestic institutional barriers, or fences, to non compliance do not depend either on rational cost–benefit calculations or normative preferences on the part of individual policymakers. He then asserts that institutional rules and the presence of lawyers in the bureaucracy of the US government contributed to push back against the interrogation program in "war on terror."

113 See Jimenez-Bacardi, *supra* note 71. See *also* Jimenez-Bacardi, *supra* note 83. Jimenez-Bacardi's excellent dissertation differs from this study in several ways. It does not focus on policymakers' perceptions regarding the reasons that states comply with international law, it discusses the State Department to a lesser extent, it does not attempt the same temporal scope and cross-administration view, and it asks some different questions. Nevertheless, his examination of the inter agency process and other agencies provides valuable insight to decision-making in the US government as a whole.

foregone conclusion: All steps involve contestation between adversarial individuals and groups. Nevertheless, to the extent that the result of greater institutionalization of international law results in greater compliance, the model describes, essentially, key self-enforcement mechanisms. Jimenez-Bacardi applies his theory to explore the extent to which six US national security agencies, including the State Department, have institutionalized the international law of armed conflict into their organizations and culture, and the effect of institutionalization on US decisions.

As these studies suggest, and as the present study confirms, the presence of lawyers in policymaking raises the profile of international law concerns and serves to nudge policy toward compliance with international law. Concentrating on the State Department, this study adds to that literature by focusing not just on the effect of law and lawyers but also on the reception by other policymakers of legal norms and their interactions with the lawyers. It also explores the effect of other factors on decision-making.

2.2.5.2 Organizational Theory, Bureaucratic Politics, and Foreign Policy

Several of these authors – Arsenault, Jimenez-Bacardi, and Dickinson – join with Sandholtz and Whytock in employing various organizational theories. The reference by these scholars to organizational theories is not surprising, as bureaucracies are simply one kind of organization, and these theories clearly have explanatory power in this context. Jimenez-Bacardi refers to organizational theories and to the literature on US foreign policy.

The basic thrust of the organizational theories is that formal governing rules and structure, as well as informal norms and informal culture, serve to guide and limit the choices of individuals within the organization.[114] A detailed description and analysis of different organizational theories is beyond the scope of this book, but the following is a very brief overview. The most significant strand[115] views the organization as a decision-making hierarchy, in which informal norms are just as important as the formal structure. Through formal structures, the organization and its leaders can provide incentives and penalties to fulfill the organization's purposes. These structures may include legal counsel and associated processes. Informal structures –

[114] *See* Dickinson, *supra* note 83, at 4; Jimenez-Bacardi, *supra* note 71, at 16.

[115] This camp consists of decision theorists, such as Herbert Simon, James March, and Richard Scott, as well as economists Oliver Williamson and Douglass North. *See* Dickinson, *supra* note 83, at 5. Dickinson, following Edward Rubin, describes several camps of organizational theorists. *See* Edward L. Rubin, *Images of Organizations and Consequences of Regulation*, 6 THEORETICAL INQ. L. 347 (2005).

shared values and meanings – are also necessary for the operation of formal organizations and influence employee behavior. Thus, the common culture and values instilled in the members of an organization matter. From these organizational literatures, Dickinson identifies a number of structural elements involving "in-house counsel" that could influence organizational behavior. Where legal advisors and lawyers operate within a bureaucracy, especially where their role is formalized and embedded in process, legal issues and concerns are likely to have an effect.

Another body of literature, the literature on bureaucratic politics and American foreign policymaking, also emphasizes the effect of institutional structure – including process, formal rules, and informal norms – on policy decisions.[116] While much of this literature is empirical, some also draws on organizational models, bureaucratic politics models, and rational actor models.[117] Some authors in the foreign policy literature address the roles of individuals and interpersonal dynamics. Others evaluate the role of individuals in policymaking more broadly, considering their background, professional experiences, and beliefs, for example.[118] Nevertheless, even when the role of the individual policymaker is relevant, institutional culture and structure constrain or shape individual or group action. Thus, "[a]s far as the bureaucratic system is concerned, the main factors that influence the outcome of the process by which issues are raised are the standing of the participants, the rules (formal and informal) that guide an issue through the system, and the information and analysis that participants use to choose among alternative positions and to argue their case."[119] As the dean of bureaucratic politics, James Q. Wilson, puts it, organization matters.[120]

All of these particular theories of domestic politics, based on the organizational theory, or bureaucratic politics, or foreign policy literatures, add to approaches based on international relations or international law in

[116] *See* Jimenez-Bacardi, *supra* note 71, at 15.

[117] *See id.* For bureaucratic, organizational, and rational actor models, *see* GRAHAM ALLISON & PHILIP ZELIKOW, ESSENCE OF DECISION: EXPLAINING THE CUBAN MISSILE CRISIS (2d ed., 1999). For a primarily descriptive account of foreign policy making that appears to apply a bureaucratic politics model, see MORTON H. HALPERIN & PRISCILLA A. CLAPP, *with* ARNOLD KANTER, BUREAUCRATIC POLITICS AND FOREIGN POLICY (2d ed., 2006). For an application of new institutionalism to the national security bureaucracy, see AMY B. ZEGART, FLAWED BY DESIGN: THE EVOLUTION OF THE CIA, JCS, AND NSC (1999).

[118] *See, e.g.*, HALPERIN & CLAPP, *supra* note 117; JAMES Q. WILSON, BUREAUCRACY: WHAT GOVERNMENT AGENCIES DO AND WHY THEY DO IT 50–90 (new edition, 2000). Wilson writes about bureaucracy in general, but his work is applicable to the foreign policy making bureaucracy and, indeed, one of the bureaucracies he examines is the State Department.

[119] *See* HALPERIN & CLAPP, *supra* note 117, at 99.

[120] WILSON, supra note 118, at 50–90.

understanding domestic compliance processes. Indeed, aspects of all of them were revealed in the interviews for this project. Process matters, the positions and personalities of bureaucratic players matter, and norms, both formal and informal, matter to decision-making outcomes.

2.2.5.3 Epistemic Communities

The constructivist notion of epistemic communities may also help us understand some aspects of the influence of Legal Advisers and Foreign Service Officers over policy development in the US government. References to the concept, or to analogous ideas, appear throughout the literatures discussed here.[121] Epistemic communities are "networks of knowledge-based communities with an authoritative claim to policy-relevant knowledge within their domain of expertise."[122] They share knowledge about social or physical phenomena, have a reputation for competence, and share a set of normative believes about which actions will benefit human welfare.[123] Epistemic communities extend domestically and internationally. They influence policymaking by leveraging their knowledge and expertise to generate legitimacy, to persuade other policymakers, and to gain bureaucratic influence and power, both internationally and domestically.[124] Key to their influence, then, is both their specialized knowledge and the extent of their bureaucratic power.

In terms of domestic policymaking, epistemic communities can be seen as stakeholder groups created by ratification of international law rules into domestic law, according to Jimenez-Bacardi, writing in the Sandholtz and Whytock tradition.[125] Attorney-advisers in the State Department are subject-matter experts and may constitute an epistemic community. Their expertise in the sometimes arcane reaches of international law may give them some

[121] *See., e.g.*, Jimenez-Bacardi, *supra* note 71, at 13; Nunez-Mietz, *supra* note 83, at 219–220; Ian Johnstone, *Treaty Interpretation: the Authority of Interpretive Communities*, 12 MICH. J. INT'L L. 371, 374 (1991); Sandholtz & Whytock, *supra* note 2, at 5; Koh, *Obey*, *supra* note 34, at 2648, 2656.

[122] Peter M. Haas, *Epistemic Communities*, *in* INTERNATIONAL ENCYCLOPEDIA OF POLITICAL SCIENCE 787 (Bertrand Badie et al., eds., 2011), *available at* http://doi.org/10.4135/9781412959636.n189 [hereinafter, Haas, *Epistemic Communities*]. *See also generally* Peter M. Haas, *Do Regimes Matter? Epistemic Communities and Mediterranean Pollution Control*, 43 INT'L ORG. 377 (1989) [hereinafter, Haas, *Do Regimes Matter?*].

[123] *See* Haas, *Epistemic Communities*, *supra* note 122, at 788. They also share the following characteristics: shared principled beliefs, shared causal beliefs or professional judgment, common notions of validity, and a common policy enterprise.

[124] *See* Haas, *Epistemic Communities*, *supra* note 122, at 789; Haas, *Do Regimes Matter?*, *supra* note 122, at 398 (emphasizing the domestic context).

[125] Jimenez-Bacardi, *supra* note 71, at 13.

influence or advantage over policymakers. They certainly have a reputation for competence. And they may well share a set of normative beliefs, at least about the virtues of respecting international law and the nature of preferred processes.

Foreign Service Officers, from whose ranks rise many career officials within the State Department, may also fit these criteria. They have specialized knowledge of regions, languages, global politics, diplomatic history, State Department precedent, international law, and related fields. They may also possess certain conceptions or preferences for international order and the role of diplomacy or international law within that order. This specialized knowledge may give them some advantages or legitimacy in internal State Department policy battles or in the interagency policymaking process. Of course, there could be perceived disadvantages: For example, the State Department may be perceived as being elitist, or as unduly influenced by diplomatic repercussions of US actions.

2.2.5.4 Ambiguity, Interpretation, and Contestation

A challenge for international law and for compliance is the problem of ambiguity, or lack of clarity in meaning. Customary law and other non-written sources obviously suffer from this problem because they tend to be stated in more general terms and lack precision, but even written treaties can be ambiguous, or fail to address contingencies. Ambiguity poses a greater challenge to treaties and international law than to domestic law because of the relative dearth of interpretive and enforcement bodies in international law and the expense, in time and political goodwill, of appealing to those bodies when they do exist. As a result, "more often than not, the contracting parties themselves have the final say about the meaning of ... the agreement in question."[126] This is the problem of auto-interpretation, where potential ambiguity or indeterminacy of meaning is coupled with the absence of an impartial interpreter.[127] As a result, states and state officials charged with interpreting international law may, not surprisingly, favor their own state's interest.

An extensive definition of ambiguity, its challenges, and its theoretical ramifications is beyond the scope of this work. But for present purposes and

[126] *See* Johnstone, *supra* note 121.

[127] *See id.* at 372. *See also* Leo Gross, *States as Organs of International Law and the Problem of Auto-Interpretation (1953) reprinted in* Essays on International Law and Organization 367 (Leo Gross, ed., 1984).

to sketch some parameters, we can describe the problem of ambiguity as consisting of several aspects. One aspect is the very indeterminacy of language: No matter how careful the drafter, language can be subject to multiple meanings.[128] And not all drafters are careful. Moreover, treaty drafters may seek to create ambiguity, or to state issues at a high level of generality, in order to paper over disagreements about the substantive terms of a treaty. In addition, there may be gaps in a treaty, issues and contingencies that a treaty simply does not address, or are left for later consideration by the parties. Put another way, from a law and economics perspective, treaties are incomplete contracts.

Complementary challenges relate to the process of interpretation. One question is whether a purported rule is legally binding.[129] This may be more of an issue with respect to customary law but can also arise in connection with treaties. A number of interview subjects noted this interpretive challenge. There can also be disputes over the proper interpretive methodology, or the proper way to apply a particular methodology.[130]

Finally, because of auto-interpretation, states will be able to adopt interpretations that favor their preferences. These interpretations may range from those that are more or less in good faith to those that are in bad faith.[131] Toward the bad faith end of the spectrum are outright attempts at evasion.[132] Thus, the standard view of ambiguity – and the view cited by many of the former officials interviewed for this project – is that it is an impediment to compliance.[133]

The international legal process school and Sandholtz and Whytock recognize the challenges of ambiguity and auto-interpretation. Chayes notes the lack of international institutions with power to make an authoritative

[128] *See* Matthew D. Adler, *Interpretive Contestation and Legal Correctness*, 53 William & Mary L. Rev. 1115, 1134 (2012).

[129] *See* Sandholtz & Whytock, *supra* note 2.

[130] *See id.* at 7, citing Adler, *supra* note 128 (discussing different approaches to Constitutional interpretation in the US context).

[131] *Cf.* Sanders, *supra* note 3, at 154 ("The ambiguous definition of torture in the Convention against Torture ... created room for good- and bad-faith interpretation.").

[132] *See* Zoltan Buzas, *Evading International Law: How Agents Comply with the Letter of the Law but Violate Its Purpose*, 23 Eur. J. Int'l Rel. (Issue 4) 857 (2016) (defining as evasion interpretations that allow states to claim technical compliance with the letter of the law while evading its purpose).

[133] The constructivists might respond that the contestation resulting from ambiguity is inevitable and also a part of a law-making, interactive process, and so compliance should be seen more as a spectrum than as a dichotomy. *See also* Meyer, *supra* note 14 (from a law and economics perspective it is more precise to say that ambiguity – resulting from treaties that are incomplete contracts – causes disputes, not non compliance, and the resulting contestation is an essential part of international law-making).

disposition, such that most disputes are resolved by the parties.[134] As for contestation, Koh highlights the role of interaction among actors (including disputes) in the process of norm interpretation and internalization.[135] For Sandholz and Whytock and their familiars, contestation arising out of ambiguity is key to norm development.[136] The process of contestation, in this account, is a normal and expected part of the application of rules, not necessarily an attempt to evade their application.

Because of ambiguity, are states free to auto-interpret international law to their own advantage, or do constraints on interpretation exist? The international legal process scholars and Sandholtz and Whytock suggest that legal norms, institutions, and processes constrain interpretation, although they explicitly do not claim that these factors can completely overcome state interest. In addition, Sanders' notion of permissive constraint adds another way to look at the contest between law and power, in which ambiguities and loopholes in the law can be manipulated to justify departure from the law while still imposing some level of constraint. Sanders' perspective provides a pragmatic, nuanced gloss on the international legal process and Sandholtz and Whytock approaches regarding the effects of ambiguity and the relationship between state interest and legality. The three approaches collectively might describe three adjacent points on a continuum of the balance between state interest and legality.

2.3 CONCLUSION: APPLICATION OF BACKGROUND LITERATURE

This chapter provides an overview of two related bodies of literature, corresponding to two prongs of this study. The first prong examines the attitudes of former officials toward compliance with international law by states, and the second addresses the role of international law in decision-making within the State Department. The literature relevant to the first part is the theoretical literature about compliance, which generally matches up with the primary

[134] *See* CHAYES ET AL., INTERNATIONAL LEGAL PROCESS, *supra* note 51, at xiv.

[135] Where that interaction results in friction because of non compliance, states may shift their behavior to avoid that friction. *See* Koh, *Transnational Legal Process*, *supra* note 43, at 203.

[136] Others, especially in the constructivist camp, also speak about this process of contestation in response to ambiguity *See, e.g.*, Johnstone, *supra* note 121; Nunez-Mietz, *supra* note 83, at 219–220. *Cf.* Meyer, *supra* note 14; Timothy Meyer, *Shifting Sands: Power, Uncertainty and the Form of International Cooperation*, 27(1) EUR. J. INT'L L. 161, 162 (2016) [hereinafter Meyer, *Shifting Sands*]. Meyer suggests that contestation is part of law-making, but he suggests that the normative, constructivist framework is unnecessary to that analysis and takes a law and economics approach instead: treaties are incomplete contracts that states constantly negotiate and renegotiate.

schools of international relations theory discussed earlier. To what extent do the observations by policymakers about compliance reflect these theories? The purpose of the literature review for the first part of the project is not to test contending theories, but to provide context for the project, and to provide conceptual tools for understanding.[137] The results may confirm or demonstrate aspects of different theoretical perspectives. The compliance theories also informed the development of some questions posed to interview subjects and the development of codes for the responses.

The second part of the project relies on the literature addressing domestic compliance mechanisms and institutions in assessing the role of international law and lawyers in State Department policymaking. It refers, in particular, to two similar approaches, one developed by legal scholars, the international legal process school, and one developed primarily by political scientists, following the work of Sandholtz and Whytock. Again, the purpose is not to test contending theories but to use them as conceptual tools for understanding.

2.3.1 *Factors Affecting Compliance by States in General and the United States in Particular*

Among the main findings related to compliance theories are the following. The overwhelming majority of former officials believed that international law constrains state behavior and that states comply to a large extent with international law. To the extent that this result reveals actual practice of policymakers and states, it supports the proposition that international law plays a significant role in international affairs. That outcome runs contrary to realist predictions and comports better with theories that recognize the role of international law in state behavior, from rationalist theories, such as liberalism or neoliberal institutionalism, to normative theories, such as constructivism. As discussed below, however, other results reveal the countervailing effect of state interest on the application of international law.

Many former officials explicitly suggested that decisions about compliance with international law, or the extent or nature of that compliance, involve a cost–benefit calculus. That might involve a balance of many factors, including legal considerations. Although the predilection of most policymakers was to follow international law, legal factors may not always win out. This cost–benefit approach suggests that policymakers – and states – tend to follow a rationalist model of decision-making. Nevertheless, policymakers were clear

[137] *See, e.g.*, SANDERS, *supra* note 3, at 25–26 (employing this approach in applying rationalist and normative theoretical traditions to understand the capacity of law to limit state violence).

that many of them included ethical or normative factors in their consideration of costs and benefits, suggesting a prominent role for those concerns.

Frequency counts were generated for the responses of former officials to an open-ended question about the reasons for state compliance with international law. The top positive factors were, in order, reputational concerns; state interest in a stable legal and institutional system; reciprocity, or the prospect of retaliation; ethical considerations, including ethical values underlying international law rules and respect for the rule of law; idiosyncratic factors, including the political culture of states and their adherence to the rule of law; and benefits flowing from participation in specific regimes. Among factors militating against compliance, the dominant factor was state interest. Accordingly, factors often included in rationalist or instrumentalist theories, such as reputation, reciprocity, and state interest, seemed to play a large role in decisions about compliance.

Two other factors played notable roles in constraining state behavior that cut against an exclusively rationalist model, however. First, normative or ethical factors played a significant role, giving a boost to normative theories about compliance. The normative values underlying legal rules matter to compliance, such as the ethical values underlying human rights laws. Respect for the rule of law – a normative factor – also mattered. In addition, a number of former officials asserted that countries with a history or culture of applying the rule of law domestically were likely to translate that respect for the rule of law to their international interactions. Again, the presence of this factor indicates the power of normative and cultural factors in compliance.

Second, former officials asserted that the benefits of specific regimes and the benefits of the international legal and institutional order provided a significant impetus to complying with international law. Regimes are worthwhile because states benefit from the collective goods that they produce. The interest in maintaining a stable international system, moreover, serves the interests of all states, and particularly the interest of powerful states. The existence of a structure to deal with problems contributes to the existence of a stable, prosperous, peaceful, and just world. Essentially, former officials supported the multilateral, institutional, and rule-based postwar international system. These findings could support a neoliberal institutionalist view of regimes, or a realist view, if we see regimes and institutions providing benefits for powerful states. The findings do not necessarily run counter to normative theories, however.

Participants provided examples of areas in which compliance by states in general and the United States in particular was more or less likely. The least likely areas for state compliance were those related to national security. The most likely areas for compliance were trade and economic law, environmental law, humanitarian law, arms control, law enforcement, and cooperative arrangements such as aviation agreements and postal unions.

These results suggest that compliance is less likely in areas of high politics and more likely in areas of low politics, reciprocity bolstered compliance in several cases, and compliance is more evident in coordination situations. That is, compliance may be better understood through an instrumentalist lens, rather than a normative one. This conclusion is at odds with the responses indicating a significant role for ethical and normative concerns in compliance. Some of the examples, moreover, potentially highlight the role of ethical and normative considerations in compliance decisions, such as in humanitarian law.

Former officials perceived states other than the United States to be more concerned with carrots and sticks offered by the international community, as opposed to ethical concerns or concerns about the maintenance of the international legal system. This perception of the behavior of other countries is consistent with realist notions regarding the effect of direct incentives. That is, powerful states may apply straightforward material inducements, either positive or negative, to encourage others to comply.[138]

The project also examined the attitudes of policymakers toward US compliance with international law in a similar fashion. The United States was motivated by considerations similar to those of other states, they said, with some notable emphases or divergences. For example, respect for the rule of law and for treaties can encourage compliance, and the existence of a stable legal and institutional system can serve the interest of the United States as a conservative, *status quo* power. At the same time, concerns about national interest and intrusions on sovereignty, among others, can exert a pull against compliance.

This assessment of attitudes is significant not only in and of itself but is also relevant to the discussion in the next section regarding the role of international law in State Department policymaking. The views of policymakers toward international law contribute to a picture of the cultural and normative context to help understand policymaking outcomes within the State Department, in keeping with the approach of international legal process and Sandholtz and Whytock.

In particular, the project assessed tensions in attitudes between the requirements of international law, on the one hand, and policy concerns or national interest, on the other. While the overall predilection of policymakers was to

[138] *See* discussion *supra* Section 2.1.1.

comply with international law, the interviews revealed a range of views regarding the tension between international law and national interest and policy. Views ranged from those who indicated that United States complied with international law almost all of the time to those who asserted that international law was subservient to policy concerns and the national interest. Most officials fell in the middle of this range, holding that the United States followed international law much of the time, but that national interest sometimes took priority.

2.3.2 *State Department Policymaking: The Role of International Law*

Broadly speaking, several theoretical perspectives could help explain the study's findings regarding the role of international law and lawyers in State Department policymaking. A realist approach would predict that international law, lawyers, and processes are dedicated solely to furthering the interest of United States. A constructivist or liberal approach would predict that law, lawyers, and process could channel or constrain the exercise of raw state interest through the operation of norms and processes.

Regarding domestic policymaking, this study focuses on the constructivist-leaning theories of the international legal process school and the Sandholtz and Whytock approach. Both the international legal process school and the Sandholtz and Whytock framework emphasize the role of internalized norms in decision-making by individuals and government organizations. Both recognize the importance of process and organizational structure in guiding political decision-making, and the potential effect of individuals inhabiting that structure and their preferences. Both recognize the challenge that ambiguity poses for the application of international law.

Neither of these approaches claim that law or institutions control the exercise of state power, but rather constrain or channel it in limited ways. Chayes saw law, lawyers, and institutions affecting policy in a subtle way: International law and domestic law operate first as a constraint on action by limiting options, second as the basis for justification of action, which must be credible, and, third, as providing organization structures, procedures, and forums for decision-making.[139] Sandholtz and Whytock assert that law and institutions do not tame power or nullify power differences, rather they mediate power and channel behavior. Law tempers power by requiring that it be exercised through institutions and by rule-defined processes.[140]

[139] *See* CHAYES, *supra* note 56, at 7.
[140] See Sandholtz & Whytock, *supra* note 2, at 7–9, 17–20.

Rebecca Sanders is more skeptical about the limits of these mechanisms to control state power. She finds both realism, on the one hand, and liberalism or constructivism, on the other, inadequate to explain the relationship between power and law. Sanders argues, instead, for a model of permissive constraint: Law is both permissive, to the extent that ambiguities can be manipulated justify a range of behavior, and constraining because law is still a measure of appropriate conduct.[141] While the notion of permissive constraint is somewhat more pessimistic about the effect of law than the international legal process and Sandholtz and Whytock, these three approaches sit adjacent to each other on a spectrum regarding accommodation between law and power.

Of course, it is challenging to apply a definitive characterization to the attitudes of almost eighty individuals with disparate views about the relationship between law and state power. Nevertheless, the collective views of former officials in this study correspond reasonably to this range of views predicted or described by the international legal process school, Sandholtz and Whytock, and Sanders. That is, law, process, and institutions may constrain or channel the policy of the United States, but not always and to varying degrees. Policymakers generally want to do the right thing and their predilection is to comply, but their job is to pursue the interest of the United States.

The culture and norms of the State Department include an appreciation for international law. In addition, bureaucratic structure and procedural requirements ensure that international law considerations play a role in decision-making, both formally and informally. Lawyers have significant clout. Indeed, State Department lawyers may constitute an "epistemic community," and so may be able to leverage their expertise and legitimacy to influence policymaking.

Some former officials stressed that arguments over policy involving legal issues could sometimes be real battles among different bureaus or individuals within State, including the Legal Adviser's Office, and among agencies within the federal government. These battles illustrate the role of bureaucratic politics and individual personalities in decision-making, as described in the organizational behavior and bureaucratic politics literature. They also illustrate the process of contestation, the idea that the application of norms will be contested at every stage of the decision-making process.

Contestation was evident in the relationship and back and forth between lawyers and policymakers. Legal advice was influential, and sometimes determinative, though not necessarily so. There seemed to be a wide agreement that when the lawyers said that a course of action was illegal, that was the final

[141] SANDERS, *supra* note 3, at 16.

word, but that may not have happened often. Otherwise, the weight of "L's" advice varied depending on the circumstances, according to policymakers.

Policymakers generally had decision-making authority on issues involving legal concerns, depending on the seniority of the policymaker and the nature of the issue at hand. The Legal Adviser's Office, on the other hand, had formal and informal mechanisms for pressing its positions, particularly against Assistant Secretaries and lower-ranking officials. While many former officials indicated that the development of policy was a collaborative process, a significant number indicated that they had pushed back against the lawyers in favor of policy interests, so that their interaction resembled more of a negotiation.

When international law conflicted with significant policy or national interests, policymakers could employ several strategies to address legal obstacles, in descending order of preference and frequency. First, they and the lawyers might attempt to identify alternative, arguably legal approaches to achieve the same ends. Second, they and the lawyers might explore alternative interpretations of international law, though this may not have been a preferred practice. The inherent ambiguity of much international law provided room to present favorable arguments for the legality of a course of action. Finally, on rare occasions, if the national interest was strong enough and after significant review at higher levels, policymakers might decide to proceed with a course of action that potentially conflicted with international law, or at least pushed against its limits.

Thus, international law has had a key role in formulating policy in the State Department. The views of the Legal Adviser's Office regarding legality were taken seriously, and its status and role in the decision-making process ensured that international law had a voice in that process. The predilection of most former officials was to follow international law, and they generally supported the multilateral, rule-based, collaborative world order and the United States' place in that order. Nevertheless, in the face of significant national interests, the application of international law can be flexible, and policymakers and lawyers have developed strategies and processes to accommodate tensions between law and policy. This may sometimes amount to an attempt to create plausible legality, in Sanders' words.

3

State Compliance with International Law

Broadly speaking, this chapter explores the views of former officials regarding the extent of state compliance with international law and the factors or considerations that affect state calculations about whether or not to comply. The overwhelming majority of former officials believed that international law constrains state behavior and that states comply with international law to a significant degree. This result, to the extent that it reveals actual state practice, provides significant support for the proposition that international law plays an operative role in international affairs. Nevertheless, this conclusion comes with caveats and qualifications. It does not mean that former officials believe that international law *controls* state behavior, nor does it mean that international law always overcomes significant state interests.

The chapter next examines the factors that former officials believe positively affect compliance. The top positive factors are, in order, reputational concerns; state interest in a stable legal and institutional system; reciprocity, or the prospect of retaliation; ethical considerations, including ethical values underlying international law rules and respect for the rule of law; idiosyncratic factors, including the history and culture of states; and benefits flowing from participation in specific regimes. This list of factors is not entirely surprising to those familiar with the compliance literature, except, perhaps, for the prominent role for ethical factors.

This prominent role gives a boost to normative theories about compliance. The importance of maintaining a stable legal and institutional system is likewise significant, especially as a consideration for compliance by big powers, including the United States. A stable legal and institutional system serves not only the interests of all states, the former officials asserted, but also the interest of the United States as a conservative, *status quo* power. The existence of a structure to deal with problems contributes to the existence of a stable, prosperous, peaceful, and just world. In other words, these officials tended to support the postwar, liberal, rule-based, international order.

Among factors militating against compliance by states, by far, the dominant factor is state interest. Rounding out the top six negative factors are the ambiguity of international law, the notion that some states (i.e., rogue states) just do not care about international law or have no interest in it, the perception that compliance by some states is shallow, the role of domestic politics, and sovereignty concerns. Several factors mentioned by former officials relate to domestic issues, including domestic legal and structural impediments, domestic budgetary concerns, and capacity issues in developing countries.

Many former officials explicitly suggested that decisions about compliance with international law, or the extent or nature of that compliance, involve a cost–benefit calculus. That calculus might consist of a comparison of the benefits versus costs of compliance, or might involve a balance of many considerations along with legal considerations. In this calculus, strictly legal factors may not always win out. This approach suggests that states follow an instrumentalist model of decision-making, but, clearly, the costs and benefits considered often include ethical issues.

The chapter then considers the former officials' perceptions about the reasons that other states take into consideration regarding compliance with international law. As for other states, former officials readily distinguished among classes of states based on, for example, size, relative power, and location. Nevertheless, former officials perceived many states to be more concerned with hard benefits and costs, including carrots and sticks offered by the international community, as opposed to systemic or altruistic concerns. Perhaps that perception reflects reality: Smaller countries may be more susceptible to pressure than big powers. But one wonders whether government officials from other countries might take a more charitable view toward their own motivations. The former officials' perceptions of US behavior will be summarized briefly at the end of this section for contrast and then will be examined extensively in the next chapter, Chapter 4.

The chapter next examines the perceptions of former officials regarding the areas of international law in which compliance is more or less likely, as assessed by frequency counts. Responses to questions on this topic were somewhat limited, primarily due to time constraints in interviews. The least likely issue area for state compliance was national security. The most likely areas for compliance were trade and economic law, environmental law, humanitarian law, arms control, law enforcement, and cooperative arrangements such as aviation agreements and postal unions. These responses tended to support an instrumentalist take on compliance: Compliance was less likely in areas of high politics and more likely in areas of low politics, reciprocity bolstered compliance in several cases, and compliance was more evident in coordination situations. Some of the examples, however, could also support a normative perspective. Other results from this study, moreover, highlight the role of ethical and normative considerations in compliance decisions.

The chapter concludes by examining potential factors that affected some of the variation in officials' perceptions about compliance. To be sure, some of that variation is explained by individual personal characteristics, but analysis revealed several predictable factors. First, differences in political affiliation affected their views. Officials appointed by Democratic presidents expressed a stronger belief that international law affects state action than officials appointed by Republican presidents. Second, former officials from different administrations held different views about the role of international law, although this result is likely due for the most part to differences in political affiliation among administrations. Other factors noted in comments by former officials included differences in culture, personnel, and process between and within administrations, noting in particular the personalities and preferences of senior officials. Competing bureaucratic interests may also affect perceptions. No quantitative difference was detected, however, in the views of career Foreign Service Officers compared to political appointees. In addition, some former officials asserted that attitudes about international law and norms can shift over broad periods of time. For example, several pointed out the increased attention to human rights norms within the State Department during and following the Carter and Reagan presidencies.

3.1 STATE COMPLIANCE WITH INTERNATIONAL LAW IN GENERAL

Former officials were asked two general questions about the propensity of states to comply with international law. First, they were asked whether they believed that international law constrained state behavior. Forty-five of seventy-four subjects, or 61 percent of valid responses, agreed that international law constrained states and an additional twenty-six officials, or 35 percent of valid responses, agreed that states were constrained maybe or sometimes. Thus, a total of seventy-one officials, or 96 percent of valid responses, agreed that international law constrained state behavior to some extent.

Furthermore, a large majority of former officials also believed that most states complied with international law much of the time. They were asked "do you believe that most states comply with international law a) most of the time; b) some of the time; c) rarely"? This question was inspired by Louis Henkin's often-cited observation that "[i]t is probably the case that almost all nations observe almost all principles of international law and almost all of their obligations almost all of the time."[1] Henkin's point was that in the ordinary course of international affairs, states routinely follow international law, and when they do violate their obligations, those violations attract attention. When asked, forty-two former officials, or 59 percent of valid responses, believed that most states complied with international law most of the time, and another twenty-eight subjects, or 39 percent of valid responses, believed that they complied some of the time. Only one former official believed that most states rarely complied with international law. Accordingly, the former officials interviewed provided strong support for the notion that most states comply with international law much of the time.

For the first question, the word *constrained* was selected on purpose in order to capture a broad array of effects international law may have on state freedom of action. Most subjects appeared to understand the term "constraint" in this way; those who asked about the intended meaning of the question were essentially given this definition. One former official specifically remarked that constrain was the correct term, as international law does not control states.[2] Whether states are *constrained* by international law does not necessarily mean they are *controlled* by it.

Some former officials reacted to the term "constrain" and sought to redefine the question in different ways to reflect their sense of international law. Several former officials, all on the conservative end of the political spectrum, objected to the idea that the United States might be constrained by international law at all, at least to the extent that international law might supersede US law.[3] Another official commented that while international law may be a constraint on state action, some states try to turn it into a defense for their actions under the banner of sovereignty.[4]

Several former officials of both parties argued that international law should not be viewed as a constraint, or at least not solely as a constraint, but also as a

[1] Louis Henkin, How Nations Behave, 47 (2d ed., 1979).

[2] *See* Interview with Phyllis Oakley, Assistant Secretary for Population, Refugees, and Migration, Clinton administration.

[3] *See, e.g.*, Interview with Lincoln Bloomfield, Assistant Secretary for Political-Military Affairs, George W. Bush administration; Interview with Ellen Tauscher, Under Secretary for Arms Control and International Security, Obama administration. Ambassador Tauscher, a Seton Hall University graduate, passed away in 2019. *See* Ellen Tauscher, *Congresswoman and Diplomat, Is Dead at 67*, NY Times (May 1, 2019), *available at* https://www.nytimes.com/2019/05/01/obituaries/ellen-tauscher-dead.html.

[4] *See* Interview with Kim Holmes, Assistant Secretary for International Organizations, George W. Bush administration.

tool to enable states to achieve their objectives.[5] One former senior official said that international law both enables and frames national action. Constraint, they said, is not the right word because international law enables a lot of what a state wants to do, such that international law has a larger role than the question suggests.[6] For example, the constraint imposed by international law is not necessarily unhelpful: In the Gulf War, the US approach of going through the United Nations arguably laid a stronger foundation in terms of political and legal support for US actions, even though to some it appeared to be a constraint. Indeed, many former officials noted that one reason for complying with international law is because states want to make use of it for their own purposes, and so violating international law undermines it and weakens its utility.

The proposition that most states comply with international law most or some of the time may prove too much. Former officials pointed out that while most states may follow international law regarding the bulk the of low-level, noncontroversial issues before them, states may be less likely to follow international law when it comes to matters that really impinge on state interests.[7] Those issues where strong state interests and international law are in stark opposition may not be common, but that is precisely where the effect of international law may be most at issue.[8] In these cases, international law may provide less constraint.[9]

In addition, some former officials noted that states, and in particular the United States, comply with their own *interpretation* of international law.[10] A state's own officials, therefore, may overstate their country's tendency to comply. Other states and outside observers might disagree with their assessment.

Moreover, because international law is so susceptible to ambiguity, the range of acceptable behavior is quite broad. Numerous former officials made

5 *See, e.g.*, Interview 8, Former Senior State Department Official; Interview 10, Former Assistant Secretary.

6 *See* Interview 8, *supra* note 5.

7 *See, e.g.*, Interview with Thomas McNamara, Assistant Secretary for Political-Military Affairs, Clinton administration, and Senior Advisor for Counter-Terrorism and Homeland Security to the Secretary of State, George W. Bush administration; Interview with Esther Brimmer, Assistant Secretary for International Organizations, Obama administration.

8 *Cf.* Interview 28, Former Official (speaking about the challenges of compliance with international law where there is no established regime (such as the WTO), especially in the case of failed states).

9 *See* discussion *infra* Section 3.2.2.1 (regarding the countervailing effect of national interest concerns on compliance). *See also* discussion *infra* Chapter 4 (regarding former officials' attitudes towards US compliance with international law when significant national interest is at issue).

10 *See* Interview 35, Former State Department Official; Interview 29, Former Assistant Secretary in a Republican Administration.

the point that the content of international law can be ambiguous and vague, especially compared to national law. Customary international law rules tend to be couched in general terms and may be contested, leaving much room for disagreement and interpretation. Though treaty provisions are generally more specific, they may not be precise and may be subject to varying interpretations. Interpretation of legal rules is usually left to states themselves. Often, states can make a colorable legal argument to support a variety of interpretations and policy positions.[11]

3.2 FACTORS THAT AFFECT COMPLIANCE

Former officials were asked several questions about the factors that favor state compliance with international law. Their responses were coded and assessed, in part, through the use of frequency counts. The top six factors most frequently mentioned that positively affect state compliance with international law were as follows:

- Reciprocity (for present purposes, the prospect of retaliation, generally or specifically, i.e., sticks)
- State interest in a stable legal and institutional system
- Reputation
- Ethical considerations, including ethical values underlying international law rules and respect for the rule of law
- Idiosyncratic
- Benefits flowing from participation in international regimes in general and specifically.

The following section examines these and other factors in greater detail. Several aspects of these results are notable. First, the dominant role ascribed to reciprocity and reputational costs suggests the dominance of factors common to rationalist theories of international law. Second, the prominent role given to ethical factors supports the idea that ethical concerns play a role in the calculation of officials regarding compliance, contrary to most rationalist theories. Third, the state interest in a stable legal and institutional international system highlights the prevailing view among these former officials in support of a rule-based, multilateral, world order.

Factors militating against compliance by states are also discussed. In the top six factors, national interest was the most frequently mentioned factor, followed

[11] *See* discussions *infra* Section 3.2.2.2 and *infra* Chapter 5 (discussing ambiguity of international law and resulting room for interpretation).

by the ambiguity of international law, the notion that some states just do not care about international law or have no interest in it states, the perception that compliance by some states is shallow, domestic political concerns, and sovereignty concerns. Several factors mentioned by former officials relate to domestic issues, including domestic legal and structural impediments, domestic budgetary concerns, and capacity issues in developing countries.

In essence, many former officials viewed compliance with international law in general and in specific circumstances as a cost–benefit, rational choice trade-off between the benefits of compliance and its costs. In this calculus, compliance with international law has an advantage, but may not always win out. Although policymakers take a cost–benefit approach, that approach does not fit neatly into a rationalist theoretical model as ethical issues play a significant role. The nature of the cost–benefit analysis followed by policymakers is discussed at the end of the section.

The interview transcripts were coded in response to the factors the subjects mentioned that favored or disfavored compliance with international law. Frequency counts in this study capture how many respondents cite certain factors unprompted in response to a general question. While they may reveal the most salient factors, they do not reveal respondents' explicit ranking of their relative significance.

The list of factors for coding was developed in the following way. An initial list of potential factors favoring or disfavoring compliance was developed by consulting the political science and international law literature regarding compliance.[12] That list was supplemented and modified during the course of coding by adding new or more specific factors mentioned by the subjects.

3.2.1 *Factors Favoring Compliance*

Table 3.1 lists the frequency of responses regarding factors that favor compliance with international law. The factors will be discussed essentially in order from higher frequency to lower frequency.

The list is not entirely surprising to those familiar with both the international relations and international law literature on compliance. For example, the responses highlight the roles of reciprocity and reputational concerns in encouraging compliance, both central factors in rationalist compliance theories. Other factors with prominent roles include maintaining a stable legal and institutional system (the second most frequently cited) and ethical factors (the fourth most cited). Diplomatic pressure, primarily but not

[12] *See infra* Chapter 2 for more detailed discussion of the compliance literature.

TABLE 3.1 *Factors favoring compliance*

	Respondents	Percentage
Reciprocity: general, unspecific	41	53.95
Self Interest: stable legal/int'l system	39	51.32
Reputation: general, unspecified	34	44.74
Ethics: general, nonspecific	30	39.47
Idiosyncratic	28	36.84
Self-interest: benefits of regime	28	36.84
Self-interest: states use law, institutions	21	27.63
Self-interest: membership in int'l society	20	26.32
Diplomatic pressure	19	25.00
Publicity, attention, awareness, shame	19	25.00
Self-interest: generally favors compliance	19	25.00
Domestic popular opinion	17	22.37
Compliance Mech: availability of interp/enforce encourages use	14	18.42
Interpretive guideline, constraint	12	15.79
Self-interest: general economic interest	12	15.79
Legitimacy	12	15.79
Self-interest: general, unspecified	12	15.79
Treaty: more important; formality	12	15.79
Self-interest: give smaller states leverage	11	14.47
Domestic politics (in favor)	11	14.47
Norms: shape state behavior	11	14.47
Coercion by powerful states	7	9.21
Habit and inertia	6	7.89
Inducement (specific)	5	6.58
Allies'/other states' view	5	6.58

exclusively exerted by powerful states on less powerful states, can also be a factor. The allure of membership in international society and international organizations also provides a motivation for leaders and states to comply with international law.

3.2.1.1 Reputation and Reciprocity

As illustrated in the first line of Table 3.1, forty-one of the former officials interviewed, or almost 54 percent, named reciprocity as a factor in favor of compliance. For the purposes of this project, reciprocity means concerns about reciprocal behavior by other states, primarily negative responses from other states, whether in response to a specific action or issue (specific reciprocity) or more generally across a range of issues (diffuse reciprocity).[13] Reciprocity includes the possibility of sanctions, potential use of force, the fear of prosecution for individuals, and general adverse consequences. Reciprocity also includes the notion that compliance begets compliance by others, that it is better "to go along to get along" with other states, and that maintaining good bilateral relations (e.g., with the United States) justifies compliance.

Related to reciprocity is the factor of inducements provided by other states to encourage compliance, often, or usually, to further the inducing state's self-interest (twenty-fourth on the list). One might include inducements in a broader conception of reciprocity, and certainly, inducements and reciprocity together represent the idea of "carrots" and "sticks." The notion of inducements includes financial or technical assistance, explicit cooperation on other issues, and maintaining or enhancing good relations with the United States.

Reputation is the third most cited reason for compliance.[14] Reputation consists not only of responses that broadly fall into that category but also includes sub-factors such as reputation connected to power status; reputation related to the desire to be a "player" among states; reputation for steadfastness, or threat credibility; reputation related to that of individuals within a government; maintaining a reputation for law-abiding behavior by avoiding criticism; reputation in the sense of internal legitimacy; and reputation for trustworthiness. Note that a related factor, "publicity, attention, awareness, shame," fell in the top ten responses, too, indicating that even greater weight should be given to reputation.

3.2.1.2 Maintaining the International Legal System

Former officials placed a high value on maintaining the international legal system, including international legal rules and international organizations. Accordingly, the second most frequently cited reason given for compliance with international law was to support the international legal and institutional system as a whole. Compliance, even if not in the short-term interest of a state,

[13] *See, e.g.*, Robert O. Keohane, *Reciprocity in International Relations*, 40 INT'L ORG. 1, 4 (1986).

[14] The table reflects the responses of former officials to the following question: former officials were asked the extent to which they thought international law constrains state behavior, how and why, or through what mechanisms, does it do so?

enhances the system and the long-term benefit of that state. National interests include the systemic interest of maintaining the system – certain constraints on action that appear limiting actually serve state interests for achieving collective goods, such as alliances and standards.[15] Noncompliance serves not only to undermine the rules directly but also may create a precedent for other states to violate rules and further degrade the system.

The former officials interviewed for this study often appeared to conflate international legal rules and international organizations and speak of them in one breath. While it may be useful analytically to distinguish between the effects of international law and the effects of international organizations on state compliance and state behavior, they are sometimes difficult to distinguish and disentangle. For one thing, international organizations are largely created through treaties and mechanisms of international law and employ international law rules in their operations; to an extent, international organizations are creatures of international law. Indeed, international relations scholars sometimes conflate international organizations and international rules in their definitions of international regimes and international institutions.[16] For purposes of this project, the terms "international regimes," "international institutions," and "international legal system" will include both international legal rules and international organizations, unless otherwise specified.

In essence, the former officials valued the multilateral, international legal, and institutional order, an order constructed after World War II under the leadership of the United States. It may not be surprising, therefore, that American officials continued to see the value of that legal order at the end of the twentieth century and into the second decade of the twenty-first century. They generally saw the international order as reflecting and furthering not only the interests of states in general but also the interests of the United States in particular.[17] Of course, attitudes in the Trump administration, and to some extent in the George W. Bush administration, shifted toward

[15] *See* Interview 36, Former Senior State Department Official.

[16] *See, e.g.*, John Duffield, *What Are International Institutions?*, 9 INT'L STUDIES REV. 1 (2007) (discussing definitions of international institutions, some including international organizations, some limited to rules); Lisa Martin & Beth Simmons, *International Organizations and Institutions*, *in* HANDBOOK OF INTERNATIONAL RELATIONS 326, 329 (Walter Carlsnaes et al., eds., 2d ed., 2012) ("While many find it convenient to use the word 'institution' to refer to both rules and organizations, for purposes of this essay we make a distinction between the two.") The term "international institution" seems to have overtaken the term "international regime" in the international relations literature, but they are now seen as essentially equivalent in meaning.

[17] *See infra* Chapter 6 (discussion regarding the liberal international order and the US interest in maintaining it).

a unilateral approach, but that shift in attitudes probably was not shared by career officials and Foreign Service Officers generally, as discussed in Chapter 6.

Many former officials stated specifically that having a structure of institutions to deal with problems contributes to the existence of a stable, prosperous, peaceful, and just world.[18] One former official said that without the international system, relations with states would be chaotic: You just do not run through a red light.[19] Thomas Pickering argued that collaboration is better than anarchy: States and officials have expectations of behavior and the ability to codify them is helpful.[20] Another former official echoed that point: Interdependence and interaction are better done with a set of rules.[21] That is, the world is more secure with a strong international order that contributes to peace and stability and would be less secure and more dangerous without one.

At least two former officials also emphasized the role of law in creating a just world.[22] Phyllis Oakley argued that the United States has promoted the rule of law for this purpose. In particular, she said that the United States has sought to prevent genocide and promote the prosecution of genocide, for example, in the Balkans and in the aftermath of Darfur.

The factor "state interest in a stable legal and institutional system" also breaks down into a number of subcategories. Collectively, the frequency with which these factors were cited indicates, again, the importance former officials placed on that interest. The main category and subcategories are listed in Table 3.2, along with the number or frequency of former officials who cited each factor.[23] Most are self-explanatory.

18 *See, e.g.*, Interview 2, Former Senior Official; Interview 15, Former Official; Interview 16, Former Assistant Secretary; Interview 27, Former Senior Obama State Department Official; Interview 1, Former Assistant Secretary; Interview with Anthony Quainton, Assistant Secretary for Diplomatic Security, Clinton administration; Interview with John Hillen, Assistant Secretary for Political-Military Affairs, George W. Bush administration.

19 *See* Interview 35, *supra* note 10.

20 See Interview with Thomas Pickering, Under Secretary for Political Affairs in the Clinton administration.

21 *See* Interview 15, *supra* note 18.

22 *See, e.g.*, Interview 2, *supra* note 18; Oakley Interview, *supra* note 2.

23 The number of respondents citing each factor is relatively small and the non-response rate is almost 50 percent. This is because Table 3.2 captures a subset of all the factors favoring compliance that respondents mentioned, and because respondents were responding to an open-ended question to which respondents gave different responses. Recall that that question was, how and why does international law constrain state behavior? Through what mechanisms? In order to check on the validity of the results, after about 90 percent of the interviews had been conducted, the responses to three similar questions were combined and

TABLE 3.2 *State interest in a stable international system*

	Frequency	Percentage	Percentage (valid)
Self Interest: stable legal/int'l system	18	23.68	46.15
Self-interest: powerful state interest in system	12	15.79	30.77
Self-interest: predictability	10	13.16	25.64
Self-interest: value of int'l institutions	7	9.21	17.95
Self-interest: allows accommodation, to mutual benefit	7	9.21	17.95
Self-interest: peace	4	5.26	10.26
Self-interest: system encourages states to comply	4	5.26	10.26
Self-interest: community interest in everyone complying	2	2.63	5.13
Self-interest: greases state interaction	0	0.00	0.00
DOCUMENTS with code(s)	39	51.32	100.00
DOCUMENTS without code(s)	37	48.68	–
ANALYZED DOCUMENTS	76	100.00	–

These subcategories complement, or further specify, the main category and some may overlap.

As indicated in Table 3.2, some former officials also separately and explicitly cited predictability as a benefit of the international legal system for all states. One former official stated that international rules make state behavior orderly: The rules you follow, and hope others do, provide predictability and consistency.[24] Thus, states can have some confidence that regimes will persist.

Other former officials highlighted the interest of maintaining peace. The international system may help states avoid bumbling into a war, with huge costs in lives and treasure. Because of their history, European states in

the analysis re-run. The three questions were (1) how and why does international law constrain state behavior?; (2) why do foreign states comply, or not, with international law?; and (3) why does the United States comply, or not, with international law? The combination of responses yielded larger frequencies and a better response rate. The results of this second analysis were very similar, with most factors in roughly the same order. The results of the second analysis are not included here because the three questions had different purposes and the study attempts to isolate here the responses to the first and broadest question. The foregoing analysis also applies to the results in Table 3.3.

24 *See* Interview 16, *supra* note 18.

particular may value the role of international law and institutions in avoiding war, and so may be more concerned about violations that undermine them.[25]

One subcategory in Table 3.2 speaks to the vested interest of powerful states, such as the United States, in the international legal and institutional system.[26] By promoting stability, predictability, order, and peace, it benefits big powers, who see the *status quo* reflecting their position on top and serving their interest in the global system. They see danger in unpredictability and relative chaos, which could lead to downturns in the global economy, to conflicts that may ensnare them, and to other disruptions that may cost them blood and treasure. In addition, as discussed below, all states and especially big powers can use international law and institutions to pursue their own ends.

Tom Shannon, former Under Secretary of Political Affairs, asserted that with power comes responsibility. As a power that is part of the ordering force in the world, creating predictability is an advantage because it promotes peaceful resolution and pacific behavior. This is an advantage to a great power like the United States because it can only deal with so many threats and issues. It is better to deal with the most important and leave less important issues to others, instead of maintaining order only through the direct application of power. Also, a great power does not want to open itself to challenge if it does not have to.[27]

Another cluster of subcategories in Table 3.2 relates to the facilitating role of the international legal system and its institutions. That is, former officials noted that the international legal system allows accommodation to mutual benefit, provides a community interest in everyone complying, and greases state interaction. States need a basis for international contracts, a system in which to speak on common ground.

Returning to Table 3.1, other factors cited by the former officials as reasons for compliance are related to the benefits of maintaining a stable legal and institutional system. They include the importance of benefits provided by regimes (the fifth most frequently cited factor overall in Table 3.1), the notion that states use law and institutions for their own ends (the seventh most frequently cited factor), and the desirability of membership in international society, often represented by membership in international organizations (the eighth most frequently cited factor).

[25] *See* Interview with Brian Atwood, Under Secretary of State for Management, Clinton administration; Administrator, USAID, Clinton administration.

[26] *See, e.g.*, Interview with Thomas Shannon, Under Secretary for Political Affairs, Obama and Trump administrations; McNamara Interview, *supra* note 7.

[27] Shannon Interview, *supra* note 26.

TABLE 3.3 *Regime benefits*

	Frequency	Percentage	Percentage (valid)
Self-interest: benefits of regime	14	18.42	50.00
Self-interest: Isolation potential	10	13.16	35.71
Self-interest: tool for collective action	6	7.89	21.43
Self-interest: use against violators	5	6.58	17.86
Self-interest: corral rogue regimes	1	1.32	3.57
Self-interest: dispute resolution as a benefit	1	1.32	3.57
Self-interest: create credible commitment	0	0.00	0.00
DOCUMENTS with code(s)	28	36.84	100.00
DOCUMENTS without code(s)	48	63.16	–
ANALYZED DOCUMENTS	76	100.00	–

Table 3.3 shows a breakdown of factors under the general category of the importance of benefits provided by regimes.

In general, realizing the goals and purposes of specific regimes provides a benefit to states. The benefit of an arms control agreement, for example, is achieving some restriction on the use or stockpiling of weaponry. A related and more specific benefit is providing a tool for collective action to achieve regime aims to overcome the difficulties of collaboration. Another benefit is the capability to enforce rules against violators to corral rogue regimes and to isolate them. Yet another potential benefit, as indicated in Table 3.1, is the provision of dispute resolution or enforcement mechanisms: The threat and availability of enforcement action encourage compliance with international law.

A number of former officials asserted that states also value international law and institutions because they can use them as vehicles for pursuing state interests. Philip Zelikow, former Counselor to the State Department and Professor at George Mason University, stated that states use the procedures and practices of international law and organizations to achieve their aims, such as in trade or to initiate sanctions.[28] To do so, however, they have to follow the accepted rules and practices, he said. Big powers, including the United States, may be in the best position to take advantage of the system in

[28] *See* Interview with Philip Zelikow, Counselor to the State Department, George W. Bush administration.

this way – one former official asserted that states can use the international system as a tool of power if they have it.[29] But less powerful states, in addition to pursuing other goals, may seek to use the international legal and institutional system to constrain big powers.[30] Having the support of international law, moreover, can strengthen a state's argument or position within the international community.[31]

One can think about state use of international law cynically: States use international law for their own ends and do not comply when it is not in their interest. Some former officials offered this perspective. Or, one can think about this in a more positive way: International law's utility makes it valuable, providing a mechanism for collective action and rallying allies and, therefore, encouraging states to comply.[32]

Some former officials cited examples in which the United States sought successfully to use international law and institutions to achieve a foreign policy goal. One former official, Arthur Dewey, recalled that "even under Reagan," the United Nations was used "for everything," such as addressing humanitarian disasters.[33] The State Department would be told to "fix it" and, in turn, would work through the United Nations to do just that. Granted, the United States had influence within the United Nations in good measure because of the level of its contributions. Another former official echoed Tom Shannon's point earlier, stating that after the Cold War, the United States did not want to be the world's policeman and relied on the United Nations to perform that role so that the United States did not have to.[34]

Sometimes, the tools of law and diplomacy can be an alternative to the use of force, highlighting the importance of having international law available for use as a tool of statecraft in diplomacy. One former official, Thomas McNamara,[35] gave the example of the United States' response to Libya after the Lockerbie bombing, a response that he helped develop.[36] In his view, a

[29] *See* McNamara Interview, *supra* note 7.

[30] *See* discussion *infra* Section 3.3 regarding the factors states other than the United States take into consideration regarding compliance.

[31] *See, e.g.*, Interview with Alexander Watson, Assistant Secretary for Western Hemisphere Affairs, Clinton administration.

[32] *See* Interview 10, *supra* note 5.

[33] See Interview with Arthur "Gene" Dewey, Assistant Secretary for Population, Refugees, and Migration in the George W. Bush administration.

[34] *See* Interview 31, Former State Department Officer and Career Senior Diplomat.

[35] See McNamara Interview, *supra* note 7.

[36] *See also* Thomas E. McNamara, *Unilateral and Multilateral Strategies against State Sponsors of Terror: A Case Study of Libya, 1979 to 2003*, *in* UNITING AGAINST TERROR: COOPERATIVE NONMILITARY RESPONSES TO THE GLOBAL TERRORIST THREAT 83, 100–105 (David Cortright & George A. Lopez, eds., 2007).

military option would not have been productive: Allies might have opposed it, especially those in Southern Europe who obtained petroleum from Libya. The other option, pursued successfully, was to make use of international law to obtain UN resolutions and sanctions against Libya. This successful strategy, among other things, resulted in the Security Council's first chapter VII resolution on terrorism.[37]

Another example involved the efforts of the Bush and Obama administrations to obtain support for UN sanctions against Iran for its nuclear efforts, as recounted by a former official.[38] These ultimately led to a diplomatic solution embodied in the Iran Nuclear Deal[39] and affirmed by Security Council resolution[40] as an alternative to military action. Thus, even beyond addressing specific issues or crises, the use of UN resolutions is a way to create international law on important security issues, the former official said.

Maintaining the benefits of the international legal system provides reasons to comply with related international legal rules. Violating the rules may jeopardize the interest in predictability and stability provided by a particular regime or by international law more generally.[41] Weakening that system by violating legal rules, or creating precedents that may be used against a state in the future, moreover, weakens the system's long-term utility for that state. Violators of international law may have a harder time using international law to their advantage.[42] In addition, one former official indicated that the systemic interest could be particularly strong when tied to an organization, for example, the United Nations, or, for European countries, European institutions.[43] Noncompliance in this case may undermine or damage the institution. In terms of US interest, a former official put it well: The United States benefits from the international legal structure, so going outside that structure weakens it and may have other consequences the state does not want to bear.[44]

37 *Id.*, at 104.

38 *See* Interview 14, Former State Department Official.

39 *See* Joint Comprehensive Plan of Action, U.S. Dep't of State (July 14, 2015), http://www.state.gov/documents/organization/245317.pdf (http://perma.cc/9DBJ-XEX4).

40 S.C. Res. 2231, UN Doc. S/RES/2231 (July 20, 2015), *available at* http://unscr.com/en/resolutions/doc/2231.

41 *See, e.g.*, Interview 20, Former Official; Brimmer Interview *supra* note 7; Interview 26, Former Official.

42 *See, e.g.*, Interview with Robert Gallucci, Assistant Secretary for Political-Military Affairs, Clinton administration (one reason for a state not to violate a treaty is that it makes it harder to use as a rationale for a state's own action).

43 *See* Interview 20, *supra* note 41.

44 *See* Brimmer Interview, *supra* note 7.

Systemic interests must be weighed against the advantages of violating or stretching a rule in a particular instance, to make an exception. The trade-off is between protecting the integrity of the system and the pressures of national interest or political reality in a particular case.[45] For example, when the George W. Bush administration concluded a nuclear cooperation deal with India, the trade-off was between standing by the Non-Proliferation Treaty, for fear that it would unravel, and engaging with India, a big country that the United States did not want to isolate[46] and that served as a counterweight to China. At least one former official cautioned that the systemic interest was "the least concern" when considering policy options.[47]

3.2.1.3 Normative Factors

The fourth most frequently cited factor favoring compliance related to ethics or normative concerns, primarily the ethical underpinnings of various international law rules and respect for the rule of law more generally. Former officials were also asked explicitly about the extent to which they thought normative considerations (ethical, moral) play a role in compliance and were provided the response options of none, some, and a lot.

- only 2, or roughly 3 percent of valid responses said none
- 53, or 80 percent of valid responses, said some
- 1, or roughly 17 percent of valid responses, said a lot.

Thus, over 97 percent responded that normative considerations played at least some role in driving compliance with international law.[48]

This result reveals the prominent role of ethical concerns but is even more significant given the theoretical dispute between rationalist and normative views of international law and compliance discussed in the literature review chapter, Chapter 2.[49] In brief, the rationalist view holds that only interests shape state action, and to the extent norms do exist, they serve states in obtaining their interests. Once norms no longer serve state interests, they are discarded. The normative view, in contrast, posits that norms may shape not only state action but also may shape state perception of interests.

The results of this study provide support for the normative view, demonstrating some role for ethical considerations in making decisions about

[45] *See* Interview 16, *supra* note 18.
[46] *See id.*
[47] *See* Interview 26, *supra* note 41.
[48] Ten interviews had no responses.
[49] *See infra* Chapter 2.

compliance with international law. A more difficult question to address is the weight of normative considerations in decision-making relative to state interests. The study did not address that question in depth. For the 17 percent of former officials who indicated that ethical factors were given a lot of weight in decision-making, we might assume that the relative role of ethical factors was substantial. But for the 67 percent who responded that ethical factors carried some weight, the answer is not so clear. Several former officials mentioned that in comparison to state interest, ethical considerations were secondary.

Former officials did discuss, however, various specific, ethical, and normative factors that they considered significant in encouraging compliance. The ten most frequently mentioned factors were as follows:

- Idiosyncratic: History, culture
- Ethics: intrinsic to norms
- Ethics: respect rule of law
- Ethics: general, nonspecific
- Reputation: appearance of good citizenship
- Ethics: of individuals
- International law reflects ideas of good behavior
- Self-interest: Costs to violating ethical rules/benefits to complying
- Norms shape state behavior
- Reciprocity
- Ethics: keep promises
- US created norms: interest in maintaining.[50]

The first five factors cited are the most significant. "Idiosyncratic: history, culture" refers to the idea that certain states may comply to a greater or lesser degree with international law because of their history and cultural background. Within that category, some former officials' comments fell into several subcategories, including one regarding the propensity of liberal states, and the United States specifically, to respect the rule of law, and one regarding the effect of the ethics of individual leaders on state behavior.

A significant number of former officials expressed the idea that liberal states – those states featuring a democratic political system based on the rule of law – were more likely than others to comply with international law rules because of that liberal tradition. Some officials linked the liberal tradition primarily to Western states. And some suggested that non-liberal states were not particularly interested in complying with international law. A significant

[50] There are more than ten because of ties in the frequency counts. Some responses were not included because they were reasons mitigating against the application of ethics.

number of former officials asserted that the United States was likely to comply with international law for various ethical reasons, such as belief in the rule of law, or belief in human rights.

"Ethics: intrinsic to norms" refers to the pull toward compliance of the ethical norms underlying legal rules. That is, one reason for compliance with a particular legal rule may be the appeal of the ethical content of that rule. Rules of human rights law are primary examples of this dynamic. In results not shown here, this category is broken down further into several subcategories, including human rights (when mentioned explicitly), well-being of people, and peace.

Respect for the rule of law *per se* was also mentioned by former officials as a reason for compliance. Indeed, respect for the rule of law is an ethical value itself. Another factor mentioned by former officials was an incentive for ethical behavior: the reputational value of keeping up the appearance of good ethical behavior, or good citizenship.

Norms, however, are subject to change. As a senior former State Department Official in the Obama administration put it, speaking of international law and norms more generally, the whole system works if people decide that it should, implying that if people and states fail to follow the norm, the norm can fall apart. The United States, for example, sees itself as a rule of law country and transposes that attitude to international law. That official drew an analogy with the force of domestic norms governing presidential action, which waned under the Trump administration.[51]

3.2.1.4 Additional Factors Favoring Compliance

As described in Table 3.1, former officials mentioned numerous additional factors favoring compliance, of which the following are the most notable. Diplomatic pressure, primarily but not exclusively exerted by powerful states on less powerful states, can also be a factor. Diplomatic pressure may be exerted by states or by the UN or its agencies. For example, states and the United Nations may bring diplomatic pressure to bear to urge compliance with human rights law, either separately or in tandem.

Former officials also cited the desire of many states for membership in international society and international organizations, or maintenance of good standing in the club, as a motivation for leaders and states to comply with international law. Not only can membership enhance credibility for states and their leaders, it can also provide a seat at the table and an opportunity to be heard.

[51] *See* Interview 18, Former Obama administration Senior State Department Official.

TABLE 3.4 *Factors militating against compliance*

	Frequency	Percentage	Percentage (valid)
Con: self or national interest, other	16	21.05	37.21
Con: interpretation or facts ambiguous	14	18.42	32.56
Con: no interest/do not care	11	14.47	25.58
Con: shallow compliance (e.g., sign only)	9	11.84	20.93
Con: domestic politics	8	10.53	18.60
Con: sovereignty concerns	6	7.89	13.95
Con: domestic law also/more constraining/takes precedence	4	5.26	9.30
Con: low cost for noncompliance	3	3.95	6.98
Con: capacity	3	3.95	6.98
Con: domestic law complications in application of IL	2	2.63	4.65
Con: rationalization about circumstances	1	1.32	2.33
Con: funding/budgeting difficulties	0	0.00	0.00
Con: second-order consequences	0	0.00	0.00
DOCUMENTS with code(s)	43	56.58	100.00
DOCUMENTS without code(s)	33	43.42	–
ANALYZED DOCUMENTS	76	100.00	–

3.2.2 *Factors Militating against Compliance*

The former officials also cited numerous factors militating against compliance by states with international law, as reflected in Table 3.4.

Among the top six factors, national interest was the most frequently mentioned factor, followed by the ambiguity of international law, the notion that some states (i.e., rogue states) just do not care about international law or have no interest in it, the perception that compliance by some states is shallow, domestic political concerns, and sovereignty concerns. Several other factors mentioned by former officials relate to domestic issues, including domestic legal and structural impediments, domestic budgetary concerns, and capacity issues in developing countries. The effect of these factors and others are discussed in more detail in the following text.

3.2.2.1 National Interest

The dominant factors militating against compliance relate to concerns about national interest being balanced against international law when the two conflict. In essence, many former officials viewed compliance with international law in general and in specific circumstances as a cost–benefit, rational choice trade-off between the benefits of compliance and its costs, or disadvantages. The nature of that trade-off will be discussed after first describing the factors former officials identified that militate against compliance.

The top-ranked factor in Table 3.4, "Con: self or national interest," directly captures the concern with national interest. That factor, or category, also contains a number of sub-factors not listed in Table 3.4, including "National security," "Big powers comply only in national interest," and "US Superpower exceptionalism." These sub-factors seem self-explanatory, except for US exceptionalism, the idea that the United States is an exceptional power because of its superpower status or leadership role in the world and should not always be bound by international law.[52] That factor is obviously unique to the United States, although it is related to the notion that big powers comply only when it is in their national interest. Other factors in the table also relate to national interest, so that broad national interest concerns may be even more significant when considered collectively. The related factors include "Sovereignty concerns," and states that have "No interest/do not care" about international law – that is, rogue states.

3.2.2.2 Ambiguity

As discussed in Chapter 2, another factor that works against compliance is the ambiguity of much international law. This ambiguity allows states appreciable "wiggle room" for interpretation and discretion in the application of international law.[53] One former official stated that law has interpretive elements in general and that international law is not black and white because much is in a gray, interpretive zone.[54]

Accordingly, international law and its application can be subject to dispute, allowing states significant discretion in the application – or evasion – of international law rules. States can often make colorable legal arguments to support their preferred policy positions and national interests. One former official put it a slightly different way. Because much international law is subject to interpretation, there might be a range of options available to

[52] The notion of US exceptionalism is explained further in Chapter 4, which addresses in greater detail US compliance with international law.

[53] *See, e.g.*, Interview 8, *supra* note 5; Interview 18, *supra* note 51; Pickering Interview, *supra* note 20; Interview 28, *supra* note 8; Interview 2, *supra* note 18; Interview 35, *supra* note10.

[54] *See* Interview 28, *supra* note 8.

policymakers, some of which might be more or less in compliance. Compliance may represent a choice among shades of gray.[55]

At the best of times, the application of international law is hardly cut and dried, one former official indicated: For example, different states sign on to different treaties or parts of treaties (e.g., the ILO Convention), or some treaty provisions codify custom and some do not, as in the case of the Law of the Sea Treaty.[56] Another former official said that international law is so esoteric and that plenty of countries do not realize they have a problem with international law until they are "cross-wise" with it.[57]

In addition, governments, and government officials, seem inclined to believe or adopt an interpretation favorable to their state. This is a subtly different point from the point that states sometimes intentionally manipulate interpretations of international law to conform to state interest. Perhaps it verges on a simplistic psychological assessment, but people generally like to believe that their side operates legally and ethically. One former US official observed that while others may think that the United States is violating international law, we do not necessarily think so.[58] Former officials mentioned the reaction of other states' officials, faced with assertions that their states had violated international law, who claimed that their state faced special considerations or that exceptions should apply.[59]

3.2.2.3 Additional Factors

In addition, some former officials noted, compliance with international law obligations may be shallow.[60] States may sign treaties to gain the reputational advantages of doing so without the intention of actually or effectively implementing them into domestic law or complying with them when potential violations arise. As one former official put it, many states have an interest to

[55] *See* Interview 36, *supra* note 15.

[56] *See* Interview 18, *supra* note 51; Constitution of the International Labour Organisation, Apr. 1, 1919, 49 Stat. 2712, 225 C.T.I.A. 373 (entered into force: 28 June 1919); United Nations Convention on the Law of the Sea, Dec. 10, 1982, 1833 U.N.T.S. 3, 21 I.L.M. 1261 (entered into force 16 Nov. 1994).

[57] *See* Interview 11, Assistant Secretary in the Bush administration.

[58] *See* Interview 35, *supra* note 10.

[59] *See* Interview 31, *supra* note 34; Interview 26, *supra* note 41; Zelikow Interview, *supra* note 28.

[60] *See, e.g.*, Interview 36, *supra* note 15; Interview 19, Former Assistant Secretary, Trump administration; Interview with Melvyn Levitsky, Assistant Secretary for International Narcotics Matters, George H. W. Bush administration, Clinton administration; Interview with Joan Spero, Under Secretary for Foreign and Agricultural Affairs, Clinton administration.

become free riders on the system and to not fully fulfill the commitments they have made.[61]

Some factors in the list relate to domestic issues, including not only domestic politics and domestic public opinion but also capacity issues in developing countries and domestic legal and structural impediments. Former officials often cited domestic legal and structural impediments when speaking of the United States. They spoke of the limits imposed by federalism, of funding inadequacies and bureaucratic budget constraints and red tape, and of occasional bureaucratic opposition in interagency discussions. In a related vein, the former officials spoke of the primacy of domestic law, both in the sense of trumping international law rules or norms in conflict with domestic law, and in terms of commanding the focus of policymakers compared to international law.[62]

3.2.3 *Cost–Benefit*

About one-third of former officials explicitly suggested that decisions about compliance with international law, or the extent or nature of that compliance, involved a cost–benefit calculus. That calculus might consist of a comparison of the benefits versus costs of compliance, or might involve a balance of many considerations along with legal considerations. The calculus would not necessarily be limited to short-term, hard interests but could include long-term systemic interests and moral considerations.

As one former official stated, there is a range of considerations for any government: A mix of political, economic, strategic, diplomatic, ethical, and legal considerations that all must be balanced in different directions.[63] Another former official, for example, declared that broadly speaking, states operated on the basis of self-interest, whether economic, political, or moral.[64] The question is whether there are other interests so serious that supersede the value and benefits of complying with international law. This is not at all to say that international law is treated lightly or routinely ignored. Chapter 4 discusses in greater detail the considerations and the weight given to them, in the calculations of US officials and the ways in which tensions between international law and other issues might be resolved.

61 *See* Interview 36, *supra* note 15.
62 *See* discussion *infra* Chapter 4.
63 *See* Interview 20, *supra* note 41.
64 *See* Interview with John Holum, Under Secretary for Arms Control and International Security, Clinton administration.

3.3 OTHER STATES

When asked specifically about the reasons other states (not the United States) comply with international law, the former officials' responses differed from their responses regarding factors favoring compliance of states in general. Table 3.5 lists the top twenty-five factors they cited favoring compliance in other countries.

Recall that the top ten factors cited favoring compliance[65] by states in general:

- Reciprocity
- Self Interest: stable legal/int'l system
- Reputation
- Ethics
- Idiosyncratic
- Self-interest: benefits of regime
- Self-interest: states use law, institutions
- Self-interest: Membership in int'l society
- Diplomatic pressure.

One significant conclusion from this comparison is that the former officials' perception of the behavior of other states focuses more on their response to carrots and sticks than on more systemic or altruistic motivations, such as an interest in a stable international system or ethical concerns. Perhaps that perception simply reflects reality: Less powerful countries may be more susceptible to pressure than big powers; big powers must have other reasons for compliance. But one wonders whether government officials from other countries might take a more charitable view toward their own motivations.

Of course, "other states" is an overbroad category, containing not only small, weaker states but also large or powerful states and every kind of state in-between. Former officials recognized distinctions between different kinds of states, especially between powerful and less powerful states. Two factors highlight the attractions of international law and institutions for smaller states. First, former officials said, the international legal system gives states leverage over bigger states, leveling the playing field. That is, international legal arguments may be used to constrain the behavior of larger states. Second, membership in the international "club" means a lot in terms of reputation, legitimacy, and prestige, for both states and their leaders. As a result, smaller states may be willing to comply in order to achieve or maintain that

[65] *See* Table 3.1, *supra*.

TABLE 3.5 *Factors favoring compliance: other states*

	Documents	Percentage	Percentage (valid)
Diplomatic pressure	32	42.11	45.71
Reciprocity: general, unspecific	31	40.79	44.29
Inducement	29	38.16	41.43
Idiosyncratic: other	25	32.89	35.71
Reputation: general, unspecified	23	30.26	32.86
Self-interest: stable legal/int'l system	22	28.95	31.43
Self-interest: membership in int'l society	22	28.95	31.43
Self-interest: smaller state leverage	19	25.00	27.14
Self-interest: states use law, institutions	16	21.05	22.86
Self-interest: benefits of regime	16	21.05	22.86
Coerced by powerful states	13	17.11	18.57
Ethics: general, nonspecific	11	14.47	15.71
Self-interest: general, unspecified	11	14.47	15.71
Self-interest: generally in favor compliance	10	13.16	14.29
Publicity, attention, awareness, shame	10	13.16	14.29
Ethics: respect rule of law	9	11.84	12.86
Self-interest: general economic interest	9	11.84	12.86
Domestic popular opinion.	6	7.89	8.57
Cost/benefit in general	6	7.89	8.57
Legitimacy of rule	5	6.58	7.14
Domestic politics (in favor)	5	6.58	7.14
Norms: shape behavior	3	3.95	4.29
Allies' view	3	3.95	4.29
Compliance mech: availability interpretation/enforcement encourages use	3	3.95	4.29

membership. Large states with control over club membership (the Co-op Board of International Affairs, as it were), may use the prospect of membership as a carrot or stick to entice compliant behavior.

Chapter 4 addresses the reasons that the United States takes into consideration regarding compliance with international law. Some observations are relevant here, however, in order to compare the views of former officials regarding states in general, other states, and the United States. The former officials' responses largely tracked the factors they listed for states in general, with a few notable exceptions. Ethical concerns played a more substantial role for the United States than for states in general, their responses indicated. Perhaps American policymakers are more likely to ascribe ethical behavior to the United States, as opposed to other countries. In a similar vein, policymakers highlighted the notion of US exceptionalism and moral responsibility, in part a responsibility for leadership, as factors favoring compliance with international law. They also pointed out the significance of treaty obligations and the importance of adhering to them in the American context.

3.4 AREAS OF LAW IN WHICH COMPLIANCE IS MORE OR LESS LIKELY

Former officials were also asked whether countries are more or less likely to comply with international law in different issue areas. There were limited responses to the question, largely because there were time constraints in many of the interviews, restricting their scope. Thirty nine out of seventy-six former officials addressed this topic, and some of those did not provide comprehensive answers. The views presented, moreover, tended to be US centric, often focusing on US behavior. The results are similar to the results presented in Chapter 4 regarding responses to questions asking for examples of the United States stretching the boundaries of international law and, conversely, taking a scrupulous or even expansive view of compliance of its international law obligations.[66]

From the specific responses provided, the clear view was that the least likely issue area for state compliance was national security. The most likely issue areas for state compliance were trade and other areas of economic law. Other areas mentioned where compliance was more likely were environment and resources, humanitarian law, arms control, law enforcement, and cooperative arrangements such as aviation agreements and postal unions. Overall, as discussed below in more depth, the responses provided some support for instrumentalist explanations regarding compliance with international law.

Around seventeen former officials mentioned national security as an area in which states, in general, and the United States, in particular, were less likely to comply with international law. Some extended that observation to areas in which a state's vital interests more broadly were at issue. Many of these comments might best be summed up in the words of Robert Gallucci, who said that, at the end of the day, there was no case related to national security where the United States went against its own interest because of international

[66] *See* discussion *infra* Chapter 4.

law. The further away an issue is from a vital interest, the more likely it is that policy is determined by international law, the closer to national security, less so.[67]

One or two former officials cautioned, however, that international law still played a role in the national security area. As discussed below, several former officials asserted that areas related to security, arms control, and humanitarian law stood out as areas of greater compliance. Compliance in these areas could be explained through the operation of reciprocity, and normative concerns could also be involved in compliance with humanitarian law, but the point still stands that security issues may not be immune to legal constraints. In addition, as one former official pointed out, both George W. Bush and Obama "did cartwheels" to get UN resolutions against Iran in an effort to create international law on important security issues.[68]

On the other side of the ledger, twenty former officials mentioned trade as an area in which states, including the United States, are more likely to comply with international law. Several more cited economic law generally, apparently including trade law, but also mentioned commercial law, banking, and finance.

Former officials gave various reasons for the assertion that states were more likely to comply in these areas. It is in states' mutual interest to comply with trade law because of the overall benefits from the trading system.[69] Economic powers, moreover, stand to gain the most from the trading system, one former official said.[70] Indeed, until the Trump administration, the United States saw itself as the driving force in the creation of the international trading system, as having an interest in maintaining it.[71] The availability of a dispute resolution and sanctions system also militates in favor of compliance.[72] In the face of third-party interpretation and potential sanctions, there are costs to noncompliance.

These conclusions about trade have been brought into doubt in the last few years, however, partly because of the Trump administration's trade policies and increased conflict over trade rules and institutions. As discussed more fully

67 Gallucci Interview, *supra* note 42.
68 *See* Interview 14, *supra* note 38.
69 *See, e.g.*, Interview 13, Assistant Secretary in the George W. Bush administration.
70 *See* Interview 14, *supra* note 38.
71 *See id.*; Interview 17, Assistant Secretary, George H. W. Bush administration (the United States advocated binding dispute resolution decision from the beginning of the Uruguay Round).
72 *See, e.g.*, Interview 14, *supra* note 38; Interview 31, *supra* note 34; Tauscher Interview, *supra* note 3; Interview 13, *supra* note 69.

in Chapter 6, the Trump administration took significant steps to weaken the international trade regime. The Biden administration, however, has continued many of the Trump administration's policies. Indeed, most of the interviews were recorded before these difficulties developed in the global trading system, so it is possible that views on trade might have shifted.

The increased skepticism about trade may turn out to vindicate the views of handful of former officials who believed that the trade area does not necessarily experience better compliance than others.[73] Some of these officials were interviewed after the Trump administration came to office, so were aware of pending trade conflicts. Former Under Secretary Tom Shannon, for example, said that trade may be the toughest area because the consequences of compliance are immediate.[74]

Some former officials mentioned other areas where compliance was more likely. Several mentioned humanitarian law and arms control. The rationale seemed to be that both areas were enforced by reciprocity, by the fear of reciprocal retaliation. Several asserted that the United States took its arms control obligations very seriously, as discussed in Chapter 4. Arms control involves many technical rules, with which compliance is straightforward, and often contains verification procedures, which also enhance compliance.[75]

Other areas mentioned included environmental and resource management, the Law of the Sea, narcotics and law enforcement, aviation law, and postal unions. Compliance in regard to postal unions and aviation can be seen as self-interested because those regimes provide coordination rules that facilitate a mutually beneficial arrangement, which, at the same time, does not require much sacrifice.[76]

In general, the responses regarding areas of greater and lesser compliance provide some support for instrumentalist explanations of compliance. Some former officials provided their own overall explanations for these results along these lines. Broadly speaking, some former officials asserted that countries tend to comply in areas that do not affect significant national interests and are less likely to comply in areas that do affect the national interest.[77] They also highlighted issue areas that lent themselves to reciprocity, such as trade, arms

[73] *See, e.g.*, Interview 18, *supra* note 51; Shannon Interview, *supra* note 26; Brimmer Interview, *supra* note 7; Interview with Herman "Hank" Cohen, Assistant Secretary for African Affairs, George H. W. Bush administration.

[74] *See* Shannon Interview, *supra* note 26.

[75] *See* Interview 36, *supra* note 15.

[76] *See id.*

[77] *See, e.g.*, Interview 32, Assistant Secretary in the Obama administration; Gallucci Interview, *supra* note 42.

control, and humanitarian law, areas where treaty regimes were clear or comprehensive, areas where third-party dispute resolution or assistance was available, and areas where regimes provided the benefits of coordination at little cost, such as postal unions. Overwhelmingly, former officials spoke of compliance as the result of a cost–benefit analysis on the part of states, of measuring state interests against the constraints imposed by international law.

Nevertheless, officials provided some significant caveats to these conclusions. Some factors like the existence of compliance mechanisms and the clarity of obligations may comport with normative theories or with both camps. Law may play a role even in the national security area, or other areas of high politics. And other responses indicate that legal and normative forces play a significant role in compliance. Recall the overwhelming view expressed by former officials about the significance of ethical factors. Ethical factors play a role in policymakers' cost–benefit analysis.

3.5 VARIATIONS IN PERCEPTION ABOUT COMPLIANCE AMONG FORMER OFFICIALS: KEY VARIABLES

Variations in views about compliance and other matters existed among the former officials. Of course, much of the variation was probably due to differences in personal background, views, and temperament. But some of the variation was also due to several predictable factors, revealed through analysis of the data and the insights of the participants. Differences in political affiliation affected their views: Officials appointed by Democratic presidents expressed a stronger belief that international law affects state action than officials appointed by Republican presidents. In spite of this difference, it is important to stress that both groups expressed overall confidence in the constraining effect of international law.

Similarly, analysis of the data showed that views about compliance differed by presidential administration, too. In their comments, former officials noted differences in culture and processes – not just in political preference – between different administrations, and sometimes even among different terms of the same administration. They noted the effect of the different mix of people in different administrations, and particularly the effect of the personalities and preferences of the most senior officials. A number of former officials noted the effect of changes in attitudes about international law over time, providing the specific example of changes in attitudes about human rights following the Carter and Reagan administrations.

Competing bureaucratic interests within the State Department could also affect the views of individuals about compliance with international law.

TABLE 3.6 *Effect of international law by presidential party*

Does IL Constrain? × Presidential Party (frequencies; column percentages)	Democrat	Republican	Total
Yes	25 (78.1)	20 (47.6)	45 (60.8)
Maybe/sometimes	5 (15.6)	21 (50.0)	26 (35.1)
No	2 (6.3)	1 (2.4)	3 (4.1)
Total	32 (100.0)	42 (100.0)	74 (100.0)

Functional bureaus, especially those more oriented to international law like Democracy, Human Rights, and Labor, might have different views from regional bureaus more inclined to take the position of those in their client states. One promising premise did not pan out: At least in the frequency counts, career Foreign Service Officers did not have a more positive attitude toward international law than noncareer appointees.

3.5.1 *Differences in Political Affiliation*

Officials appointed by Democratic presidents expressed a stronger belief that international law affects state action than officials appointed by Republican presidents. The difference was reflected in responses to the question whether former officials thought that international law constrained states. Their responses were coded into the categories of yes, sometimes or maybe, and no (Table 3.6).

As we can see, officials appointed by Democratic presidents were more likely than officials appointed by Republican presidents to believe that international law constrains states, as opposed to sometimes or maybe constraining states. This result is statistically significant[78] and conforms to expectations: We would expect more "Democratic" officials to have internationalist, multilateral perspective than "Republican" officials because the two parties differ as a whole along those lines. While these results were striking and robust, it is important to note that overall, both Republican appointees and Democratic appointees consistently and uniformly indicated that international law constrained state behavior. All but one of the Republican appointees and two of

[78] These differences according to political affiliation are significant, with a p value less than .01 (.008). A Cramer's V analysis shows the result to be moderately strong. Caveat: the results may not be completely accurate because two of the cells have counts of less than 5.

TABLE 3.7 *Frequency of state compliance*

States Comply Most of the Time?	Democrat	Republican	Total
Most of the time	21 (72.4)	20 (47.6)	41 (57.7)
Some of the time	8 (27.6)	20 (47.6)	28 (39.4)
Rarely	0 (0.0)	1 (2.4)	1 (1.4)
Never	0 (0.0)	1 (2.4)	1 (1.4)
Total	29 (100.0)	42 (100.0)	71 (100.0)

the Democratic appointees said that international law constrained states most or some of the time.

In response to another question, namely, whether they believed that most states comply with international law most of the time, Democratic officials appeared more likely to say that states complied most of the time than some of the time than Republicans (Table 3.7).

These results were not as robust as the results from the previous question and were not statistically significant.[79] When asked about the extent to which the United States complied with international law, moreover, there was clearly no distinction between Democrat-appointed officials and Republican-appointed officials.[80] The overall results demonstrate an essential consensus in the views of former officials regarding the international legal system: International law plays a role in the behavior of states.

3.5.2 *Differences among Presidential Administrations*

Clearly, different administrations have held different views about the role of international law, probably due to differences in political affiliation. As Table 3.8 reveals, responses to the question whether international law constrains states differed significantly by presidential administration, although those results are muddied somewhat by the relatively small number of respondents from the first Bush 41 administration and the Trump administration.

Comparing results from the Clinton and Bush 43 administrations reveals that former Clinton officials believed more strongly that international law constrains states. Results from the Bush 41 and Obama administrations are

[79] However, if we remove the categories "rarely" and "never," with only two cases between them, and re-run the analysis, the result barely misses out on significance, with a p value slightly greater than .05, at .06.

[80] The relevant question asked, "to what extent did the US comply with international law?" Response categories were Never, Rarely, Some of the time, Most of the time, Always.

TABLE 3.8 *Effect of international law by presidential administration*

IL Constrains?	Bush I	Clinton	Bush II	Obama	Trump	Total
Yes	5 (62.5)	17 (85.0)	12 (40.0)	7 (63.6)	4 (80.0)	45 (60.8)
Maybe/ sometimes	3 (37.5)	2 (10.0)	18 (60.0)	3 (27.3)	0 (0.0)	26 (35.1)
No	0 (0.0)	1 (5.0)	0 (0.0)	1 (9.1)	1 (20.0)	3 (4.1)
Total	8 (100.0)	20 (100.0)	30 (100.0)	11 (100.0)	5 (100.0)	74 (100.0)

comparable to one another. Overall, the results in this cross-tabulation are statistically significant.[81] These results are not surprising, given the earlier results assessing differences in views by political affiliation. Qualitative analysis provides a more nuanced view of differences in process and in attitude among administrations, as discussed in the following sections.

3.5.2.1 Differences in Culture

In their open-ended responses, several former officials noted that the State Department in different administrations, and even from one term of the same administration to the other,[82] exhibited differences in culture.[83] Administrations also may work differently, with different processes.[84] Differences in culture and processes are distinct from differences in political affiliation, though sometimes it may be difficult to tease the two apart. Accordingly, cultural differences among administrations may play a role in explaining differences in officials' perceptions about attitudes in the State Department toward international law and its role and their perceptions about processes.

3.5.2.2 Differences in Personnel

Differences in culture and process among administrations are partly due to the different mix of people in general,[85] and in particular to the different personalities and preferences of the most senior officials, including the President, the

[81] Chi-square analysis showed a p value of .008. The results were moderately strong, with a Cramer's V value of .37. The relatively small number of Bush 41 and Trump officials, and the existence of several cells with less than five responses, may limit the validity of this result.

[82] *See* Interview 29, *supra* note 10.

[83] *See* Bloomfield Interview, *supra* note 3.

[84] *See* Interview 29, *supra* note 10; Pickering Interview, *supra* note 20.

[85] *See* Bloomfield Interview, *supra* note 3.

Secretary, and the Legal Adviser.[86] For example, one former official made the observation that Secretary Powell elevated more Foreign Service Officers than other Secretaries to politically appointed positions, and they tended to be more risk averse and more likely to defer to the Legal Adviser's Office.[87] Another former official pointed out that there was a big difference between the first and second George W. Bush administrations, in that during the first Bush administration, the Secretary of State was only one of several decision-makers, whereas in the second, the Secretary could often make decisions on their own.[88] Another former official observed that both times he was in the State Department, the Secretary was a lawyer, inclined to take counsel from the lawyers. He contrasted this approach with Kissinger's (for whom he had worked), who was less inclined to take the lawyers' advice.[89]

Much also may depend on the character and preferences of the Legal Adviser. Different Legal Advisers tend to have different views about international law and can be more or less flexible or doctrinaire in its application.[90] In addition, Legal Advisers see their overall roles differently: Some see themselves partly as policymakers and some see themselves more as general counsels dispensing mostly legal advice. The "policymaker" types may be more flexible regarding the role of international law.[91] The stature of the Legal Adviser may also matter, that is, the extent to which they are respected and trusted may affect their influence.[92] Finally, some Legal Advisers may have more forceful personalities than others. At least two former officials mentioned former Legal Adviser Harold Koh in this regard.[93]

Finally, much may depend on the personalities and preferences of other individuals in influential positions in the Department during any particular administration. Those preferences include political preferences but may also include other preferences. Under Secretary John Bolton is going to have a different view of international law than, say, Under Secretary John Negroponte or Under Secretary Thomas Pickering, said one former official.[94]

86 *See* Interview with Richard Moose, Under Secretary for Management, Clinton administration; Assistant Secretary for African Affairs, Carter administration.

87 *See* Bloomfield Interview, *supra* note 3.

88 *See* Interview 29, *supra* note 10.

89 *See* Moose Interview, *supra* note 86.

90 *See, e.g.*, Interview 7, Former Assistant Secretary; Interview 27, *supra* note 18; Interview 1, *supra* note 18.

91 *See* Interview 7, *supra* note 90.

92 *See* Interview 29, *supra* note 10.

93 *See* Atwood Interview, *supra* note 25; Interview 15, *supra* note 18.

94 *See* Interview with Richard Solomon, Assistant Secretary for East Asian and Pacific Affairs, George H. W. Bush administration.

The role of law in decision-making may also depend on the attitudes and skills of the different lawyers involved in a particular issue.

3.5.3 *Changes in Attitudes over Time*

Over time, attitudes about the nature and extent of international law can shift among policymakers and among international lawyers. In no area or aspect of international law has there been more of a shift in attitudes among US policymakers in the last forty-five years than in human rights. In the 1970s, policymakers did not pay as much attention to human rights concerns. The prominence of human rights in US policymaking has grown significantly since then, though it may have waned somewhat in the last twenty years, with the war on terror and with less emphasis on human rights in the Trump administration.

A number of long-serving former officials remarked upon the shift since the 1970s in attitudes toward human rights law among policymakers from skepticism to growing institutionalization and significance.[95] Former officials mentioned two precipitating factors in this shift in attitudes. The first was the emphasis placed on human rights by President Carter. The second was the leverage against the Soviet Bloc provided by the inclusion of human rights in the Helsinki Final Act.[96]

When President Carter began pressing human rights concerns in the late 1970s, policymakers resisted.[97] One former official recalled that when President Carter pressed South Korea on human rights, that official's seniors thought President Carter was crazy.[98] In particular, they thought that the American conception of human rights did not fit in other contexts. Carter, nevertheless, asserted that international law gave the United States the right to comment on the human rights records of other countries.

At that time, the State Department under the Carter administration also began producing human rights reports regarding the performance of countries around the world. The State Department hated this development, according to one former official.[99] Over time, however, those reports became the gold standard for human rights observation, they asserted.

95 *See, e.g., id.*; Moose Interview, *supra* note 86; Interview 31, *supra* note 34; Interview 8, *supra* note 5.

96 Conference on Security and Cooperation in Europe: Final Act, Aug. 1975 [hereinafter cited as Helsinki Final Act], reprinted 14 INT'L L. MATERIALS 1292 (1975).

97 *See* Solomon Interview, *supra* note 94; Interview 31, *supra* note 34; Interview 8, *supra* note 5.

98 Interview 31, *supra* note 34.

99 Interview 8, *supra* note 5.

The other precipitating event was the signing of the Helsinki Final Act, a nonbinding agreement in which Western states essentially accepted the territorial boundaries established at the end of World War II and Soviet Bloc states pledged to respect human rights. Because of that pledge, the Soviet Bloc countries had difficulty claiming that national sovereignty precluded criticism of their human rights records. Western countries, accordingly, pressed human rights claims against the Soviet Bloc nations at follow-up conferences and at other times.[100]

As a result, human rights, generally speaking, appealed not only to the liberal Carter administration but also to the conservative Reagan administration as a weapon in the Cold War to put pressure on the Soviets.[101] Thus, the Reagan administration built on the achievement of the Carter administration, though redirected it. The bipartisan appeal of human rights, it may be argued, contributed to the institutionalization of human rights in the State Department and the US government more generally. In addition, the existence of the Helsinki Final Act also contributed to the appeal of human rights on a grassroots level, which then percolated upward. One former official recalled traveling in Europe with John Whitehead, Deputy Secretary of State in the Reagan administration, and encountering resistors carrying copies of the Helsinki Final Act and the UN Charter.[102] Thus, the views of policymakers regarding specific areas of international law and international law more generally can shift over time.

3.5.4 *Competing Bureaucratic Interests*

Views among policymakers with regard to international law generally and with regard to the legality of particular issues are not monolithic. Individuals, obviously, may have different views. Policymakers in every government and in every agency within governments also operate within the structure and cultures of their bureaucracies, which invariably have varying and competing interests and positions. Bureaucratic competition within the State Department can serve as an example of this wider dynamic.

Bureaus within the State Department may take different positions at times, several former officials pointed out.[103] In the State Department, conflicts most

[100] *See* Sean D. Murphy, Principles of International Law 128 (3d ed., 2018).
[101] *See* Solomon Interview, *supra* note 94.
[102] *See* Interview 8, *supra* note 5.
[103] *See, e.g.*, Pickering Interview, *supra* note 20; Holmes Interview, *supra* note 4; Brimmer Interview, *supra* note 7; Interview 32, *supra* note 77; Interview 13, *supra* note 69.

often arise between the functional and regional bureaus.[104] As a result, any final position developed within the State Department reflects a consensus opinion, masking some variation. Similarly, the final position of the US government as a whole may represent on some issues the results of a negotiation and discussion between state and other agencies, including the White House. These dynamics are addressed more extensively in Chapter 5.

3.5.5 *Career v. Political Appointees*

One promising hypothesis is that career Foreign Service Officers appointed and confirmed to senior leadership positions have a more positive attitude toward international law than noncareer appointees. Some of this study's results lean in that direction, though they are mixed. On other measures, there did not appear to be much distinction between the views of career and noncareer appointees.

Career appointees consist of officials appointed from the ranks of the Foreign Service, while noncareer appointees are those appointed from outside. Many noncareer appointees come from outside government (e.g., from think tanks, from business, from academia, or from NGOs). Many may have governmental experience in other departments (e.g., the Defense Department) or in the legislative branch (e.g., current or former members of Congress, Senators, or Congressional staffers).

There might be several reasons to think that there would be a difference in the views of career and noncareer appointees. Foreign Service Officers may have greater experience in government and often have greater experience in foreign affairs. They have had more occasions to observe and think about the role of international law in international relations and, thus, may be more inclined to believe in its effectiveness. A contrary hypothesis is that Foreign Service Officers, through their training and professional experience, have become acculturated to a belief in international law and its effectiveness, a view not necessarily shared by those with different backgrounds.

In any event, as indicated earlier, there is some indication that career appointees believe more strongly in the authority of international law. On two questions regarding state compliance with international law, career appointees appeared to believe more strongly that states comply with international law. The two questions were whether international law constrains state behavior and whether most states comply with international law most of the time, some of the time, or rarely. Responses to the two questions were

[104] *See* Holmes Interview, *supra* note 4.

TABLE 3.9 *Does international law constrain states?*

IL Constrains?	Career	Noncareer	Total
Yes	18 (78.3)	27 (52.9)	45 (60.8)
Maybe/sometimes	4 (17.4)	22 (43.1)	26 (35.1)
No	1 (4.3)	2 (3.9)	3 (4.1)
Total	23 (100.0)	51 (100.0)	74 (100.0)

Valid cases: 76; missing cases: 2 (2.6 percent)

distributed similarly, with similar statistical results. For illustrative purposes, Table 3.9 shows the distribution of responses to the first question, whether international law constrains state behavior.

On a percentage basis, more of the career appointees than the noncareer appointees believed that international law constrains state behavior, as opposed to constraining state behavior sometimes, or not at all. This result just misses statistical significance[105] but is at least suggestive. On other metrics – the weight of the Legal Adviser's position, the role of normative factors, and compliance by the United States – there is little distinction between the views of career and noncareer officials.

3.6 CONCLUSION

Most former officials expressed the opinion that international law constrains state behavior and that states generally comply with international law. To the extent that this observation reflects actual state behavior, it supports the proposition that international law plays a role in international affairs. The former officials collectively identified various factors that encouraged or discouraged states to comply with international law. The top positive factors, in order of the frequency cited, were reputational concerns; state interest in a stable legal and institutional system; reciprocity, or the prospect of retaliation; ethical considerations, including ethical values underlying international law rules and respect for the rule of law; idiosyncratic factors, including the political culture of states and their adherence to the rule of law; and benefits flowing from participation in specific regimes. Among the factors militating against compliance by states, state interest was the most significant factor, followed by the ambiguity of international law; the notion that some rogue

[105] A chi-square analysis/test reveals a p score of .097, just slightly above the usual .05 threshold for significance.

states do not comply; the perception that compliance by some states is shallow; the role of domestic politics; and sovereignty concerns.

Two aspects of these results are significant. The emphasis of policymakers on ethical factors supports normative theories about compliance. These normative factors included the ethical values underlying legal rules, such as human rights, as well as respect for the rule of law. A number of officials asserted that countries with a history or culture of respecting the rule of law domestically were more likely to respect the rule of law in international affairs as well.

A large proportion of former officials, moreover, emphasized the value of the international legal system and the value of maintaining it. The interest in maintaining a stable international system serves the interests of all states, particularly powerful states. In general, it seems that the worldview of most of the former officials interviewed was multilateralist, institutionalist, and rule of law-oriented.

Many former officials indicated, however, that decisions about compliance with international law involved a cost–benefit calculation. Though the predilection of most policymakers was to follow international law, legal considerations might not always prevail in that calculation. This calculation involved a balance of considerations, together with legal concerns, which might include state interest, political calculations, moral concerns, and bureaucratic obstacles, among others. Chapter 4 discusses in greater detail competing considerations and their weight in the calculations of US officials. Chapter 4 then examines the ways in which tensions between other concerns and international law might be resolved.

The chapter then explored former officials' perceptions about the reasons *other* states (not the United States) take into consideration when making decisions about compliance. Former officials tended to perceive other states to be more concerned with hard benefits and cost, including carrots and sticks, as opposed to systemic or altruistic concerns. They perceived the United States, in contrast, as motivated in part by those systemic and altruistic concerns. Perceptions of US compliance will be examined more thoroughly in the next two chapters, Chapters 4 and 5.

Next, the chapter examined the areas of international law in which compliance is more or less likely. The least likely area for state compliance was national security. The most likely areas for compliance were trade and economic law, environmental law, humanitarian law, arms control, law enforcement, and cooperative arrangements such as aviation agreements and postal unions. These responses tended to support an instrumentalist take on compliance. The overall perception was that compliance was less likely in areas of high politics related to national security issues and more likely in areas of low politics, where compliance is easier in the face of competing interests. In the same vein, compliance was more likely in areas potentially subject to reciprocity: humanitarian law, arms control, and economic law. Some compliance could also be explained by the dynamics of simple coordination situations, such as in postal unions. The results of this analysis are similar to the analysis in Chapter 4 regarding examples of minimal and maximal compliance by the United States.

These results are in tension with the results regarding ethical factors, described earlier. Recall the significant weight given by former officials to ethical factors and to other normative considerations. Still other factors former officials cited as contributing to compliance, such as the existence of compliance mechanisms and the clarity of obligations, may comport with normative theories or with both theories. While decisions about compliance with international law may involve a cost–benefit framework, that framework seemingly contains both instrumentalist and normative elements.

4

Compliance by the United States

The perception of former officials was that US compliance with international law was robust. Eighteen percent of former officials said that the United States always followed international law, 72 percent said the United States followed international law most of the time, and 10 percent said the United States followed international law some of the time. Of course, this result could reflect some inflation due to wishful thinking, but it demonstrates a least a positive assessment of overall US compliance.

When asked about the reasons that the United States complies or does not comply with international law, the former officials' responses tracked many of the factors they listed for states in general, with a few differences. Some factors cut both ways. Noteworthy factors that generally favored US compliance included the following: First, ethical concerns play a role in favoring compliance with international law but sometimes can also justify noncompliance. Second, the United States has an interest in maintaining the international order, including existing international law. Third, the views of allies can support US compliance but can also sometimes aid the United States in taking action when international law is murky or even in opposition. Fourth, the concern to set desirable precedent and avoid setting a negative precedent can affect decisions. Finally, the United States' commitment to treaties can encourage the United States to comply. Notable factors that militated against compliance by the US included national interest, sovereignty concerns, domestic law complications in the application of international law, bureaucratic or budgeting difficulties in complying with international law, domestic politics, and the ambiguity of a particular legal obligation.

Former officials were clear that while international law was generally followed, it was not always dispositive. Legal issues were considered as one factor among a variety of factors, essentially involving a cost–benefit analysis.

The salient considerations driving compliance or noncompliance, as revealed in the interviews, appeared to be the nature of the national interest or policy at stake; the nature and significance of the international legal rule involved, including ethical considerations; the views of allies; the ambiguity or precision of the legal obligation; and the weight of domestic political and bureaucratic concerns. Another consideration, not mentioned explicitly by interview subjects, is the State Department's policymaking process generally and the role of international law and of Department lawyers in that process, addressed extensively in Chapter 5.

The two most important of these salient considerations are the nature of the national interest or policy at stake and the nature and significance of the relevant international legal rule. These categories represent aggregations of several factors to simplify the analysis. "The nature of the national interest or policy at stake" refers to the constellation of national interest factors, including national security concerns, and sovereignty concerns. The "nature and significance of the international law rule involved" includes the nature of the legal rule itself, the systemic interest in complying with that rule, the ethical values favoring compliance, and other pressures to comply with international law.

These two considerations are self-evidently in tension with one another. Qualitative examination of former officials' interviews revealed a range of views regarding this tension. While the majority of former officials indicated their predilection to follow international law, responses varied regarding the ultimate balance between the two. The responses fell into three loose categories. The first category consisted of a small group of former officials who indicated that they and the United States complied with international law as a matter of course, almost all the time. In the second category, the largest, former officials suggested that while the United States followed international law much of the time, there were occasions when significant national interests took priority. In the third category, some former officials argued that international law was subordinate to policy and national interest considerations. The majority of the time, extreme tensions between policy goals and international obligations do not arise and compliance is the default position. Nonetheless, as one former official put it, while policymakers always want to do the right thing and there is a predilection to comply, their job is to pursue the interest of the United States, to know the options, and to decide.

Chapter 4 concludes with a description of examples of instances where the United States violated or bent international law and examples where the United States acted scrupulously in complying with international law. The discussion also complements and extends the discussion in Chapter 3 regarding areas of law where compliance is more or less likely, in general.

Examples of potential US overreach included military interventions, the NATO bombing of Kosovo, and enhanced interrogation or torture after 9/11. Areas of the law in which the United States has been more scrupulous include arms control, humanitarian law, diplomatic relations, and trade (until recently). As in Chapter 3, these results, overall, tend to buttress an instrumentalist take on compliance but also include examples of the role of ethical and normative concerns in decision-making. Recall the significant weight policymakers gave here and in other instances to normative and ethical concerns.

4.1 UNITED STATES COMPLIANCE WITH INTERNATIONAL LAW

Officials expressed a perception that the United States exhibited a high degree of compliance with international law. Of those who responded to the relevant question, 18 percent of former officials said that the United States always followed international law, 72 percent said the United States followed international law most of the time, and 10 percent said the United States followed international law some of the time.[1] Thus, on the face of it, former officials perceived a robust level of compliance by their government. Of course, there may not be an exact match between the perception of compliance and objective reality. Some former officials pointed out that the United States and states in general tend to define compliance from their own perspective, based on their own subjective understanding or interpretation of international law norms.[2] States, moreover, tend to advocate their own, self-regarding, interpretation of international law rules when asserting their own adherence to those rules.[3] The ambiguity of much international law lends itself to this subjectivity and flexibility.[4]

[1] One caveat: of seventy-six subjects, forty-nine responded to this question and twenty-seven did not, a high non-response rate. We cannot know, of course, how those who did not respond would have answered. Nonetheless, the lop-sided nature of the result suggests the validity of the overall point.

[2] *See, e.g.*, Interview 29, Former Assistant Secretary in a Republican Administration; Interview with Thomas McNamara, Assistant Secretary for Political-Military Affairs, George H. W. Bush administration; Interview 19, Former Assistant Secretary, Trump administration; Interview 3, Former Assistant Secretary, Trump administration.

[3] *See, e.g.*, Interview with John Shattuck, Assistant Secretary for Democracy, Human Rights and Labor, Clinton administration; Interview 10, Former Assistant Secretary; Interview 35, Former State Department Official; Interview with John Hillen, Assistant Secretary, Political-Military Affairs, George W. Bush administration; Interview with Phyllis Oakley, Assistant Secretary for Population, Refugees, and Migration, Clinton administration; Interview 1, Former Assistant Secretary.

[4] *See* discussion *infra*, Chapter 5.

4.1.1 *Factors Relevant to Compliance*

Former officials were asked about the factors US policymakers take into account when thinking about why, or whether, or the extent to which, the US should comply. They were encouraged to discuss their own experiences in this regard. In the following discussion, as in Chapter 3, we first examine factors that policymakers said contribute to compliance – this time by the United States rather than states collectively – and then examine factors that tend to discourage compliance. Even though the factors are divided neatly into these two categories for simplicity of analysis, some cut both ways. For example, the views of allies sometimes support or encourage compliance by the United States, but sometimes can encourage the United States to take action when legality is murky because staunch allies are willing to provide support. The analysis then assesses the most salient factors that affect compliance, including a deeper assessment of a primary tension, the tension between national interest, broadly defined, and considerations relevant to international law, broadly defined.

4.1.2 *Factors That Favor Compliance*

When asked about the reasons the United States complies with international law, the former officials' responses tracked many of the factors they listed for states in general, with a few notable exceptions. The following table lists the top twenty-five factors former officials cited encouraging compliance in the United States. The table lists the frequency of responses by former officials regarding those factors. Frequency counts, once again, capture how many respondents cite a certain factor and do not necessarily reveal respondents' individual or collective ranking of the relative significance of factors.

To the extent that the frequency counts for all states and for the United States track each other, we can speculate that former officials thought that many of the factors that lead all countries to comply with international law also apply to the United States. Perhaps these results are similar because US officials project their perceptions of US considerations onto other countries. In any event, the similar factors include the roles of reputation, reciprocity, ethics, interest in a stable international system, general self-interest favoring compliance, regime benefits, and avenues provided by law and institutions to further state interests.

Noteworthy similarities and differences between the factors motivating states in general and the factors motivating the United States include the following. First, ethical concerns of US policymakers can play a roles favoring

TABLE 4.1 *Factors favoring US compliance*

	Documents	Percentage
Ethics: general, non-specific	37	49.33
Reputation: general, unspecified	32	42.67
Reciprocity: general, unspecific	25	33.33
Self-interest: stable legal/int'l system	24	32.00
Treaty: more important; formality	23	30.67
Allies' view	17	22.67
Self-interest: states use law, institutions	16	21.33
Self-interest: benefits of regime	15	20.00
Self-interest: generally in favor of compliance	14	18.67
Self-interest: set desirable precedent/avoid negative precedent	14	18.67
Self-interest: US exceptionalism; moral responsibility	14	18.67
Self-interest: general, unspecified	10	13.33
Domestic popular opinion	10	13.33
Idiosyncratic: other	9	12.00
Domestic politics (in favor)	8	10.67
Self-interest: US created institutions; serves interest	8	10.67
Legitimacy or illegitimacy of rule	8	10.67
Diplomatic pressure	6	8.00
Interpretive guideline, constraint	6	8.00
Publicity, attention, awareness, shame	5	6.67
Habit and inertia	5	6.67
Domestic: treaties are US law	4	5.33
Compliance mech: Availability of interp/enforce may encourage use	4	5.33
Domestic law coincides/enforces	3	4.00
Self-interest: saves US from having to take on problems	3	4.00
Self-interest: affect domestic policy/law	3	4.00
Self-interest: general economic interest	3	4.00
Self-interest: US tries to work w/in system (or change)	2	2.67
Domestic: pressure from elites/bureaucracy	2	2.67
Efficiency of following rule	2	2.67
Inducement (specific)	1	1.33
Norms shape state behavior	1	1.33
Diplomatic pressure: NGOs	0	0.00
DOCUMENTS with code(s)	75	100.00
DOCUMENTS without code(s)	1	–
ANALYZED DOCUMENTS	76	–

compliance with international law, but sometimes can also justify non-compliant actions. Second, the United States has a particular interest in maintaining the international order, including existing international law. Third, the views of allies can support US compliance, but can also sometimes aid the United States in taking action when international law is murky or even in opposition. Fourth, the concern to set desirable precedent and avoid setting a negative precedent can affect decisions involving international law. Finally, the United States' commitment to treaties can encourage the United States to comply.

4.1.2.1 Ethics

The role of ethics is listed as the most significant factor favoring compliance, as it was in the list of factors for states generally in Chapter 3. This conclusion is somewhat misleading because factors reflecting various aspects of self-interest appear separately and if aggregated would dominate. Nonetheless, ethical factors evidently play a strong role and are also reflected in two other factors in the top ten or eleven factors on the list in Table 4.1: the notion of US exceptionalism and moral responsibility and the significance of treaty obligations and the importance of adhering to them. Neither of these factors ranked as highly in the list of factors for states generally. Perhaps American policymakers are more likely to ascribe ethical behavior to the United States, as opposed to other countries.

In a related vein, some former officials emphasized the role of law in creating a just world and the interest of the United States in promoting it. Phyllis Oakley,[5] for example, argued that the United States has promoted the rule of law for this purpose. In particular, the United States has sought to prevent genocide and promote prosecution of genocide, for example, in the Balkans and in the aftermath of Darfur.

Several former US officials viewed ethical concerns as a main factor driving compliance with international law. Several mentioned ethical matters explicitly when discussing the factors that policymakers considered, together with international law, in making a policy decision. One former official said that foreign policy is informed not just by national interest – ethics and values play a big part, including human rights concerns.[6] The United States does not want to see a genocide, for example, that official said.

Some former officials suggested that ethical concerns could sometimes even trump international law. Apparently speaking about US decisions to

[5] *See* Oakley Interview, *supra* note 3.

[6] *See* Interview 32, Assistant Secretary in the Obama administration.

use force, Richard Boucher[7] said that there is a hierarchy of considerations, including moral or ethical concerns (e.g., stop Hitler) and self-defense issues, broadly speaking, including protecting civilians, as in Grenada and Panama. At least one other former official asserted that human rights and ethical concerns were particularly salient in the determination of whether to go ahead with the bombing of Kosovo in 1999 without a Security Council blessing.[8] In the face of a potential genocide, that official said the administration was not going to be constrained. Secretary Albright may have made the winning argument, this former official said: we are not going to have boxcars for the second time in the twentieth century.

Some former officials even seemed to conflate ethical factors and legal factors. Richard Boucher's statement about a hierarchy of considerations suggests as much. In the debate regarding the air campaign against Kosovo, the former official cited before also seemed to suggest some equivalence between moral and legal arguments. The argument in favor of proceeding was, they said, based on the notion of the Responsibility to Protect, a "sort of" international law justification. Before the Kosovo air war, certainly, it would have been very difficult to claim successfully that the Responsibly to Protect reflected international law.

4.1.2.2 Systemic Interest

The fourth most frequently cited factor in favor of US compliance was its interest in a stable legal and institutional international system. As discussed in Chapter 3, that system promotes a stable, prosperous, peaceful, and just world, a benefit for all states. States can use the international legal system to pursue various goals, facilitating accommodation and reducing tensions, providing a tool for collective action and for realizing the other benefits of regimes, enforcing rules against violators, corralling rogue regimes.

Many former officials viewed the international order as reflecting and furthering not only the interests of states in general but the interests of the United States in particular. Tom Shannon, cited in Chapter 3, asserted that as a power that is part of the ordering force in the world, creating predictability is an advantage because it promotes peaceful resolution and pacific behavior.[9]

7 See Interview with Richard Boucher, Assistant Secretary for South and Central Asian Affairs, George W. Bush administration; Assistant Secretary for Public Affairs, George W. Bush administration.

8 *See* Interview 8, Former Senior State Department Official.

9 *See* Interview with Thomas Shannon, Under Secretary for Political Affairs, Acting Secretary, Acting Deputy Secretary, Obama and Trump administrations.

The United States can only deal with so many threats and issues, so it is better to deal only with the most important and leave less important issues to others, he said. Also, as discussed in Chapter 3, the United States has been able to use international law and institutions to achieve foreign policy goals.[10] For example, the United States has been able to "outsource" certain tasks to the United Nations, such as providing humanitarian relief or generating peace operations that serve US interests in stability.

A number of former officials explicitly mentioned the United States' role in establishing the post–World War II international legal order and, hence, its interest in maintaining that order.[11] One put it succinctly, if a state sets up a system, it has an interest in continuing it, so that failure to comply with its rules weakens that system.[12] Another former official in the George H. W. Bush administration pointed out that international law reflects US interest because the United States has been in the forefront of establishing its rules.[13] One former official characterized the United States as the "Liberal Leviathan," quoting international relations scholar John Ikenberry.[14] That is, following World War II, the United States was the system operator, setting up new postwar international institutions after the previous world order had collapsed.[15] Still another official recalled a relatively recent and telling example of US leadership in developing international law: The United States pushed for a more legally rigorous international trading regime in the Uruguay Round leading to the World Trading Organization agreement, including a more rigorous dispute resolution system.[16]

One former official stated that because of the US position as a dominant conservative power, the United States has a long-term interest in stability that extends not just to particular areas of international law but also to the maintenance of the entire rule-based system.[17] Another former official argued that it is in the US interest as a *status quo* power to promote international law, and that the United States is interested in all forms of international obligation

[10] *See supra* Chapter 3.

[11] *See, e.g.*, Interview with Melvyn Levitsky, Assistant Secretary for International Narcotics Matters, George H. W. Bush administration; Interview 28, Former Official; Interview 2, Former Senior State Department Official; Interview 14, Former State Department Official; Interview 18, Senior State Department Official, Obama administration.

[12] *See* Interview 18, *supra* note 11.

[13] *See* Levitsky Interview, *supra* note 11.

[14] *See* Interview 2, *supra* note 11, citing G. JOHN IKENBERRY, LIBERAL LEVIATHAN: THE ORIGINS, CRISIS, AND TRANSFORMATION OF THE AMERICAN WORLD ORDER (2011).

[15] *See* discussion of the post war international order, *infra* Chapter 6.

[16] *See* Interview 17, Former Assistant Secretary, George H. W. Bush administration.

[17] *See* Interview 10, *supra* note 3.

because it bolsters the US position and strengthens the United States compared to rising nations, such as China and Brazil.[18] The system of rules was designed, another official stated, to ensure that others comply.[19]

Nevertheless, some former officials asserted that the United States' systemic interest would be outweighed in specific cases involving national security interests.[20] While the United States has an interest in the systemic benefits of the international legal system – that is, an interest in supporting and maintaining that system – in cases involving an overriding reason of national security, the intrinsic cost to national security outweighed the systemic cost of violating international law.[21]

In addition, questions have arisen regarding the continuation of the postwar international order and, hence, the degree of its continuing value to the United States. The Trump administration raised these questions on the American side and took active steps to disregard or undermine the existing international system, shaking the faith of its allies about American steadfastness. The rise of China and the renewed threat of Russia may have ushered in the end of post-Cold War American hegemony. These developments and their effects are discussed further in Chapter 6.

4.1.2.3 View of Allies

Another factor ranked more highly for the United States was the effect of the view of allies. Policymakers indicated that the views of allies sometimes favored compliance with international law.[22] Getting the support of allies for a particular course of action may depend on the consistency of that action with international law. Having allies on board, in turn, may make it easier to get domestic US support for an action, such as humanitarian interventions.[23] In general, the United States takes the views of other states we care about

[18] *See* Interview with Richard Moose, Under Secretary for Management, Clinton administration.

[19] *See* Interview 26, Former State Department Official.

[20] *See* Interview with Robert Gallucci, Assistant Secretary for Political-Military Affairs, Clinton administration, Former President, MacArthur Foundation, Former Dean, Walsh School of Foreign Service, Georgetown University.

[21] *See Id.*

[22] *See, e.g.*, Interview with Ellen Tauscher, Under Secretary for Arms Control and International Security, Obama administration; Interview with Philip Zelikow, State Department Counselor, George W. Bush administration; Interview 27, Former Senior Obama administration; Interview with James Dobbins, Assistant Secretary for European Affairs, Clinton administration and George W. Bush administration; Interview 31, Former State Department Officer and Career Senior Diplomat; Interview 10, *supra* note 3.

[23] *See* Gallucci Interview, *supra* note 20.

seriously; these states may include not only traditional allies but other partners, states neighboring a situation, and other interested parties.[24] The views of allies may even pull the United States toward respect for norms in treaties to which the United States is not a party, but to which the allies are. Accordingly, the role of friendly states in US decision-making is underrated.[25]

At other times, the views of allies provided support for going forward – or not – when international law was not necessarily clear.[26] The allied bombing of Kosovo and the 2003 United States invasion of Iraq, for example, each rested on shaky legal foundations. The support of allies in both cases made a determination to go forward easier.[27]

4.1.2.4 Precedent

Another factor that appeared in the top eleven for the United States but not for states in general was the concern to set a desirable precedent and avoid setting a negative precedent. This concern seemed more related to the politically constraining effect of precedent than a concern about law-creating state practice, but the latter concern may also have played a role. That is, the concern seemed related to violating a precedent the United States had previously set, or creating a precedent that might limit the United States in the future, or even creating a precedent that other states might take advantage of to the United States' detriment. Seemingly, violating its own precedent could lead to credibility problems for the United States and provide opponents with ammunition.

4.1.2.5 Role of Treaties

Another area in which frequency counts differed with respect to states generally and the United States specifically involved the role of treaties. The predominant view among many former officials appeared to be that the United States takes treaty obligations seriously. One former official, for example, stated that treaties are "different" for the United States because they

[24] *See* Interview with Esther Brimmer, Assistant Secretary for International Organizations, Obama administration.

[25] *See Id.*

[26] *See, e.g.*, Interview with Tim Wirth, Under Secretary for Democracy and Global Affairs, Clinton administration; Interview with Tara Sonenshine, Under Secretary for Public Diplomacy and Public Affairs, Obama administration; Interview with Richard Boucher, *supra* note 7; Interview with John Hillen, *supra* note 3; Interview 3, *supra* note 2; Interview 33, Former Assistant Secretary with Experience in Trump administration.

[27] *See* Boucher Interview, *supra* note 7.

are in the Constitution and they are "pretty damn clear."[28] Accordingly, the United States operates within them and cannot violate them, they said. Treaties can be interpreted, but the United States must be careful in doing so. For that reason, said other former officials, the United States enters into fewer treaties and is reluctant to do so unless it is willing to comply with them. Some former officials also compared US behavior with regard to entering treaties to that of many other countries, which may treat treaties as more aspirational, rather than binding. Several former officials indicated that the time to consider whether an international rule is too constraining is when deciding whether to enter into an agreement; once the US enters into an agreement, it should comply.[29]

On a related note, the predominant view among many former officials appeared to be that the United States is more likely to comply with treaty norms than with non-treaty norms. Unfortunately, there was not enough time in an already packed interview protocol to explore systematically the differences in compliance between treaty and non-treaty norms. Some former officials, however, discussed levels of compliance with different types of norms on their own initiative. Non-treaty norms might include customary law, non-treaty United Nations documents or practices, and manifestations of soft law. Those former officials that made a distinction between different types of norms expressed a greater respect for treaty law, as illustrated by the discussion above. With non-treaty norms, in contrast, there could be more weighing of other factors and more room for interpretation, one official said.[30] Others also indicated that custom or other non-treaty norms were seen as less formal, or as subjective and relative, or as lacking American buy-in.[31] For example, most states will comply most of the time with treaties and extensions of treaties, such as UN Security Council resolutions, whereas they comply with customs and norms on a case-by-case basis, in part because customs are more subjective, both nationally and internationally, whereas treaties are comparatively objective.

4.1.3 *Factors Militating against US Compliance*

The factors that former officials cited that militate against compliance by the US are similar to the factors they cited as militating against compliance

[28] *See* Interview 6, Former Assistant Secretary. *See also, e.g.*, Interview with J. Brian Atwood, Under Secretary for Management, Clinton administration; Administrator, USAID, Clinton administration; Interview 25, Assistant Secretary in the George W. Bush administration.

[29] *See, e.g.*, Interview 15, Former Under Secretary; Interview 24, Former Official.

[30] *See* Interview 6, *supra* note 28.

[31] *See, e.g.*, Interview 7, Former Assistant Secretary; Interview 28, *supra* note 11.

TABLE 4.2 *Factors militating against US compliance*

	Documents	Percentage	Percentage (valid)
Con: self or nat'l interest, other	43	56.58	62.32
Con: interpretation or facts ambiguous	26	34.21	37.68
Con: sovereignty concerns	18	23.68	26.09
Con: bureaucratic infighting	16	21.05	23.19
Con: domestic political opposition/ concerns	15	19.74	21.74
Con: domestic law complications in application of IL	15	19.74	21.74
Con: domestic law also/more constraining/takes precedence	13	17.11	18.84
Con: funding/budgeting difficulties	7	9.21	10.14
Con: second-order consequences	7	9.21	10.14
Con: existing pattern noncompliance	4	5.26	5.80
Con: US already complies; no oversight	4	5.26	5.80
Con: low cost for noncompliance	1	1.32	1.45
Con: if have allies with you, legality less important	1	1.32	1.45
Con: diplomatic pressure other side	0	0.00	0.00
DOCUMENTS with code(s)	69	90.79	100.00
DOCUMENTS without code(s)	7	9.21	–
ANALYZED DOCUMENTS	76	100.00	–

by all states. Table 4.2 lists these factors. The cause of the overlap may be that these officials, when thinking about noncompliance in general, were focused on the view from the United States. Nevertheless, a few specific factors in the US context are worth discussing here, such as national interest, sovereignty concerns, domestic law complications in the application of international law, bureaucratic or budgeting difficulties in complying with international law, domestic politics, and the ambiguity of the particular legal obligation and its context. As with the factors militating against compliance in general, the most commonly cited factor was "self or national interest."[32]

32 The role of national self-interest in US decision-making involving international law concerns is discussed more extensively *infra*, Section 4.1.4.2.

TABLE 4.3 *Elements of US national interest*

	Frequency	Percentage	Percentage (valid)
Con: national security	17	22.37	68.00
Con: US a superpower; exceptionalism	7	9.21	28.00
Con: short-term interest/cost	5	6.58	20.00
Con: cost to economy	1	1.32	4.00
Con: big powers comply only in national interest	1	1.32	4.00
DOCUMENTS with code(s)	25	32.89	100.00
DOCUMENTS without code(s)	51	67.11	–
ANALYZED DOCUMENTS	76	100.00	–

4.1.3.1 National Interest

The category of national interest contains several subcategories relevant to the US perspective, as listed in Table 4.3, including "national security" concerns, and "US a superpower; exceptionalism." A significant number of former officials (seventeen) mentioned national security specifically as a sub-factor that could militate against the strict application of international law. A number of former officials (seven) also mentioned American exceptionalism. American exceptionalism reflects the idea the United States, as a superpower, or as an exceptional power because of its leadership role, should not always be bound by international law as a prescriptive matter, or does not view itself as bound as a descriptive matter. A related idea mentioned by former officials is that since the United States already complies with most international law, no oversight is necessary at the international level. That position represents a rather sanguine view of US compliance.

4.1.3.2 Sovereignty Concerns

The third-ranked factor in Table 4.2, "sovereignty concerns," is related to national interest and seems particularly relevant for the United States, as opposition to international law in domestic politics often centers around sovereignty concerns. Indeed, sovereignty concerns, or anti-internationalism, has played a historic role in American political history. In the last thirty years or so, this view gained adherents among a group of largely conservative scholars, academics, and policymakers who became known as the "New Sovereigntists."[33] Of course, expressions of concern about intrusions on US sovereignty from global governance or the international legal order are not necessarily linked or limited to conservatives.

Most former officials who discussed sovereignty concerns described them as a factor that the United States and policymakers take into account when considering entering into international commitments and sometimes when complying with them.[34] Karl Inderfurth, a former Clinton official, described the mainstream view involving respect for international law, but also described a competing narrative involving a phobia about signing treaties because of possible restraints on US freedom of action.[35] This skepticism toward treaty commitments has also been reflected in Congress' unwillingness to ratify various conventions, he said. Others also noted this tension between international law and sovereignty, as well the historical roots of sovereignty concerns in the United States. Several former officials mentioned, in particular, US reluctance to join the International Criminal Court as a reflection of sovereignty concerns.[36] Inderfurth emphasized that issues of sovereignty have not just been a democratic versus republican issue.

Nevertheless, some former officials noted the rise in conservative skepticism about international law. One former official said that the George W. Bush administration marked a break in the common foreign policy view in support of international law. That official identified a growth of suspicion about treaties, international organizations, and other aspects of international law and organizations.[37] Another former official also noted the philosophy in the George W. Bush administration: All international law is too constraining, as demonstrated by "unsigning" the Kyoto Protocol and leaving the ABM Treaty.[38] Tom Shannon, former Under Secretary of State for Political Affairs in the Trump administration, noted that the Trump administration's salient

[33] *See e.g.*, Peter J. Spiro, *The New Sovereigntists: American Exceptionalism and Its False Prophets*, 79(6) FOREIGN AFF. 9 (2000).

[34] *See, e.g.*, Interview with Karl Inderfurth, Assistant Secretary for South Asian Affairs, Clinton administration; Interview 17, *supra* note 16; Interview 11, Former Assistant Secretary, George W. Bush administration; Interview with Lincoln Bloomfield, Assistant Secretary for Political Military Affairs; Interview 20, Former Official; Tauscher Interview, *supra* note 22; Interview 33, *supra* note 26; Interview 25, *supra* note 28; Shannon Interview, *supra* note 9.

[35] *See* Inderfurth Interview, *supra* note 34.

[36] *See, e.g.*, Interview with Alexander Watson, Assistant Secretary for Western Hemisphere Affairs, Clinton administration; Gallucci Interview, *supra* note 20; Interview 17, *supra* note 16; Interview 32, *supra* note 6.

[37] *See* Interview 17, *supra* note 16.

[38] *See* Interview 11, *supra* note 34.

quality or belief was that sovereign nations get to act as such and only reluctantly admit to any limits, including those imposed by treaty and international law.[39]

4.1.3.3 Domestic Law, Politics, and Process

In a related vein, former officials spoke of the primacy of domestic law, both in trumping international law rules or norms that conflicted with domestic law and in commanding the focus of policymakers. Complying with US law appeared to be the main concern. One former senior official stated, for example, that policymakers pay more attention to the laws passed by Congress.[40] International law is important, but US law is in front of policymakers all the time. One reason, another former official said, is that international law tends to be more vague.[41] All who spoke specifically on the matter made it clear that in a conflict between national law and international law, national law would take priority.

Former officials also cited domestic legal and structural impediments to complying with international law. They spoke of the limits imposed by federalism, of funding inadequacies, and of bureaucratic budget constraints and red tape. They also mentioned occasional bureaucratic opposition and turf wars in interagency discussions.[42]

Another factor in US decision-making mentioned by a number of former officials was domestic political pressure, including Congressional opinion or reaction to State Department or executive action.[43] Former Under Secretary Joan Spero stated that policy does not exist in a vacuum, but always in a political context.[44] While compliance with international law is in US interest, international law exists within the context of politics of international relations and the politics of the nation-state. For example, she said, trade decisions

39 *See* Shannon Interview, *supra* note 9. Shannon recalled negotiations about the language of the communique from the Toronto G7 meeting. The administration wanted a statement to assert sovereign control over who crosses borders. Most states agree on restrictions, except for refugees. But the only way to get agreement was to add the clause "in accordance with international law." The White House was unhappy because it saw a limit to sovereignty in that formulation. Shannon pointed out that the United States had exercised its sovereignty in accepting limits.

40 *See* Interview 8, *supra* note 8.

41 *See* Interview 27, *supra* note 22.

42 *See* discussion *infra*, Chapter 5.

43 By a rough count, at least fifteen former officials mentioned the impact of political considerations.

44 Interview with Spero, Under Secretary for Economic, Business, and Agricultural Affairs, Clinton administration.

related to the steel industry obviously have domestic political ramifications, as would discussions about taking action in Syria. One disincentive to complying with trade regulations more broadly, another former official said, was the lack of domestic support for them.[45] Another former senior official stated that the United States tries to comply, but when it does not, there is often a domestic political issue involved.[46] Indeed, that former official said, most countries comply with international law, but sometimes domestic politics wins.

One particularly striking example of a domestic budget and bureaucratic hurdle involved State Department decision-making related to the US response to the Rwandan genocide: According to two former officials, one factor was that there simply was no money in the State Department budget to take action and the military was not interested in doing so.[47] Another reported incident related to Rwanda involved the UN Mission's request for troops before the killing took place. That would have required a US airlift, which meant that the State Department would have had to "rent" the necessary forces from the Pentagon.[48]

4.1.3.4 The Ambiguity or Precision of the Legal Obligation

As discussed previously, the ambiguity of much international law lends itself to subjectivity and flexibility in application.[49] States often have a some "wiggle room" or a zone of discretion in which to act and still argue that they remain in compliance with international law. Accordingly, the greater the generality or imprecision of the legal rule at issue, the greater the latitude for states in applying the rule.

By the same token, the relative precision of a legal obligation can enhance compliance, primarily because precise obligations are less subject to plausible, alternative interpretations that allow wiggle room for states. Brian Atwood noted that if the legal issue is more black and white, law carries the day: Having to explain variation to the international community is embarrassing.[50] A former Assistant Secretary in the Trump administration said that where the

[45] *See* Interview 29, *supra* note 2.

[46] *See* Interview 18, *supra* note 11.

[47] *See* Interview with Thomas Fingar, Assistant Secretary for International Research, George H. W. Bush administration; Wirth Interview, *supra* note 26.

[48] *See* Fingar Interview, *supra* note 47.

[49] *See* discussion *supra* Chapters 2 (the nature of ambiguity in international law) and 3 (ambiguity as a challenge for state compliance). *See also* discussion *infra* Chapter 5 (ambiguity allowing wiggle room for US compliance).

[50] *See* Atwood Interview, *supra* note 28.

law is really clear, you'd have to have a good reason not to comply, suggesting that clarity falls along a spectrum. That former official qualified their response by saying that encountering a crystal clear rule on that end of the spectrum rarely happens and that they had never run into it.[51]

This point obviously relates to the comparison between treaties and other forms of international law because treaties are likely to contain more precise obligations than customary law or other norms. Of course, even treaty obligations are often ambiguous, or subject to alternative interpretations, and so the degree of precision is relative to other forms of international law and relative among treaties.

As noted previously, several former officials cited arms control as an area in which the United States took pains to comply, some indicating the precise nature of arms control treaties as a factor. Arms control is an area where the rules are more cut and dried than in other areas, and compliance is more easily determined by others. Arms control involves many technical rules embodied in treaties, with which compliance is straightforward. Of course, the United States also has a strong interest in complying with arms control treaties to generate reciprocal compliance from others, so precision may not be the only reason for US compliance.

A related factor in US compliance mentioned by a number of former officials was the availability of a body to interpret international law, or to provide adjudication, or conflict resolution.[52] Examples of such bodies include the WTO, the IAEA, and NAFTA.[53] The availability of dispute resolution reduces ambiguity and limits the discretion of states to interpret rules to their advantage. The availability of such a body also increases the likelihood that issues would be raised about noncompliance. Dispute resolution bodies that can impose sanctions, such as the WTO, carry more weight.[54]

4.1.4 *Weight of Factors in Decision-Making*

A number of former officials emphasized that international law was considered as one factor among a variety of factors in making a decision on a course of action, one that was sometimes, but not always, determinative. That

[51] *See* Interview 3, *supra* note 2.

[52] *See, e.g.*, McNamara Interview, *supra* note 2; Interview 28, *supra* note 11; Wirth Interview, *supra* note 26; Brimmer Interview, *supra* note 24; Shattuck Interview, *supra* note 3; Tauscher Interview, *supra* note 22; Interview with John Hillen, *supra* note 3.

[53] *See* McNamara Interview, *supra* note 2.

[54] *See id.*

is, these decisions involve a cost–benefit analysis of factors.[55] Indeed, the statements of policymakers who commented on the role of multiple factors were remarkably consistent.

Nevertheless, out of all the factors discussed earlier, some appeared to be more salient than others. Any or all of these factors may have been relevant to a decision on any particular issue, but significant factors across issues appeared to include the following: the nature of the national interest or policy at stake; the nature and significance of the international law rule involved, including the ethical considerations involved; the views of allies; the ambiguity or precision of the legal obligation; and the weight of domestic political and bureaucratic concerns. The identification of these salient factors is somewhat impressionistic but is based on assessment of the frequency counts discussed in the previous sections and on qualitative assessment and comparison of the interviews.

The two most important salient factors represent an aggregation of several factors to simplify the analysis. Most importantly, "the nature of the national interest or policy at stake" refers to the constellation of national interest factors, including national security concerns, and sovereignty concerns. The "nature and significance of the international rule involved" refers to the nature of the legal rule itself, the systemic interest in complying with that rule or legal rules in general, the rule of law or ethical values favoring compliance, and other pressures to comply with international law. Aggregating the factors broadly in this way made it easier to examine the most fundamental and significant tension, the tension between pursuing national interest, or policy, and complying with international law.

Another salient factor, the effect of the policymaking process, will be discussed in the next chapter, Chapter 5, which will address policymaking in the State Department and in the US government as a whole and how that affects policy outcomes, focusing particularly on the dynamics of the interaction between policymakers and lawyers. In short, the role of international law and lawyers in policymaking guaranteed them a high profile in that process.

4.1.4.1 Law as One Factor among Many

To begin with, it should be emphasized that former officials expressed a basic respect for international law, as noted at the beginning of the chapter, albeit with some caveats and allowing for some variation in views. For example,

55 *See* discussion *supra* Chapter 3.

many former officials indicated that when international law rules were clear, they would be followed. One typical former official stated that no policymaker wants to do something that is flatly illegal.[56] A number of former officials also said that they never heard anyone say that the United States should follow a proposed course of action that would violate international law; no one would say international law is clear and we should ignore it.[57] Thomas Pickering said that he never saw a Secretary knowingly choose an option so contrary to international law.[58] In addition, on the relatively rare occasions that the Legal Adviser's Office determined that a course of action was precluded by international law, that would be determinative, a number of former officials said.[59]

Nevertheless, that does not mean that the United States did not push the envelope when international law was ambiguous or controversial, when other legal means were available to achieve the same policy ends, when a favorable interpretation was available, or when significant interests were at stake. For these reasons, and because the State Department is an agency of the US government pursuing its interests, former officials applied a cost–benefit analysis in decision-making, in which international law was one significant factor.

A selection of statements by former officials provides a sense of these views and their range. Former Assistant Secretary Thomas McNamara asserted that while international law frequently matters, it rarely matters by itself. Rather, it is an element in an overall picture.[60] Nonetheless, he could not conceive of situations entirely devoid of recourse to international law. Another former official stated that while compliance with international law is in US interest, international law exists within the context of politics of international relations and the politics of the nation-state, implying that legal and political issues are necessarily entwined.[61] Another former official stated that law is not determinative because issues are not structured that way for consideration by policymakers: There are lots of inputs or factors and issues are not necessarily

56 *See* Interview 27, *supra* note 22.

57 *See, e.g.*, Wirth Interview, *supra* note 26; Interview 1, *supra* note 3; Interview 14, *supra* note 11; Interview with Herman J. "Hank" Cohen, Former Assistant Secretary for African Affairs, George H. W. Bush administration; Interview 35, *supra* note 3.

58 *See* Interview with Thomas Pickering, Under Secretary for Political Affairs, Clinton administration; Ambassador to the United Nations and Multiple Countries; Assistant Secretary for Oceans and International Environment, Carter administration. *See also* Interview with Arthur "Gene" Dewey, Assistant Secretary for Population, Refugees, and Migration, George W. Bush administration.

59 *See, e.g.*, Interview 16, Former Assistant Secretary; Interview 8, *supra* note 8. *See also* discussion *infra* Chapter 5.

60 *See* McNamara Interview, *supra* note 2.

61 *See* Spero Interview, *supra* note 44.

black and white because much international law is subject to interpretation.[62] Another former official said that international law creates constraints, but those can be overridden and reshaped: Ultimately, states decide on interests, political pressures, and values.[63]

Former Assistant Secretary for Political Military Affairs John Hillen stated that the best decisions were considered seamlessly with both international law and policy considerations in mind.[64] As in a business decision, many interests are interwoven and there are always trade-offs, he said. When that happens, policymakers must look to the North Star, which is US interest. Sometimes, he added, international law fails because the government needs to do what it needs to do. In that context, international law does not have a national constituency.

Two former senior officials seem to have captured the consensus view. Tom Shannon, former Under Secretary of Political Affairs, stated that generally speaking, the United States complies when it can, and if it decides not to it is because of extraordinary factors and consequences that overwhelm.[65] Similarly, another former senior official said, policymakers always want to do the right thing and their predilection is to comply with international law, but their job is to pursue the interest of the United States.[66] That former official went on to say that 99 percent of policymakers ask, what is the right thing to do? There may be many right things to do, however. What is the position of Congress? What is the law? What are the human rights concerns? Human rights and ethical concerns were particularly salient in the determination of whether to go ahead with the bombing of Kosovo in 1999, this former official said. The higher you are, this former official said, the more challenging and harder it is to make choices. All options may be horrible or sensible and the high-level policymaker has to decide. At the President/Secretary of State level, it is constantly a balance of what is right and legal, and what can be justified in public.

4.1.4.2 Law v. National Interest and Policy

The major contextual factor affecting the application of international law for former policymakers was, not surprisingly, considerations of the national interest. Former officials were asked a number of questions about the role of

[62] *See* Interview 27, *supra* note 22.
[63] *See* Interview 36, Former Senior State Department Official.
[64] *See* Hillen Interview, *supra* note 52.
[65] *See* Shannon Interview, *supra* note 9.
[66] *See* Interview 7, *supra* note 31.

international law in State Department decision-making to assess the competing demands, or tensions, between the requirements of international law, on the one hand, and policy concerns or national interest, on the other. This section assesses the nature of these substantive concerns and the balance between them.

The more specific question is how and the extent to which policymakers in the State Department balance these competing concerns. The short answer is that most former policymakers applied a cost–benefit assessment. This part of the study attempts to examine the nuances of former policymakers' views in two ways. In the first, former officials' views were coded, and then those results were subject to frequency counts. In the second, former officials' views were compared qualitatively.

The views of former officials were grouped into several categories, ranging from those who ascribed more deference to international law to those who asserted that policy concerns or national interest generally took priority. The majority of former officials fell in the middle of this spectrum or slightly to one side or the other. That is, they believed that officials have a predilection to comply with international law but are flexible in applying it and believe that there are times when policy concerns or national interest take priority, particularly in the case of national security. Sometimes law controls and sometimes it does not.

CODED VIEWS: INTERNATIONAL LAW V. POLICY Subjects' overall views were assessed and coded on a scale from one to five, with one representing greater adherence to international law and five representing greater deference to national interest or policy concerns. More specifically, the first category represented the view that international law always controls; the second posited that international law usually controls, except in cases of high national interest; the third posited that officials have a predilection to comply, but interpretation of the law is flexible and law is only one factor; the fourth represented the notion that national interest often trumps international law; and the fifth represented the idea that policy almost always trumps, even when decisions are justified in terms of international law.

From Table 4.4, we can see a bell-shaped distribution of views, with the highest number of respondents (42 percent) bunched in the third, middle category, representing the perception that officials have a predilection to comply with international law but are flexible in applying it. At the same time, the number of respondents holding views on either side of the midpoint declines as we approach the poles. Thus, most of the respondents are clustered around the midpoint: Some 85 percent of the respondents fall into categories

TABLE 4.4 *International law v. policy*

	Frequency	Percent	Percent (valid)
1. IL almost always controls	5	6.60	6.80
2. IL usually controls, except hi-interest	18	23.70	24.30
3. Predilection, but flexibility	31	40.80	41.90
4. Predilection, but policy often trumps	15	19.70	20.30
5. Policy almost always trumps	5	6.60	6.80
TOTAL (valid)	74	97.40	100.00
MISSING:	2	2.60	
TOTAL	76	100.00	

TABLE 4.5 *International law v. policy (collapsed)*

	Frequency	Percent	Percent (valid)
[1 and 2] International law tends to control]	23	30.30	31.10
[3] Predilection, but flexibility	31	40.80	41.90
[4 and 5] Policy tends to control	20	26.30	27.00
TOTAL (valid)	74	97.40	100.00
MISSING: 99	2	2.60	
TOTAL	76	100.00	

two, three, and four, with only 7 percent in each of categories one and five. This distribution of views regarding the balance between law and policy does not vary much according to political affiliation, career versus non career appointment, or other factors.

Accordingly, for greater simplicity and ease of analysis, the distribution of frequencies will be rearranged into three groups, rather than five. Categories one and two, as well as four and five, will be collapsed, as in Table 4.5. The first category consists of former officials who indicated that they and the United States complied with international law almost all of the time, or that it controls, except in cases of high national interest. In the second, middle category, former officials suggested that while the US followed international law much of the time, there were occasions when national interest took priority and the application of international law could be flexible. In the third category, former officials argued that considerations or policy and national interest were generally superior to international legal considerations.

This arrangement of the results loses some nuance because it does not illustrate the extent to which the views at the poles have few adherents and the views in the middle predominate. Even so, this distribution of the data still captures the essential picture and simplifies further analysis. The middle category – predilection to follow the law but with flexibility – still represents the largest group, again demonstrating the predominance of that view.

One or two further caveats are in order here, which may blur the distinction between the views of the first group, asserting that the United States almost always or usually complies, and the middle group, asserting that the United States has a predilection to comply, but may not always. Because former officials indicated that clear conflicts with international law were not that common, it could simultaneously be true that policymakers deferred to international law in a relatively smaller number of clear matters but also sought maneuvering room in the many cases where international law was not so clear-cut. In addition, a number of former officials indicated that while the United States almost always complied with international law, it complied with its own interpretation of that law.[67] Real conflicts between national interest and international law, therefore, may be blurred, making it superficial to say the United States always, or almost always, complies with international law. Nonetheless, this description seems to characterize the range of views discussed by former policymakers.

QUALITATIVE COMPARISON OF RESPONSES: INTERNATIONAL LAW V. NATIONAL INTEREST/POLICY The statements of former officials regarding the relationship between international law and policy were reviewed and compared with the aid of qualitative coding software. In this way, the views of those falling into the three aforementioned categories could be teased out and examined in more detail.

To begin with, the analysis confirms that former officials possessed a baseline level of respect for international law. Fifty-four of seventy-four former officials, or 73 percent of valid responses, fell into the first or second category. Twenty-four, or 32 percent, moreover, volunteered in their interviews that the baseline assumption was that the United States would comply with international law.[68] Thomas Pickering, for example, stated that the assumption that the United States is going to comply with international law is

[67] *See* discussion *supra* Section 4.1.3.4 and *infra*, Chapter 5.

[68] *See, e.g.*, Pickering Interview, *supra* note 58; Moose Interview, *supra* note 18; Levitsky Interview, *supra* note 11; Interview 8, *supra* note 8; Interview 24, *supra* note 29.

understood.[69] Another said that the presumption is that the United States would always act consistent with international law unless there was an overriding reason of national interest and, in that case, would try to interpret international law to be consistent.[70]

In examining the three categories of responses in more detail, we will proceed in the following order: the first category, the third category, and then the middle category. The first category consists of those who expressed the view that international law almost always controls, except possibly in cases of high national interest. One former official said that the United States was not going to pursue policy contrary to its obligations: There was no à la carte attitude toward international law.[71] In the perception of another former official, although there were exceptions to the proposition that the United States almost always followed international law, they occurred on the margins and involved regimes the United States had shared in creating.[72]

Former Deputy Secretary Richard Armitage said that it was very unlikely the United States would act against international law and that he could not remember ever going against the advice of his Legal Advisor, Will Taft.[73] Similarly, a number of former officials said that they deferred to the judgment of L attorneys.[74] One former senior official said, for example, that not being a lawyer, he or she had great dependence on the attorneys, so he or she often deferred to them.[75] Several former officials said that when L said no, that meant no,[76] although that might be a rare occurrence,[77] or arise after exploring other options. In addition, as noted before, a number of former officials stated that no one ever says explicitly "let us go violate international law."

Interestingly, many of those who felt most strongly that international law concerns prevailed over national interest or policy considerations were Republicans, as demonstrated in Table 4.6.

69 *See* Pickering Interview, *supra* note 58.
70 *See* Gallucci Interview, *supra* note 20.
71 *See* Inderfurth Interview, *supra* note 34.
72 *See* Interview with John Holum, Under Secretary for Arms Control and International Security, Clinton administration.
73 *See* Interview with Richard Armitage, Deputy Secretary of State, George W. Bush administration.
74 The interaction between policymakers and the attorneys in "L" is more fully described in Chapter 5.
75 *See* Interview 2, *supra* note 11.
76 *See, e.g.*, Interview 33, *supra* note 26; Interview 6, *supra* note 28; Interview 16, *supra* note 59 (with rare exceptions, L's decision is determinative; if "L" says no, it's hard to fight); Tauscher Interview, *supra* note 22. *See also*, discussion *infra*, Chapter 5.
77 *See* Boucher Interview, *supra* note 7.

TABLE 4.6 *Party identity and international law v. policy*

	Democrat	Republican	Total
Int'l law tends to control	8 (25.0)	15 (35.7)	23 (31.1)
Predilection, but flexibility	16 (50.0)	15 (35.7)	31 (41.9)
Policy tends to control	8 (25.0)	12 (28.6)	20 (27.0)
Total	32 (100.0)	42 (100.0)	74 (100.0)

Valid cases: seventy-six; missing cases: two (2.6 percent)

Perhaps that is because Republicans more than Democrats tended to express the belief that the United States takes its treaty obligations very seriously. Of those former officials who volunteered that one factor leading the United States to comply with international law in general was the US predilection for complying with treaties, fifteen were Republicans and eight were Democrats.

At the other end of the spectrum, in the third group, former officials emphasized the primacy of national interest and policy considerations. Some former officials insisted that policy goals or national interest are primary and that legal justifications are found or adjusted to support them.[78] For example, Richard Solomon stated that the general approach of policymakers was to say this is what I want, and the job of support staff, including the lawyers in the Legal Adviser's Office, was to figure out how to make it happen.[79] In general, he said, L worked backward from the policy goal, taking legal constraints into account. Some former officials explicitly said that they could not recall any situation where international law concerns prevented the pursuit of policy goals, although it might shape the manner in which those goals were pursued.[80] Legal constraints, said at least one former official, influence how the United States does something, not the decision whether or not to do it in the first place.[81]

78 *See, e.g.*, Interview with Richard Solomon, Assistant Secretary for East Asian and Pacific Affairs, George H. W. Bush administration, Past President, United States Institute of Peace; Gallucci Interview, *supra* note 20; Wirth Interview, *supra* note 26.

79 Solomon Interview, *supra* note 78. Mr. Solomon speculated, however, that in recent years international law has been brought more to the fore in the consciousness of policymakers.

80 *See* Solomon Interview, *supra* note 78; Gallucci Interview, *supra* note 20; Interview 31, *supra* note 22; Interview with Anthony Quainton, Assistant Secretary for Diplomatic Security, Clinton administration; Hillen Interview, *supra* note 3.

81 *See* Brimmer Interview, *supra* note 24. *See also* the extensive discussion in Chapter 5, *infra*, regarding interactions between attorneys and policymakers.

Some former officials in this group, and one or two in other groups, indicated that the primacy of national interest and policy goals holds particularly for issues of national security, and perhaps other issues of compelling national interest.[82] Robert Gallucci[83] stated that the presumption is that the United States would always act consistent with international law unless there was an overriding reason of national security and, in that case, would try to interpret international law to be consistent. At the end of the day, however, he said that there was no case related to national security where the United States went against its own interest because of international law. On issues of national security, the United States is not going to be driven by international law. International law, Gallucci said, may take on more weight when the policy issues are not as significant.[84]

Others expressed similar views. One former official said that when international law is in conflict with national security, no president would jeopardize national security to comply with an international body's interpretation, even the Security Council's.[85] While the United States follows international law most of the time, this official had no doubt that if international law conflicted with national security, the United States would side with national security. Former Assistant Secretary Anthony Quainton said, in regard to national security issues, that the United States would like to be consonant with international law and would try to find a way to remain consonant through interpretation but will essentially do what it wants.[86] Anything that a country can describe in existential terms, it will do, he said. Another former official indicated that when it comes to issues involving the use of American power – for example, in cases where the United States wants to intervene – the United States is less rigorous in complying with UN resolutions.[87] Another former official stated that when there is debate about circumstances in which national security interests might override international law concerns, the United States may have a more expansive notion of the latitude provided under international law.[88]

[82] *See, e.g.*, Gallucci Interview, *supra* note 20; Quainton Interview, *supra* note 80; Brimmer Interview, *supra* note 24; Interview 1, *supra* note 3; Interview 14, *supra* note 11; Interview 24, *supra* note 29.

[83] *See* Gallucci Interview, *supra* note 20.

[84] *See id. See also* discussion, *infra* Section 4.2, regarding the relative weight of international law concerns in different issue areas.

[85] *See* Interview 1, *supra* note 3.

[86] *See* Quainton Interview, *supra* note 80.

[87] *See* Interview 24, *supra* note 29.

[88] *See* Interview 14, *supra* note 11.

Others were less emphatic about the primacy of national interest or policy but, nonetheless, indicated that legal concerns often took a backseat to significant policy interests. Policymakers, they said, would push the envelope to meet policy objectives.[89] While compliance is always an element in the decision-making process, said one former official, the importance of an overriding interest will trump compliance, though legal analysis may determine how a policy is implemented.[90]

Along the same lines, James Dobbins said that international legality is taken into account when considering US action.[91] The United States has a generalized interest in adhering to international law and encouraging others to do likewise. The United States never went ahead knowing a course of action was illegal. Nonetheless, he said that the United States would go forward when a course of action was controversial, arguing that what we were doing was lawful. The weight of legal arguments in these instances mostly related to efficacy in achieving the political goal. If an activity is illegal, then it stiffens resistance or can weaken a coalition of countries.

Former officials in the second, most numerous, group while generally expressing respect for international law, indicated that national interest took priority at times. As discussed earlier, many former officials across all groups indicated that the predilection of officials was to follow international law. Nonetheless, officials in this group indicated that sometimes law does not control. Moreover, law is only one factor in a calculation of US behavior. Policymakers can push the envelope when policy is in tension with the law. These officials also emphasized the inherent ambiguity of much international law, which can allow for flexibility in compliance. The ambiguity of international law and the room it gives for flexibility are discussed in greater detail in Chapter 5.

One former senior State Department official said that most State Department officials fall in this middle group: State Department people are option B people, practical, and moderate.[92] Policymakers always want to do the right thing, and their predilection is to comply, but their job is to pursue the interest of the United States. They wanted to understand it all: What did the law mean? What was its intent? How much flexibility is there? They wanted to find a way to comply, but when they chose not to do so, they wanted to make an informed choice. An example, this former official said, is when the

89 *See* Brimmer Interview, *supra* note 24; Interview 26, *supra* note 19.
90 *See* Interview 31, *supra* note 22.
91 *See* Dobbins Interview, *supra* note 22.
92 Interview 8, *supra* note 8.

United States decided to go forward and participate in the bombing campaign in Kosovo without Security Council blessing.

In a similar vein, Thomas Pickering emphasized that in State Department decision-making, the focus is on policy, with the assumption that the United States is going to comply with international law as it understands it.[93] All perspectives would be taken into account, including the legal perspective. He never saw a Secretary knowingly choose an option completely contrary to international law.

One former Assistant Secretary indicated that part of the interest calculation in determining a course of action includes the international costs of potentially violating a legal norm.[94] Most states believe they comply all the time, but there is an elasticity to international law that allows the legal framework to adjust to accommodate state interests. In US practice, they said, an argument would not be made solely on the basis of legality: Other factors would be introduced, such as eroding constraints on treaty parties, or exposing the United States politically as a result of the potential illegality, among others. Systemic and reputational interests could also play a role in a decision. The position going in when considering an issue is to identify the national interest, believing that pursuing it will be legal. Then, it is necessary to determine whether any tactical ideas are consistent along political, legal, and moral lines, and to adjust. The better way to look at the tension between law and national interest, this official suggested, is that law does not compel action, it permits it, allowing the United States and others to employ international law as a tool for implementing policy.

STRATEGIES AND OPTIONS WHEN INTERNATIONAL LAW AND NATIONAL INTEREST CONFLICT When significant national interest took priority over international law, former officials indicated that they might follow several general strategies to address the tension, in descending order of preference. These are described in more detail in Chapter 5. The first strategy was to attempt to determine whether alternative approaches were available that were colorably legal. The second strategy, if necessary, was to explore, together with the lawyers, alternative interpretations of the law that might frame US action in a more favorable light. Two other strategies were mentioned by a few participants but seem less likely options: Policymakers might engage in lawyer shopping to find a more amenable legal recommendation, or the United States might itself attempt to shift international law to suit its policies. When

[93] *See* Pickering Interview, *supra* note 58.

[94] *See* Interview 10, *supra* note 3.

there was a compelling national interest and when these coping strategies were not available, the United States might act contrary to international law. Still, there was a sense among former officials that acting in a legally questionably manner was rare, and certainly not a first choice.

4.2 EXAMPLES OF THE UNITED STATES TAKING A MINIMALIST OR MAXIMALIST APPROACH TOWARD INTERNATIONAL LAW

In response to specific questions or volunteering of their own accord, the former officials interviewed for this project provided examples of instances where the United States violated or bent international law and examples where the United States acted scrupulously in complying with international law. Some of these examples have been discussed elsewhere in the book; most are widely known. As will become apparent, the examples of US compliance and noncompliance overlap with the areas of overall state compliance and noncompliance examined in Chapter 3. The consistency of policymakers' responses to similar questions may indicate their validity but may also indicate that former policymakers tended to focus on the US experience when assessing the global situation.

Not all interview subjects were systematically asked to provide or discuss examples because of time constraints in the interviews. Accordingly, the number of former officials consulted was limited, and the extent and nature of the examples they provide are somewhat impressionistic and anecdotal, rather than the result of systematic examination. Nevertheless, this section provides discussion of these examples in one place and in greater depth; some limited observations can be based on them.

The former officials provided numerous examples of US overreach. The characterization of those examples may be subject to dispute: The United States at the time asserted that it complied with international law. Other people – including other former officials – may dispute whether a particular example represents a violation of international law. Nonetheless, it is at least safe to say that these examples engendered legal criticism from other states, from academics, and from the foreign policy community more broadly.

Examples of potential US overreach included various military interventions of the past sixty years, the NATO bombing of Kosovo in 1999, and enhanced interrogation or torture after 9-11. Areas of the law in which the United States has tended generally to be more scrupulous include arms control, humanitarian law, diplomatic relations, and trade (until recently). Specific examples of the United States' scrupulous compliance include the application of CITES and at least one incident involving interception of a ship on the high seas.

Some of these examples provide discrete lessons, while others generate some overall observations. One discrete lesson is that the areas where the United States was less compliant all relate to national security, supporting rationalist contentions that interests are likely to prevail in that context. A lesson provided by the example of the Kosovo bombing, however, is the potential effect of ethical concerns in driving US and state behavior more generally. Even though the NATO action potentially violated the UN Charter's prohibition on the use of force, the ethical argument was influential in the US decision to go ahead, according to some former officials. The Kosovo bombing also provides an example of the role of allied support for deciding to take action when legal justification is cloudy.

Turning to the positive examples of US behavior, it is striking that many of the areas cited by policymakers for more scrupulous adherence to law – arms control, humanitarian law, diplomatic relations, and even trade – involved the potential for reciprocity in response to US violations. Reciprocal responses would harm the US interest in maintaining those regimes. Another striking feature is that most of these areas involve extensive, specific treaty obligations. That result suggests the importance for compliance of precision in international obligations, which increases the difficulty for states to wiggle out of their obligations. It may be a challenge to untangle the degree to which reciprocity or precision contribute to greater compliance in these areas.

Finally, as noted previously and as discussed in Chapter 3, these examples tend to buttress an instrumentalist take on compliance, although not entirely. The United States was less likely to comply on issues of high politics that touch on national security. Many of the positive examples support the instrumentalist prediction that reciprocity plays a significant role in enhancing compliance with international law. Nevertheless, ethical factors played a role in some of the examples and the instrumentalist tinge of these observations contrasts with the weight given to normative factors in response to explicit questions on the subject.

4.2.1 *Examples of the US Stretching the Boundaries of International Law*

4.2.1.1 Interventions

Several former officials expressed skepticism regarding the legal justification for some of the US armed interventions of the last sixty years, including the Iraq War.[95] One former Assistant Secretary of State said that others think the

95 *See, e.g.*, Dobbins Interview, *supra* note 22; Interview 10, *supra* note 3; Cohen Interview, *supra* note 57; Pickering Interview, *supra* note 58; Watson Interview, *supra* note 36; Interview 17, *supra* note 16.

United States is self-serving when it comes to interventions. The United States disputes that characterization and asserts a different view of international law, that person said.[96] James Dobbins stated that the United States may go forward with intervening when the legal issues are controversial, suggesting that the United States will make a legal argument to justify its action.[97] Dobbins stated that some interventions have had more legal support than others, such as those in Afghanistan, Haiti, and Bosnia. Others have not, including Iraq, Panama, Granada, and the Dominican Republic. In the Cold War, no interventions had clear-cut support, he said. Other former officials expressed doubts about Panama and Grenada, in particular.

IRAQ Some former officials mentioned the decision to go to war in Iraq as a potential example of the US acting in violation of international law. James Dobbins thought that the basis for the Iraq War was "dubious." One former official said that Iraq was a tough issue but that the United States probably did not have the right to depose Saddam Hussein.[98] Melvyn Levitsky identified the Iraq War as an instance where the United States was not necessarily complying with international law, but at least the United States made a resort to a legal justification.[99]

Thomas McNamara, Assistant Secretary for Political Military Affairs in the George W. Bush administration, pointed out that while the United States argued that the US invasion of Iraq complied with international law, half the states in the world disagreed. In the same vein, another former official indicated that the fact that two-thirds of Security Council members were not aligned with the United States demonstrated the extent of the legal debate.[100] Even if the action fell on the side of legality, others perceived it as illegal or questionable. As a result, the United States paid a price in its relationships with countries that count for the United States in Europe and in the Middle East. The ability of the United States to convince others to go along was less successful in other contexts as a result. For these reasons, McNamara quoted Talleyrand: worse than a defeat, it was an error.[101]

96 *See* Interview 10, *supra* note 3.
97 *See* Dobbins Interview, *supra* note 22.
98 *See* Niles Interview 17, *supra* note 16.
99 *See* Levitsky Interview, *supra* note 11.
100 *See* Interview 14, *supra* note 11.
101 *See* McNamara Interview, *supra* note 2. McNamara slightly misquoted the quip. The actual quip is even more apropos: "It's worse than a crime, it's a blunder." The quip is usually attributed to the French diplomat Charles-Maurice de Talleyrand, describing the summary execution of the Duc d'Enghien on Napoleon's orders. *See* Robert Zaretsky, *Trump's Napoleon Moment: When Crimes Become Blunders in an Acquiescent Court*, FOREIGN AFF. (Jan. 9, 2020), *available at* https://www.foreignaffairs.com/articles/france/2020-01-09/trumps-napoleon-moment.

McNamara was present in debates regarding the Iraq War and indicated that he and Deputy Secretary of State Richard Armitage largely argued against intervention, arguing that the UN inspectors should be allowed to continue their work instead of pursuing the use of force. He said that international law arguments were made, but they did not carry much weight. In contrast, President George H. W. Bush took international law seriously, looking for the nonmilitary option first. President George W. Bush was not listening to his father, but wanted to go to war, in McNamara's estimation. In Iraq, there were nonmilitary options, but the administration chose not to pursue them.

Nevertheless, some former officials felt that US action in Iraq was legally justified or, at least, that its legality was unclear. One former Assistant Secretary not involved in the decision said that he thought that a legal case could be made.[102] Gene Dewey, Former Assistant Secretary in the George W. Bush administration, stated that the Iraq War was tough to criticize from an international law perspective, even though he pushed back at the time against the lack of planning for the occupation after the invasion.[103] Richard Boucher made a similar point, saying that US reliance on the existence of weapons of mass destruction, though not a lie, was not "well-founded."[104]

PANAMA AND GRENADA A number of former officials found the justifications for the US invasion of Panama and Grenada questionable,[105] most notable among them Thomas Pickering, former Under Secretary for Political Affairs in the Clinton administration. In Pickering's view, these were not actions in self-defense but were wars of choice, and the use of force to short-circuit relations was a mistake.[106] Another former official characterized the justifications for those actions as "legal legerdemain."[107]

Another former official, Otto Reich, appeared clear-eyed about the legal justifications for both invasions but seemed to favor them as a policy matter.[108] As for the invasion of Grenada, he said, the United States' mixed political and legal justifications included a genuine concern for the safety of American

[102] *See* Interview 6, *supra* note 28. *See also* Zelikow Interview, *supra* note 22 (restating the administration's position on international law, but also indicating that the role of international law was not as prominent as the role of domestic law).

[103] *See* Dewey Interview, *supra* note 58.

[104] *See* Boucher Interview, *supra* note 7.

[105] *See, e.g.*, Dobbins Interview, *supra* note 22; Cohen Interview, *supra* note 57; Pickering Interview, *supra* note 58; Watson Interview, *supra* note 36.

[106] *See* Pickering Interview, *supra* note 58.

[107] *See* Watson Interview, *supra* note 36.

[108] *See* Interview with Otto Reich, Assistant Secretary for Western Hemisphere Affairs, George W. Bush administration.

students at a medical school on the island. In addition, the Organization of East Caribbean States had appealed for American help. Thus, there were practical, military, and moral arguments on both sides. Very few other countries objected at the time, he said, although he asserted that the British were not informed in advance.[109]

In Reich's recollection, there was an intense but short debate within the State Department and the rest of the government about the extent of the invasion, with lawyers on both sides. The conflict was almost between the State Department, on the one hand, and the White House and National Security Council, on the other. State, as usual, was more cautious, diplomatic, and risk averse. State wanted to abide by a narrower interpretation – just rescue the American students but do not engage in regime change. State argued that the United States did not have the right to change the government. Another group, to which Reich belonged and which included advisers to the President, believed that if the United States was going to use military force, it should not leave Granada in the hands of the Marxist coup forces. Those forces had killed the previous leader and had allowed Cuba to develop a significant airfield on the island. In addition, the coup group was anti-American and would turn Granada into a base for subversion of the region. The decision to invade was strictly a political one, made by the NSC and the President, Reich said. While international law may have been one factor considered, the determining factor was overriding national security.

Although, as indicated earlier, several former officials expressed skepticism about the legality of the Panama invasion, other officials were more sanguine about it.[110] One former Assistant Secretary characterized international law in this case as a tool that helped facilitate what the United States wanted to do.[111] That is, the US legal justification for invading Panama provides an example of international law not as a constraint for states but as a tool that can empower a state to do what it wants to do, as an umbrella for legitimacy or authority. Earlier, the United States had gone to the Organization of American States to pass a resolution condemning Panamanian President Noriega's nullification

[109] Note, however, that the UN General Assembly condemned the invasion as a violation of international law. G.A. Res. 38/7, UN Doc. A/RES/38/1 (Nov. 2, 1983). The vote was 108 to 9, with 27 abstentions. A similar resolution before the Security Council had been vetoed previously by the United States. *See* Michael J. Berlin, *U.S. Allies Join in Lopsided U.N. Vote Condemning Invasion of Grenada*, Washington Post (Nov. 3, 1983), https://www.washingtonpost.com/archive/politics/1983/11/03/us-allies-join-in-lopsided-un-vote-condemning-invasion-of-grenada/5d979c34-41c2-4ddb-826b-eb6e5425749d/.

[110] *See* Interview 1, *supra* note 3; Interview 14, *supra* note 11.

[111] *See* Interview 1, *supra* note 3.

of election results, the former official said.[112] That created some legitimacy for the US opposition to Noriega but in the end appeared ritualistic: There was an understanding that a multilateral approach had failed. The US claim of self-defense provided a justification for the invasion, based on the need to protect American citizens, some of whom had been attacked, said the official. The Panama Canal treaties gave the US the justification to be in the country and the obligation to defend the canal until the 2000 turnover. Moreover, a loophole in the treaties allowed the US to conduct exercises, to swoop in on the Panama Defense Forces to rattle them, to convince them to get Noriega. In spite of the use of legal arguments as justification, this former official stated that there was not so much of an appetite for legal concerns, in comparison to the policy justifications for the action. There was no debate between US interests and justification under international law.

Another former official stated that he believed that the Bush administration's attention to the legality of the invasion demonstrated a conscientiousness about international law.[113] In the preparation process for the invasion, there were two NSC-led groups, one deliberating about military matters and the other about legal issues. The former official at first wondered why lawyers were involved so heavily. On reflection, he thought it was necessary because the United States is a country focused on the opinions of mankind and President Bush understood that international support would depend on how fastidious the United States was in making its case.

KOSOVO The Kosovo bombing campaign provides another example of the United States pushing the boundaries of international law. Two former officials took contrasting positions regarding whether the United States crossed the line. One, James Dobbins, characterized the US position as controversial but essentially justifiable.[114] In general, while the United States never went ahead knowing a course of action was illegal, it did go ahead where it was controversial, he said. In the Kosovo campaign, he asserted, the United States could make an argument that its action complied with international law. In any event, international law arguments played a role in the Kosovo example

[112] The former official is probably referring to an OAS resolution of May 17, 1989, linking Noriega to abuses of the electoral process in Panama and calling for a democratic transfer of power in the country. *See* Jim Anderson, *OAS Resolution Accuses Noriega of Crisis in Panama*, UPI ARCHIVES (May 17, 1989), https://www.upi.com/Archives/1989/05/17/OAS-resolution-accuses-Noriega-of-crisis-in-Panama/1148611380800/. After the invasion in December 1989, the OAS roundly condemned the invasion.

[113] Interview 13, Former Assistant Secretary in the George W. Bush administration.

[114] *See* Dobbins Interview, *supra* note 22.

because the United States had to persuade NATO that the campaign was consistent with international law, even though, in the end, each NATO member constructed its own argument and justification for the action.

Another former official characterized the Kosovo decision as falling on the other side of the line of legality but for good reason.[115] The United States may sometimes make a choice not to comply, as in the Kosovo air war, undertaken without Security Council authorization. The discussion, at the level of the President and the Secretary of State, involved a mix of moral, legal, and political arguments. A Security Council authorization would have been good but was not required. In the Kosovo case, the President decided to go ahead, based primarily on moral arguments. The United States was facing a genocide and was not going to be constrained in responding. As noted previously, the Kosovo decision may be an example of the appeal of ethical considerations in decision-making, and their potential role in mitigating legal concerns. The Kosovo decision may also have been a reaction to US lack of reaction in response to the Rwanda genocide, discussed below.

4.2.1.2 "Enhanced Interrogation" and Torture

A full review of the torture debate within and without the US government is beyond the scope of this book and has already been addressed extensively elsewhere. The opposition of Secretary Colin Powell, Legal Advisor Will Taft, and much of the State Department as an institution to enhanced interrogation and to other aspects of Bush counterterrorism policy is well known.[116] The views expressed by the majority of the former officials who expressed a view about the legality and wisdom of enhanced interrogation are consistent with that characterization.

Former officials from the George W. Bush administration seemed somewhat reluctant to discuss enhanced interrogation, or torture, following 9-11. Nonetheless, some former officials, in and out of the George W. Bush administration, mentioned enhanced interrogation as an example of the United States pushing the boundaries of international law and norms.[117] One former official, who was not involved in decisions or official discussions about interrogation techniques, asserted that some of the interrogation techniques used

[115] *See* Interview 8, *supra* note 8.

[116] *See also, e.g.*, Shannon Interview, *supra* note 9.

[117] *See, e.g.*, Interview 13, *supra* note 113; Interview 4, Former Official; Interview 16, *supra* note 59 (torture was an area, along with renditions, in which the United States did not comply with international law); Dobbins Interview, *supra* note 22. Shannon Interview, *supra* note 9 (the decision regarding interrogation was a political decision).

were torture and that the United States did not comply with international law.[118] Similarly, not all of the renditions the United States effected were consistent with international law, this former official contended.

US actions, moreover, had negative consequences, that former official said. They undermined the international standard regarding torture, in part because other countries still looked to the United States to set that standard. In addition, US actions did not make it easier for the United States to promote democracy: Other countries simply threw US behavior back in the face of US officials. Another former senior official made similar points.[119] The United States should comply with laws it has signed on to and should adhere to ethical precepts, they said. In addition, US actions went against US self-interest: The United States risked reciprocal behavior toward its own soldiers, harmed US credibility, and limited its influence.

At least four former officials asserted that the United States interpreted the law on torture to suit its own ends.[120] Robert Gallucci said that torture or enhanced interrogation was not consistent with the law. In fact, he indicated that a former Director of National Intelligence had suggested to him that waterboarding was torture.[121] But, he indicated, if they (presumably, policy-makers) believe that it is essential to national security, the lawyers will make it legal and, in fact, policymakers will tell them to do so. Another former official also indicated that the administration interpreted the law on torture and interrogation so that the United States was not bound.[122] As far as this former official was concerned, waterboarding was torture, and everybody who has gone through it will say that. This is an example of one of the rare times that the United States has not followed the rules. At every opportunity in discussions about torture this former official raised constant concern about the fact that torture was ineffective and wasted time.

James Dobbins, clearly speaking about the treatment of detainees in the conflict against Al Qaeda, noted that there were cases in the Bush administration where the State Department told the administration that steps it wanted to take were illegal.[123] Within the administration, however, these questions were unresolved and, according to him, did not reach the

[118] *See* Interview 13, *supra* note 113.

[119] *See* Interview 2, *supra* note 11.

[120] *See* Gallucci Interview, *supra* note 20; Interview 4, *supra* note 117; Interview 24, *supra* note 29; Interview 32, *supra* note 6.

[121] *See* Gallucci Interview, *supra* note 20.

[122] This former official wished to remain anonymous regarding specific comments and further information could serve to identify them.

[123] *See* Dobbins Interview, *supra* note 22.

President. So, for example, the Justice Department might issue a decision and the CIA might follow it, but other agencies like the FBI might decide not to follow. Dobbins was clearly speaking of decisions by the Justice Department's Office of Legal Counsel regarding enhanced interrogation techniques.

Tom Shannon, former Under Secretary for Political Affairs, said that it was a political decision to undertake interrogation (some would say torture) because of the threat and political costs of another attack. That decision invoked means and mechanisms that are rarely used. But even then, Shannon said, lawyers at State, the NSC, the White House, and the Department of Justice tried to define what was allowable and legal. There was an extraordinary effort to bound and explain the policy, as well as to ensure that the officials who did it were not exposed to liability. A fair reading of Shannon's comments is that the decision to engage in enhanced interrogation was political and not legal; that there was a strong effort to limit interrogation and to explain the policy in legal terms; but that a partial explanation for this legal effort was the desire to insulate participants in interrogation from liability. Insulation of personnel from liability would be essential in order to encourage or at least not discourage participants from carrying out the policy. This is not a new observation, but it is striking to hear it from a career, high-level diplomat like Shannon.

4.2.2 *A Mixed Example of US' Compliance with International Law: The Rwandan Genocide*

The United States was loathe initially to declare the 1994 mass killings in Rwanda a genocide, for fear that it would be legally and politically obligated to intervene with military force or humanitarian aid to prevent further killings and atrocities there. The United States, just six months before, had undergone the trauma of the "Black Hawk Down" incident in Somalia,[124] in which eighteen US servicemen were killed and seventy-three wounded during a United Nations peace operation to stabilize the country.[125] The Clinton administration was criticized extensively for those casualties, and was not about to embark on another peace operation that might put US soldiers' lives at risk, whether or not a genocide was occurring. Estimates on the number of

[124] *See generally* Mark Bowden, Black Hawk Down (2000).

[125] *See* Samantha Power, *Bystanders to Genocide*, The Atlantic (Sept. 2001), https://www.theatlantic.com/magazine/archive/2001/09/bystanders-to-genocide/304571/.

deaths that occurred in Rwanda during the genocide vary, but a commonly accepted number is 800,000.[126]

A number of former officials interviewed for this project participated in, or witnessed, the debate within the State Department regarding the US response to the Rwandan genocide.[127] The debate was mirrored in the US government as a whole, with some State Department and NSC officials favoring greater action and others, as well as the Defense Department and the military, generally opposed.[128] An extensive discussion of the Rwandan genocide and the US response is beyond the scope of this project and has been extensively conducted by others.[129] The following discussion attempts to capture the impressions of the former officials interviewed for this project, while exploring one or two points of interest.

One former State Department official was actually in Rwanda at the beginning of the genocide in early April, 1994, and knew many people who were killed.[130] That former official said, "all you have to do is watch one person killed in front of your eyes ...," suggesting that the experience was enough to convince anyone of the horror of the situation. But there was nothing the official could do, they said, indicating that the official US government position was that it was not an American problem.

One side of the debate within the State Department consisted of those, like John Shattuck, Assistant Secretary for Democracy, Labor, and Human Rights at the time, who believed that doing more was a moral and legal obligation; part of that obligation could have been to call the Rwandan killings a genocide.[131] The Assistant Secretary for Intelligence and Research, Toby

[126] *See* Alison des Forges, *Leave None to Tell the Story: Genocide in Rwanda*, 24 (1999), https://www.hrw.org/sites/default/files/media_2020/12/rwanda-leave-none-to-tell-the-story.pdf. That estimate includes all deaths, not just Tutsi.

[127] *See, e.g.*, Shattuck Interview, *supra* note 3; Atwood Interview, *supra* note 28; Fingar Interview, *supra* note 47; Dewey Interview, *supra* note 58; Inderfurth Interview, *supra* note 34.

[128] *See* William Ferroggiaro, ed., *The US and the Genocide in Rwanda 1994: Evidence of Inaction*, The National Security Archive (Aug. 20, 2001), https://nsarchive2.gwu.edu/NSAEBB/NSAEBB53/.

[129] This debate and US government actions are described more extensively and thoroughly by Samantha Power. *See* Power, *supra* note 125; Samantha Power, "A Problem from Hell:" America and the Age of Genocide, 329–389 (2002). *See also* the commentary and official documents assembled by the National Security Archive. Ferroggiaro, *supra* note 128. The National Security Archive is a non-profit research group that, in part, collects government documents through Freedom of Information Act requests and lawsuits. https://nsarchive.gwu.edu/about (last accessed Dec. 31, 2022).

[130] This official is being cited anonymously because they participated in this project on background and further information could serve to identify them.

[131] *See* Shattuck Interview, *supra* note 3. *See also* John Shattuck, Freedom on Fire: Human Rights Wars and America's Response (2005).

Gati, wrote a memo on or about May 18 regarding the facts on the ground in Rwanda,[132] from which a conclusion of genocide seemed warranted. One former official pointed out that like other treaties ratified by the United States, the Genocide Convention was the law of the land.[133] Nevertheless, he had instructions not to refer to the situation in Rwanda as a genocide to avoid the obligation to prevent it. To those who asserted that labeling the killings a genocide would require the United States to take further action on the ground, Shattuck believed this was the wrong interpretation and that the whole question could be determined later – now was the time to act to save lives.

On the other side were those opposed to US intervention. The political issues were the main hurdle, as indicated earlier: The real reason for the reluctance to call the genocide a genocide was that then the United States might have to do something.[134] Article 1 of the Genocide Convention provides that the Contracting Parties "undertake to prevent and to punish" the crime of genocide. Nevertheless, the United States had no intention of launching or participating in a humanitarian mission five months after the Black Hawk Down episode in Somalia, indicated several officials.[135] Brian Atwood called this attitude "Somalia Syndrome."[136] As Tim Wirth stated, the United States was not about to go into Rwanda, regardless of what international law said.[137] At the Secretary's morning staff meeting when Rwanda was discussed, Wirth recalled, there were those who called for taking various steps on the ground. Secretary of State Christopher said nothing; he and perhaps others had obviously made the decision that it would go nowhere, Wirth said.

There were also a number of bureaucratic, military, and budget hurdles to taking significant action. Shattuck's perception was that the genocide unfolded so quickly that there was no time. As US policy moved toward evacuation of its personnel, momentum shifted away from taking action within Rwanda. To say, "wait a minute" called into question that existing policy, Shattuck said.

132 *See* Memorandum from Assistant Secretary for Intelligence and Research Toby T. Gati to Assistant Secretary of State for African Affairs George Moose and Department of State Legal Adviser Conrad Harper, "Rwanda – Geneva Convention Violations" (n.d.), https://nsarchive2.gwu.edu//NSAEBB/NSAEBB53/rw051894.pdf. The memo has no date, but the National Security Archive speculated that the memo was written circa May 18, 1994. *See* Ferroggiaro, *supra* note 128.

133 *See, e.g.*, Dewey Interview, *supra* note 58; Atwood Interview, *supra* note 28.

134 *See, e.g.*, Atwood Interview, *supra* note 28.

135 *See id.*; Inderfurth Interview, *supra* note 34; Interview 32, *supra* note 6.

136 Atwood Interview, *supra* note 28.

137 *See* Wirth Interview, *supra* note 26

The military challenges were both operational and tactical.[138] Gene Dewey was out of government in 1994 but took steps to push the US toward action. He provided a minor but telling example: The United States agreed to a request from the UN force commander on the ground for Armored Personnel Carriers, but there was a delay because of the need to train the drivers. It was agonizing because there was no response and a lack of responsibility, as well as a lack of foresight and creativity, he said.[139] Thomas Fingar gave another example: When additional troops were requested before the killing began, the US would have had to airlift them, which would have meant that the State Department would have to "rent" them from the Pentagon.[140] Tim Wirth concluded that there was no military support for the venture and no State Department resources available to dedicate to the effort.[141]

The Legal Adviser's Office was involved in decision-making regarding whether or not the killings could be characterized as genocide under the Genocide Convention. Subsequent reporting has made clear that officials in the State Department and elsewhere in the US government were aware of the nature and likely extent of the killings soon after they began on April 6, 1994.[142] But officials "shunned the G-word."[143] On May 1, more than three weeks after the killings began, a Defense Department discussion paper stated "[b]e careful. Legal at State was worried about this yesterday – Genocide finding could commit USG [United States Government] to 'do something.'"[144]

By the middle of May, the Legal Adviser's Office and the State Department had a more definitive but still nuanced, position. A May 16 draft legal analysis by then Assistant Legal Adviser for African Affairs Joan Donahue concluded that the facts in Rwanda met the criteria for genocide under the Convention.[145] On May 20, referring to that legal memo and to the May 18 Gati memo regarding the factual situation on the ground, four senior State Department officials, including John Shattuck and Legal Adviser Conrad

[138] *See, e.g.*, Dewey Interview, *supra* note 58; Fingar Interview, *supra* note 47.

[139] *See also* Power, A Problem from Hell, *supra* note 129, at 379–380 (describing this incident in greater detail).

[140] *See* Fingar Interview, *supra* note 47.

[141] *See* Wirth Interview, *supra* note 26.

[142] *See, e.g.*, Power, A Problem from Hell, *supra* note 129 at 354–357.

[143] *See id.* at 359.

[144] Discussion Paper, Office of the Deputy Assistant Secretary of Defense for Middle East/Africa Region, Department of Defense (May 1, 1994), https://nsarchive2.gwu.edu//NSAEBB/NSAEBB53/rw050194.pdf.

[145] Draft Legal Analysis, Office of the Legal Adviser, Department of State, Drafted by Assistant Legal Adviser for African Affairs Joan Donoghue (May 16, 1994), https://nsarchive2.gwu.edu/NSAEBB/NSAEBB53/rw051694.pdf. Donahue was later appointed as a judge to the International Court of Justice, and is now the Court's President.

Harper, declared in a memo to the Secretary that they believed that Department officials should be authorized to state that "acts of genocide have occurred."[146] They noted that this language would be consistent with the language used to describe the situation in Bosnia. The memo went on to conclude that a statement that acts of genocide have occurred would not have any particular legal consequences, presumably including a requirement to intervene to prevent genocide. Such a statement could, however, the memo said, increase pressure for the United States to act. Shortly thereafter, Secretary Christopher issued muddied guidance allowing the use of the terms "genocide" or "acts of genocide."[147] Whether the terminology "acts of genocide" had any different legal effect than the term "genocide" is not fully explained in these memos. Nonetheless, the legalistic parsing generated skepticism.

This episode sheds light on the role of international law in decision-making. Plainly, legal concerns and the view of the Legal Adviser's Office played a role in the policy discussion. In Shattuck's view, the extensive debate within the US government demonstrated how seriously the United States takes international law.[148] How much of a role legal concerns played is more difficult to tell. Early on, the legal view seems to have been one of wariness about the possible repercussions of labeling the killings a genocide. Later, the Legal Adviser's Office and some senior policymakers in the State Department were willing to make the connection to genocide but determined that a finding of genocide would not create legal pressure to act further, even if it might create political pressure.

The genocide determination seems significant in the sense that it represented an assertion of international law that was inconvenient for the position of many, and perhaps most, US officials, who were reluctant to become involved. Yet even the ultimate position of the Legal Adviser's Office was a cautious one. This caution may have reflected the overall caution of policymakers and their conflicted views, and one can speculate whether the Legal Adviser's role reinforced those attitudes and vice versa, in a kind of feedback loop. In any event, the legal conclusion does not seem to have significantly swayed the course of State Department or overall US policymaking in

[146] Action Memorandum from Assistant Secretary of State for African Affairs George E. Moose, Assistant Secretary of State for Democracy, Human Rights and Labor John Shattuck, Assistant Secretary of State of International Organization Affairs Douglas J. Bennet, and Department of State Legal Adviser Conrad K. Harper, through Under Secretary of State for Political Affairs Peter Tarnoff and Under Secretary of State for Global Affairs Tim Wirth, to Secretary of State Warren Christopher, "Has Genocide Occurred in Rwanda?" (May 21, 1994), https://nsarchive2.gwu.edu/NSAEBB/NSAEBB53/rw051694.pdf

[147] *See* POWER, A PROBLEM FROM HELL, *supra* note 129, at 361–364.

[148] *See* Shattuck Interview, *supra* note 3.

Rwanda, except at the margins. Even if it had swayed US policy, the legal determination may have come too late in the course of the genocide to make a great deal of difference. Some former officials have asserted that whether mass killings qualify as genocide, or crimes against humanity, or some other category of atrocity is beside the point in the moment, and dithering about the correct legal characterization can serve to delay effective action.[149]

As discussed below, however, the precedent of US inaction in Rwanda, and the ultimate horror of the genocide there, led many State Department and US policymakers to believe later that they and the United States had an ethical obligation, if not a strictly legal obligation, to take action in the face of mass atrocities in the future. This sense seems to have contributed to the US decision to take action in Kosovo, to declare the situation in Darfur a genocide, and to take action against Qaddafi in Libya. It may be more telling, therefore, to view the role of legal and ethical concerns in the Rwanda episode from this longer-term perspective.

4.2.3 *Examples of Strong Compliance by the United States*

As noted earlier, former officials expressed their perception that the United States generally exhibited a high degree of compliance with international law, especially in comparison to other countries. Some former officials said, moreover, that the United States has been particularly scrupulous in complying in certain areas, going beyond the letter of the law. These areas include arms control, humanitarian law, and diplomatic relations. Note that reciprocity provides an incentive to comply in all of these areas. Officials also provided one or two additional, specific examples in which the United States complied with international law despite incentives not to.

4.2.3.1 US and Arms Control

A number of former officials mentioned that the US was punctilious about complying with its arms control commitments, taking those obligations very seriously.[150] Arms control is an area where the rules are more cut and dried

[149] *See* Remarks of David Scheffer, Conference on International Decision-Making in the Age of Genocide: Rwanda 1990–1994 (June 1–3, 2014), 2nd day transcript at 2–88, https://francegenocidetutsi.org/20150325-rwanda-transcript-day-two.pdf. Scheffer said "the legal analysis . . . delays and obfuscates what actually needs to be done by policy makers." Regarding the irrelevance of the label for mass atrocities, see also Shattuck Interview, *supra* note 3; Interview 32, *supra* note 6.

[150] *See, e.g.*, Holum Interview, *supra* note 72; Interview 18, *supra* note 11; Interview 10, *supra* note 3; Interview 36, *supra* note 63; Sonenshine Interview, *supra* note 26; Interview 33, *supra* note 26.

than in other areas and compliance is more easily determined by others.[151] Arms control agreements also often contain verification procedures, which also enhance compliance.[152] Some former officials also pointed out, however, the evident self-interest of the United States in taking arms control agreements seriously: The United States complies because it wants others to comply.[153] That is, reciprocity, or the fear of reciprocal action, plays a role.

John Holum, Under Secretary for Arms Control and International Security in the Clinton administration, shared that view.[154] According to him, the State Department in general tended to be strict constructionists, and the Arms Control bureau was the strictest of all. The basic justification for a strict approach was that the United States did not want others taking liberties with arms control agreements and that the United States had agreed to the standard in the treaty because it was in the US interest and the United States had ratified that treaty. Thus, in order to hold others to a strict standard, it was necessary for the United States to do the same. Added to that, Holum seemed to suggest, was the power of a treaty obligation for the United States.

Nevertheless, Holum said, there would sometimes be push back within the US government against a strict interpretation, primarily on the basis of national security concerns. In addition, sometimes disputes developed over technical issues or ambiguities that became matters for a technical determination regarding the boundaries of acceptable behavior. Regional or country-specific concerns also could outweigh legal interpretations.

Holum asserted that country-specific political considerations won the day when the George W. Bush administration decided to enter into the United States–India Civil Nuclear Agreement,[155] designed to lead toward civil nuclear cooperation with India in spite of India's status as a nuclear weapons power that was not a party to the Non-Proliferation Treaty.[156] He believed that this step represented a violation of previous agreements, including the

[151] *See* Interview 10, *supra* note 3. *See also* Interview 36, *supra* note 63 (compliance more likely in arms control than other areas because it is technical and detailed, there are verification systems, and so a breach is discoverable and creates problems that undermine the reason for the regime).

[152] *See* Interview 36, *supra* note 63.

[153] *See* Holum Interview, *supra* note 72; Interview 18, *supra* note 11.

[154] *See* Holum Interview, *supra* note 72.

[155] Agreement for Cooperation between the Government of the United States of America and the Government of India Concerning Peaceful Uses of Nuclear Energy (Oct. 10, 2008). *See also* Office of the Press Secretary, *Joint Statement between George W. Bush and Prime Minister Manmohan Singh*, WHITE HOUSE (July 18, 2005), http://georgewbush-whitehouse.archives.gov/news/releases/2005/07/20050718-6.html.

[156] Treaty on the Non-Proliferation of Nuclear Weapons, July 1, 1968, 729 U.N.T.S. 161. *See generally*, Jayshree Bajoria & Esther Pan, *Council on Foreign Relations Backgrounder: The*

Non-Proliferation Treaty, even though the International Atomic Energy Agency (IAEA) later approved the relationship.

Other former officials thought this case was a harder call. Richard Boucher thought the challenge was not only compliance with the NPT but also how to work politically to get approval through a body of the IAEA.[157] Another former Assistant Secretary thought this was a difficult case of international law versus political reality, where the issue was to defend the NPT or accept that India is a big power and accommodate and help it.[158] Another former official asserted that if the gray legal area had been more black and white, the deal would not have happened.[159]

4.2.3.2 Humanitarian Law

A number of former officials cited humanitarian law, or the law of armed conflict, as an area in which the United States generally was scrupulous in complying with international law.[160] One former official said that the military tries hard to comply with the law of armed conflict, and that the United States investigates every case and convicts. Few other countries are as aggressive, failing, for example, to pursue violations by peacekeepers in UN peacekeeping operations.[161] A former Assistant Secretary in the Bush administration highlighted several areas within the law of armed conflict where they thought the United States was particularly scrupulous.[162] In treatment of combatant casualties on the battlefield, US forces provide equivalent care to enemy soldiers, the former official said. US forces also go to extraordinary lengths regrading collateral damage to civilians or civilian objects. Nevertheless, one former official countered, the United States was scrupulous in complying with the Geneva Conventions – until we were not.[163] It is unclear what the former official was referring to, but an obvious example would be the US application of the Geneva Conventions to detainees and, possibly, to targets of drone strikes in the war on terror.

U.S.–India Nuclear Deal, COUNCIL ON FOREIGN RELATIONS (last updated Nov. 5, 2010), https://www.cfr.org/backgrounder/us-india-nuclear-deal.

[157] *See* Boucher Interview, *supra* note 7.

[158] *See* Interview 16, *supra* note 59.

[159] *See* Interview 22, Former Assistant Secretary in the George W. Bush administration.

[160] *See, e.g.*, Interview 16, *supra* note 59; Interview 12, Assistant Secretary, G. W. Bush administration; David Stillwell, Former Assistant Secretary for East Asian and Pacific Affairs, Trump administration; Interview 33, *supra* note 26.

[161] *See* Interview 16, *supra* note 59.

[162] Interview 12, *supra* note 160.

[163] *See* Interview 33, *supra* note 26.

4.2.3.3 Diplomatic Relations

Another area that several former officials cited for greater US compliance was diplomatic relations.[164] Roberta Jacobsen, for example, said that the United States took the broadest possible interpretation of obligations regarding diplomatic relations.[165] The United States complies almost to a fault regarding other nations' diplomats, she said, partly because of reciprocity concerns regarding treatment of US diplomats. For example, the United States does not prosecute foreign diplomats for violations of US law, instead allowing them to be recalled. David Stillwell, former Assistant Secretary in the Trump administration, agreed, expressing frustration at the level of deference accorded foreign diplomats compared to treatment of US diplomats.[166]

4.2.3.4 Genocide in Darfur

A noteworthy example of the United States taking an expansive view of international law occurred when Secretary Powell chose to declare atrocities committed by the Sudanese government and Janjaweed militia in Darfur a genocide. The US response to the genocide in Darfur stands in stark contrast to its response the Rwandan genocide roughly ten years before. Indeed, the failed US response in Rwanda may have served to motivate the different decision regarding Darfur.[167]

Secretary Powell described the situation in the following way in email comments provided to the author: "One difficult issue arose when I became concerned with the situation in Darfur. Did it constitute a Genocide? I sent a team to examine the situation. My lawyer said it was a close call and he could defend whatever I decided. I called it a Genocide. The UN did not agree with what was now also the President's position."[168] On a legal question and facts

[164] *See, e.g.*, Interview 33, *supra* note 26; Stillwell Interview, *supra* note 160; Interview with Roberta Jacobsen, Assistant Secretary for Western Hemisphere Affairs, Obama administration and Ambassador to Mexico, Obama and Trump administrations; Boucher Interview, *supra* note 7.

[165] *See* Jacobsen Interview, *supra* note 164.

[166] *See* Stillwell Interview, *supra* note 160.

[167] *See* Interview 32, *supra* note 6; Shattuck Interview, *supra* note 3. *See* also Rebecca Hamilton, *Inside Colin Powell's Decision to Declare Genocide in Darfur*, The Atlantic (Aug. 17, 2011), *available at* https://www.theatlantic.com/international/archive/2011/08/inside-colin-powells-decision-to-declare-genocide-in-darfur/243560/.

[168] Email from Former Secretary of State Colin Powell, conveyed to the author by email from Secretary Powell's assistant, July 30, 2018.

that may not have been absolutely clear, Secretary Powell chose to take an expansive view of the Genocide Convention.[169]

Powell made this decision in his capacity as Secretary of State, consulting only minimally with the White House and other agencies.[170] The State Department memo to Powell discussing the options regarding Darfur and possible genocide asserted that the Secretary of State typically makes a determination on genocide within a particular country.[171] This illustrates the primacy of the State Department in making many determinations related to international law.

Others interviewed recalled the incident similarly.[172] Thomas Fingar, then Assistant Secretary for Intelligence and Research, recalled that he was asked to interpret the facts in Darfur and was part of the discussions regarding the application of the Genocide Convention.[173] Fingar also recalled discussion regarding potential consequences for the United States if Darfur was labeled as a genocide, which were similar to the potential consequences faced when considering the question in Rwanda. The content of these discussions illustrates the complex weighing of factors involving questions of international law. The legal consequences were discussed, namely the potential requirements for action under the Convention, but the main concern was the political consequences, he indicated. These concerns were related to potential Congressional mandates for action and to the budget cycle. Congress might attach a rider to a bill, requiring the United States to take, or not take, certain action. A declaration could trigger the need for peacekeeping, for which the United States would be responsible for onethird of the cost, when it was the fourth quarter of the fiscal year when funds were scarce.

Fingar said that the ultimate determination to call it genocide was mostly a factual one, rather than a policy decision. Once the facts were checked off – through statisticians and polling, recalled Fingar – Powell said yes, call it a genocide. Secretary Powell made his decision even though it might have opened the United States to calls for additional action, both on moral and legal grounds. Richard Boucher, an Assistant Secretary in the George W. Bush

[169] Convention on the Prevention and Punishment of the Crime of Genocide, Dec. 9, 1948, 78 U.N.T.S. 277.

[170] *See* Hamilton, *supra* note 167.

[171] Memo from William H. Taft, Lorne W. Craner, Pierre R. Prosper, Donald Y. Yamamoto to The Deputy Secretary (June 25, 2004), at 2–3, https://nsarchive2.gwu.edu/NSAEBB/NSAEBB356/20040625_darfur.PDF.

[172] *See* Fingar Interview, *supra* note 47; Dewey Interview, *supra* note 58; Boucher Interview, *supra* note 7; Shattuck Interview, *supra* note 3.

[173] *See* Fingar Interview, *supra* note 47.

administration, pointed out that the moral implications of naming the situation a genocide would be particularly acute after Rwanda.[174] Presumably, he meant that there could be increased pressure to act in Darfur after the failure to act in Rwanda.

In terms of legal consequences, the decision conceivably could have incurred legal obligations for the United States to take action in Darfur under the Genocide Convention, similar to the situation in Rwanda. In facing the potential legal consequences, Powell may have taken comfort in the opinion of his Legal Adviser, Will Taft, and other bureau heads, who stated in a memo that "[a] determination that genocide has occurred in Darfur would have no legal – as opposed to moral, political, or policy – consequences for the United States." The memo explained that the State Department had rejected in the past an "expansive reading of article 1 that would impose a legal obligation on all contracting parties to take particular measures to 'prevent' genocide in areas outside their territory."[175] Accordingly, Powell may have had some confidence that the United States would have a credible response to claims that international law would obligate the United States to take further action. Nonetheless, there was a risk and Powell could have made a safer decision.

As noted before, the Darfur declaration may have broader implications for the US' role in international law. Phyllis Oakley asserted that it serves as an example of US efforts over time to stop genocide by relying on spreading respect for the rule of law.[176] Other examples, she said, include efforts against genocide in the Balkans[177] and support for prosecution of genocide through the international tribunals established for the former Yugoslavia and for Rwanda. A former senior official in the Obama administration supported this view, asserting that foreign policy is informed not just by national interest but by ethics and values. More particularly, we do not want to see a genocide, they said.[178] The failure to react in Rwanda galvanized the United States on the issue, and so we jumped on the genocide in Darfur.[179]

[174] *See* Boucher Interview, *supra* note 7.

[175] *See* Information Memorandum from William H. Taft et al., *supra* note 171; Hamilton, *supra* note 167.

[176] *See* Oakley Interview, *supra* note 3.

[177] The failure to respond to Rwanda was also influential in the US decision to intervene in Bosnia, reported John Shattuck, Assistant Secretary for Democracy, Human Rights, and Labor in the Clinton administration. Shattuck Interview, *supra* note 3.

[178] *See* Interview 32, *supra* note 6.

[179] *See id.*; Shattuck Interview, *supra* note 3.

4.2.3.5 CITES

A former official,[180] who maintained that the United States took its international obligations seriously and complied with them most of the time, gave the example of US compliance with the Convention on Trade in Endangered Species.[181] They mentioned occasions when the United States enforced CITES requirements even when doing so was disadvantageous to US interests. In general, enforcement of CITES restrictions involved tough issues, which could include economic harm to importers, industry sectors, and family businesses. One case involved a multi-million dollar shipment of Brazilian mahogany that US importers had already paid for. The Brazilian government had issued paperwork, but the government changed and decided the shipment was not legal. In spite of significant political and private pressure to allow the shipment, it never entered the United States.

4.2.3.6 Boarding of Ships at Sea

Robert Gallucci[182] recalled an incident involving the boarding of a ship in international waters by a close US ally, Spain. No doubt, he was speaking of an incident in December, 2002, in which two Spanish naval vessels boarded a flagless North Korean cargo ship in international waters off the coast of Yemen.[183] Allied naval forces were engaged in patrolling the Indian Ocean watching for Al Qaeda flights fleeing from Afghanistan. Fifteen Scud missiles were found hidden under stacks of cement, apparently destined for Yemen. While the boarding of a flagless vessel would have been acceptable under the Law of the Sea, the carrying of such weapons probably was not a violation of international law. Hence, they could not be seized, and the vessel was released. In these circumstances, the United States and its allies were willing to respect international law, in spite of the fact that the missiles were being transported from an "unfriendly state into a volatile part of the world."[184]

[180] *See* Interview 34, Former Official.

[181] Convention on International Trade in Endangered Species of Wild Fauna and Flora, Mar. 3, 1973, 27 U.S.T. 1087; 993 U.N.T.S. 243.

[182] See Gallucci Interview, *supra* note 20.

[183] See Frederic L. Kirgis, *Boarding of North Korean Vessel on the High Seas*, 7(14) ASIL Insights (Dec. 12, 2002), www.asil.org/insights/volume/7/issue/14/boarding-north-korean-vessel-high-seas

[184] *Id.*

4.2.3.7 Various

Some former officials cited various other areas of international law in which they thought that the United States tended to comply beyond the letter of the law. Several former officials mentioned trade, especially US compliance with WTO dispute resolution rulings. Interviews with many of these officials, however, occurred before the Trump administration began pulling back from the international trade regime, policies that the Biden administration has largely maintained, albeit more politely.[185]

A handful of other officials cited human rights, but their comments tended to focus on US promotion of human rights standards, as opposed to US compliance *per se*. Some of these former officials cited the US pushing for a declaration of genocide in Darfur and other efforts to promote the norm against genocide, discussed earlier. Some of the other examples that former officials cited reflected efforts by particular administrations that were at odds with the policies of other administrations. One former official mentioned this dynamic explicitly.[186] Citing Obama's executive order and other efforts to prohibit torture, that former official pointed out that the United States had no fixed point on this issue and that American policy wandered back and forth. Obama prohibited torture in response to Bush administration policies and Trump campaigned against Obama's position.

4.3 CONCLUSION

This chapter addressed the views of former officials regarding US compliance with international law and examined ways in which it compared with their views about the compliance of states more generally. Their conclusion was that the United States complied substantially with international law, with almost 90 percent saying that the United States complied all or most of the time.

The United States was motivated by considerations similar to those of other states, with some differences. First, the role of ethics was the most frequently cited factor favoring compliance. Ethical considerations were also reflected in two other factors cited by former officials: the notion of US exceptionalism, in the sense of moral responsibility and leadership, and the significance of treaty

[185] *See* James McBride & Anshu Siripurapu, *Council on Foreign Relations Backgrounder: What's Next for the WTO?*, Council on Foreign Relations (last updated June 10, 2022), https://www.cfr.org/backgrounder/whats-next-wto.

[186] *See* Interview 8, *supra* note 8.

obligations and the importance of adhering to them. Second, the United States has an interest in maintaining the international order, including existing international law. Third, the views of allies can support US compliance but can also sometimes aid the United States in taking action when international law is murky or even in opposition. Fourth, the United States is concerned about setting desirable precedent and avoiding a negative precedent that can affect other states' decisions involving international law. Finally, the United States' commitment to treaties can lead it to comply.

The factors that former officials cited that militate against compliance by the United States included national interest, ambiguity of legal obligations, sovereignty concerns, domestic law complications in the application of international law, bureaucratic or budgeting difficulties in complying with international law, and domestic politics. Another factor in decision-making not mentioned explicitly by former officials was the State Department's policy-making process generally and the role of international law and of Department lawyers in that process. That process is discussed in the next chapter, Chapter 5.

The project assessed tensions in US decision-making between the requirements of international law, on the one hand, and policy concerns or national interest, on the other. The predilection of former officials was to follow international law, but as indicated earlier, legal issues were considered as one factor among a variety of factors, essentially involving a cost–benefit analysis. Former officials displayed a range of views regarding the tension between international law and national interest. The views ranged from those who indicated that the United States complied with international law almost all the time, to those that argued that international law was subordinate to policy and national interest considerations and that legal justifications are found or adjusted to support them. Most former officials fell in the middle, asserting that while the United States followed international law much of the time, there were occasions when significant national interests took priority. A few former officials indicated that the primacy of policy goals holds especially for issues of national security and that, conversely, international law takes on more weight when the policy issues are not as significant. Others were less emphatic about the primacy of policy or national interest but, nonetheless, indicated that legal concerns often took a backseat to significant policy interests. Policymakers, they said, would push the envelope to meet policy objectives.

Chapter 4 concludes with a description of examples of instances where the United States violated or bent international law and examples where the United States acted scrupulously in complying with international law. To a large extent, these examples are similar to the description by former officials of areas of greater or lesser compliance of states overall in Chapter 3. Examples of potential US overreach included various military interventions of the past sixty years, the NATO bombing of Kosovo in 1999, and enhanced interrogation or torture after 9-11. Areas of the law in which the United States has tended to be more compliant include arms control, humanitarian law, diplomatic relations, trade, and, to some extent, environment.

These examples tend to buttress an instrumentalist take on compliance, although not entirely. Regarding the negative examples, the United States was less likely to comply on issues that touch on national security. Similarly, many of the positive examples support the instrumentalist prediction that reciprocity plays a significant role in enhancing compliance with international law.

Another striking feature, however, is that most of these areas involve extensive, specific treaty obligations. That result suggests the importance for compliance of precision in international obligations, a result associated more with normative approaches, or with both camps. The example of the Kosovo bombing demonstrates the potential effect of ethical concerns behind US behavior. The example of Rwanda offered a mixed story, demonstrating the dominance of state interests in the short term but also illustrating the attention to legal and ethical concerns in the debate at the time and in subsequent policy decisions in Kosovo and Darfur. Overall, these examples demonstrate the tension between instrumentalist and normative explanations offered by policymakers. Of course, both things can be true: Both instrumentalist and normative factors can play a role in decision-making.

5

The Role of International Law in State Department Policymaking

This chapter explores the role of international law in State Department decision-making. Bureaucratic structure, procedural requirements, and cultural norms within the Department ensure that international law considerations play a significant role, both formally and informally. Nevertheless, that role is not necessarily determinative, and the weight of legal advice varies, depending on the circumstances.

The chapter focuses on the role of international lawyers in the Department, which reflects the significance of international law in Department decision-making more generally. The Office of the Legal Adviser, for example, plays a formal role in decision-making, signing off on relevant policy recommendations as part of a clearance process. In addition, attorney-advisers are assigned to every functional and regional bureau in the Department, making them and their advice ubiquitous. The formal role of lawyers in the process makes it necessary to address their concerns. The lawyers also have various informal means of influencing the direction of policy. The Legal Adviser exercises substantial influence because of his or her formal position as an Assistant Secretary and their role in advising the Secretary and the higher echelons of the Department. State Department lawyers also may constitute an "epistemic community," able to leverage their expertise and legitimacy to influence policymaking.

State Department lawyers fulfill a number of roles, perhaps best described broadly as a general counsel role, assisting their "clients" to achieve their policy objectives, and an objective counselor or "judge" role regarding the content of international law. These two roles are obviously in tension. State Department lawyers must consider a number of factors in giving advice, including, for example, the content of international law, the objectives of a proposed policy, the past practice of the Department, and the positions of other government agencies.[1] These other roles constrain the lawyers' ability to act simply as an advocate for policymakers.

Policymakers generally have decision-making authority on the legal advice presented to them, depending on the seniority of the policymaker and the nature of the issue at hand. Significant matters are decided ultimately at higher levels. Even so, almost all former officials said that the advice of the Legal Adviser's Office was highly influential and sometimes determinative. When asked specifically, 21 percent of former officials said the advice of the Legal Adviser's Office was determinative regarding US compliance with international law, 68 percent said it was significant, and 11 percent said it was of moderate weight or less.

An examination of former officials' qualitative comments reflects more nuanced attitudes toward the role of advice from the Legal Adviser's Office. Views about the deference given to the views of the Legal Adviser's Office fell into three categories. The first group viewed the advice of the Legal Adviser's Office as essentially determinative. The second group – by far the largest – viewed legal advice as significant but not necessarily determinative. The third group viewed legal advice as of moderate importance, or less. In a related vein, a number of other former officials expressed various views about the weight of L's advice but strongly asserted that legal advice was subordinate to policy concerns and to policymakers' judgment.

Thus, when the lawyers said that some course of action was definitely illegal, that generally was the final word, at least within the State Department. Some former officials indicated that the lawyers rarely made such a categorical determination, however. Otherwise, L's advice was influential, but its weight varied depending on the circumstances. Policymakers, moreover, could sometimes change the lawyers' minds. Policy concerns could sometimes overcome legal objections, especially at higher levels.

This is not to suggest that decisions were presented as a stark choice between law and policy. Rather, a situation would be presented in the following manner: these are the circumstances, these are the options, and these are the legal implications. Thus, there may be a range of options available to policymakers, and compliance may represent a choice among shades of gray. The ambiguity of international law may have allowed the lawyers to provide some wiggle room regarding options. Good lawyers might present those options, identify ambiguities, and present the risks of particular interpretations or options.

In addition, decisions on issues involving international law, like all bureaucratic decisions, were subject to bureaucratic politics and the influence of

[1] *See* Ashley Deeks, *Inside "L": Some Thoughts on the Office of the Legal Adviser*, 2 CH. J. INT'L L. 503, 505 (2001).

powerful individuals, as described in the organizational behavior and bureaucratic politics literature. Turf battles might be especially keen among the regional and functional bureaus of the State Department. These conflicts also illustrate the process of contestation, the notion that norms will be contested at every stage of a decision-making process, as described by Whytock and Sanders and the international legal process school.

Some contestation was also evident in the relationship between lawyers and policymakers. Many former officials indicated that the development of policy was a collaborative and constructive process. The lawyers were often willing to work with policymakers and they were usually willing to find alternative courses of action within the law. A significant number of former officials indicated that they pushed back against the lawyers regarding the interpretation or application of the law, or other issues, in favor of policy concerns. For this group, the interaction between policymakers and lawyers resembled more of a negotiation.

When international law conflicted with significant policy or national interests, policymakers could sometimes seek to overcome those obstacles. Former officials indicated three general strategies to do so, in descending order of preference. First, they or the lawyers might identify alternative, legal approaches to achieve the same result. Second, they and the lawyers might explore alternative interpretations of international law. Finally, on rare occasions, if the national interest was strong enough, and after significant review at higher levels, policymakers might decide to proceed with a course of action that pushed against the limits of international law.

The ambiguity of much international law and the resulting opportunity for interpretation could provide a broad umbrella to justify a variety of actions. As a result, several former officials indicated, the United States rarely was unable to pursue its policy goals, though it might have to take different means to achieve them. Because of ambiguity, compliance potentially could involve a variety of acceptable courses of action, some more or less legally acceptable than others. From the weight of interviews with former officials, calculated and blatant reinterpretation of obligations after the lawyers provided their initial advice did not appear to be the norm, however.

Thus, at least in the face of significant national interests, the application of international law could be flexible, and policymakers and lawyers have developed strategies and processes to accommodate tensions between law and policy. Nevertheless, the predilection of most former officials was to follow international law, and they generally supported the multilateral, rule-based, collaborative world order and the United States' place in that order. The views of the Legal Adviser's Office regarding legality were taken seriously, and L's status and its role in the decision-making process ensured that international law had a voice in that process.

5.1 THE ROLE OF THE LEGAL ADVISER'S OFFICE IN DECISION-MAKING

The lawyers in the State Department operate out of the Office of the Legal Adviser, or "L." The Legal Adviser is politically appointed, holds a rank equivalent to Assistant Secretary of State, and reports directly to the Secretary of State.[2] The Legal Adviser's Office is staffed by about 200 attorneys, who are organized into some twenty-two sections, each of which generally corresponds to the one of the various regional and functional bureaus within the State Department.[3] An organizational chart of the Legal Adviser's Office is contained in Figure 5.1.

The relationship between L attorneys and the policymakers in the bureaus to which they are assigned is complex. On the one hand, L attorneys clearly view policymakers in their bureaus and elsewhere as their "clients" and describe them as such in their conversation. Two of the three former L officials interviewed used this terminology. Policymakers also characterized their relationship with the lawyers as a lawyer–client relationship.[4] Some policymakers asserted that as the client, the policymaker takes advice and makes the decision, not always following the lawyer's advice. On the other hand, L attorneys report to the Legal Adviser and not the bureau to which they are assigned, so they maintain a certain level of independence from political pressure by their clients. Some policymakers specifically noted that the lawyers worked for L, rather than for their bureau, implicitly highlighting the lawyers' independence.[5]

2 US Department of State, *Practicing Law in the Office of the Legal Adviser*, https://www.state.gov/s/l/3190.htm (last accessed Jan. 3, 2019) [hereinafter, *Practicing Law*].

3 *Id.* Those bureaus are, in turn, are generally headed by an Assistant Secretary, or by another high-ranking official. The regional bureaus include the Bureau of African Affairs, the Bureau of European and Eurasian Affairs, the Bureau of South and Central Asian Affairs, and the Bureau of International Organizations. The functional bureaus include, for example, Human Rights and Refugees, Political and Military Affairs, and Economics and Business Affairs.

4 *See, e.g.*, Interview 31, Former State Department Officer and Career Senior Diplomat; Interview with Esther Brimmer, Assistant Secretary for International Organizations, Obama administration; Interview 8, Former Senior State Department Official; Interview with John Shattuck, Assistant Secretary for Democracy, Human Rights, and Labor, Clinton administration.

5 *See, e.g.*, Interview 16, Former Assistant Secretary.

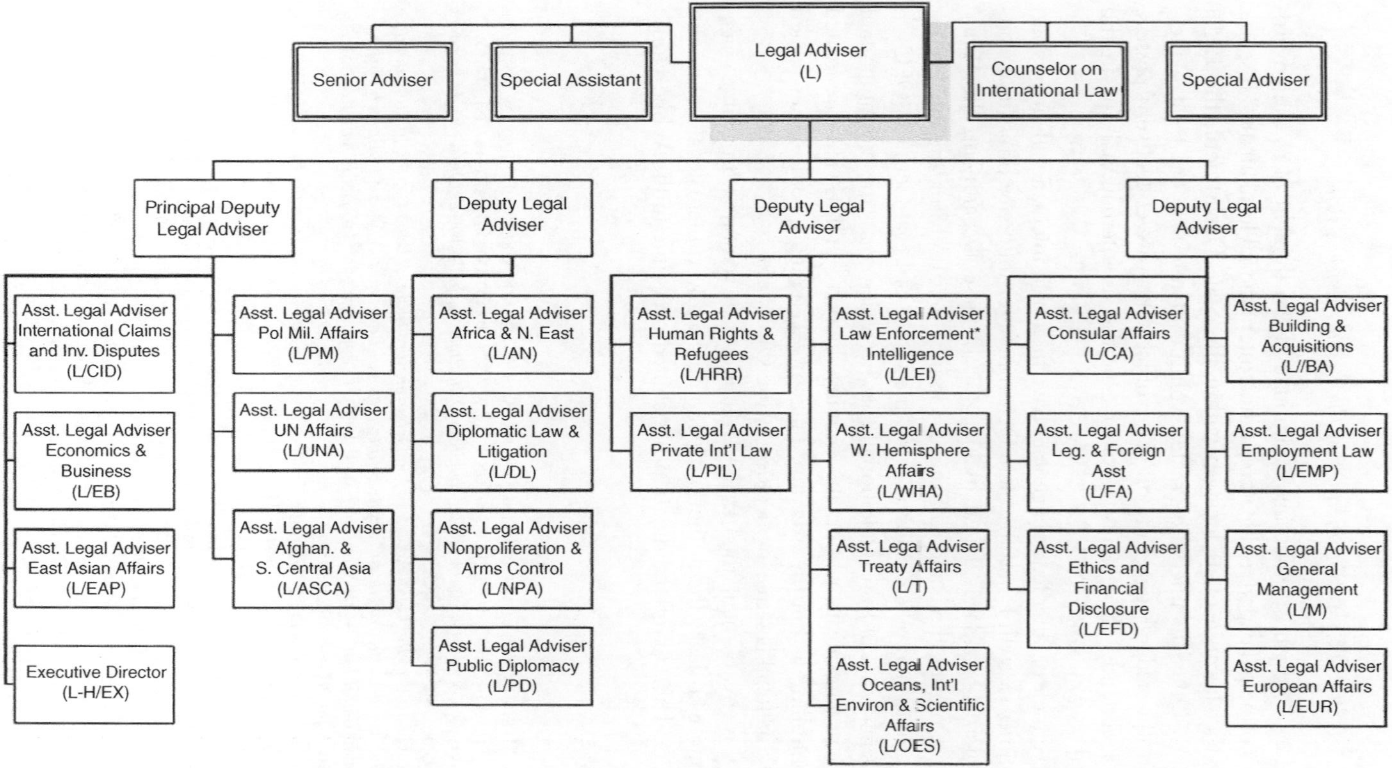

FIGURE 5.1 Office of the Legal Adviser.
Source: 1 Foreign Affairs Manual § 240: Office of the Legal Adviser (May 25, 2018), https://fam.state.gov/fam/01fam/01fam0240.html

5.1.1 *Significance of the Legal Adviser's Role*

The Legal Adviser's Office has traditionally been thought of as the government's principal expert and lead regarding international legal affairs.[6] It seems likely that because of its location within the State Department, the Legal Adviser's Office handles the greatest volume of international legal matters within the federal government. The office's lawyers collectively possess, almost certainly, the greatest level of expertise in international law in the federal government.

Nevertheless, other federal agencies have their own international lawyers and sometimes vie with L and the State Department for influence on issues involving international law.[7] These include the Defense Department, the White House Counsel, the National Security Council Legal Advisor, the intelligence community, and others. Most notably, the Office of Legal Counsel (OLC) in the Department of Justice traditionally has been viewed as "the most important source of legal advice withing the executive branch"[8] and its views are treated as controlling within the executive branch.[9] Accordingly, some issues related to international law may be decided by the OLC.

In this environment, the Legal Adviser is one lawyer, one with a large voice, but one who lacks the authority to coordinate government legal policy and lawyers. The task of coordination has shifted over time to the White House

6 *See* Michael P. Scharf & Paul R. Williams, Shaping Foreign Policy in Times of Crisis: The Role of International Law and the State Department Legal Adviser xix (2010); Harold Koh, *The State Department Legal Adviser's Office: Eight Decades in Peace and War*, 100 Geo. L.J. 1747, 1757 (2012).

7 *See The Role of the Legal Adviser of the Department of State: A Report of the Joint Committee Established by the American Society of International Law and the American Branch of the International Law Association*, 85 Am. J. Int'l L. 358, 364–366 (1991) [*hereinafter* ASIL-ABILA Joint Committee Report].

8 Trevor Morrison, *Libya, "Hostilities," the Office of Legal Counsel, and the Process of Executive Branch Legal Interpretation*, 124 Harv. L. Rev. F. 62, 63 (2011) [hereinafter Morrison, *Libya*]. For discussions of OLC's role, see also Trevor Morrison, *Stare Decisis in the Office of Legal Counsel*, 110 Colum. L. Rev. 1448, 1458–1470 (2010) [hereinafter Morrison, *Stare Decisis*]; Eric Messinger, *Transparency and the Office of Legal Counsel*, 17 N.Y.U. J. Legisl. & Pub. Pol. 239, 245–249 (2014); Cornelia T. L. Pillard, *The Unfulfilled Promise of the Constitution in Executive Hands*, 103 Mich. L. Rev. 676, 710–717 (2005).

9 Memorandum from David J. Barron, Acting Assistant Att'y Gen., Office of Legal Counsel, to Attorneys of the Office, Re: Best Practices for OLC Legal Advice and Written Opinions 1 (July 16, 2010), http://www.justice.gov/olc/pdf/olc-legal-advice-opinions.pdf. OLC opinions may be overruled by the Attorney General or the President, but that is extremely rare. Morrison, *Libya*, *supra* note 8, at 63.

Counsel's Office and the NSC Legal Adviser's Office.[10] Thus, some decisions may be made in the interagency decision-making process or elsewhere.

5.1.2 *Functions of the Legal Adviser's Office*

The attorneys in the Legal Adviser's Office perform a variety of specific legal tasks. They spend most of their time researching and advising on international law issues and the effects of international law on domestic law and vice versa. They also provide clearance on behalf of L on memos regarding policies to be presented to policymakers; attend internal and interagency meetings in order to develop those policies; negotiate and draft international agreements; handle personnel, building, and acquisitions issues; and address compliance with rules and regulations.[11] The State Department needs legal assistance not only to serve its function as an executive agency but also to manage its own operations.[12]

More generally, attorneys in L act as counselor, draftsman, advocate and negotiator, judge and international law expert.[13] Former Legal Adviser Harold Koh asserts that the attorneys in L should embody the following characteristics, among others. They should be independent, nonpartisan experts on, and scholars of, international law; have a wide-ranging remit across the entire Department; provide legal advice sensitive to the clients' policy objectives; take the long view, advancing the best long-term interests of the State Department as an institution, as opposed to the interests of a particular individual or administration; and balance the concerns of politics and the law.[14]

It is readily apparent that there is a tension between the role of L attorneys as general counsel, assisting their "clients" to achieve their policy objectives, and their other roles, especially their role as objective counselors and "judges" regarding the content of international law. Put another way, attorneys in the Legal Advisor's Office must balance many considerations that do not concern

[10] *See* Neomi Rao, *Public Choice and International Law Compliance: The Executive Branch Is a "They," Not an "It,"* 96 MINN. L. REV. 194, 233–235 (2011).

[11] Michael K. Young, *The Role of the Attorney-Adviser in the U.S. Department of State: Institutional Arrangements and Structural Imperatives*, 61 L. & CONTEMP. PROBS. 133 (1998). See also *Practicing Law*, *supra* note 2; 1 Foreign Affairs Manual § 240, Office of the Legal Adviser (L) (May 25, 2018), https://fam.state.gov/fam/01fam/01fam0240.html (last accessed Nov. 23, 2018).

[12] *See* Deeks, *supra* note 1, at 504.

[13] Richard Bilder, *The Office of the Legal Adviser: The State Department Lawyer and Foreign Affairs*, 56 AM. J. INT'L L. 644 (1962). Professor Bilder's article is the classic source on the work of the Legal Adviser's Office, referred to by authors even today. *See, e.g.*, Koh, *supra* note 6, at 1753.

[14] *See* Koh, *supra* note 6, at 1757.

the private attorney.[15] At a firm, a lawyer has a specific client, who has sought his or her counsel. A State Department lawyer may have no clearly defined client, or multiple clients with different agendas. A private lawyer is, within the bounds of the law, primarily a zealous advocate of the client. In contrast, the various goals pursued by lawyers in the Legal Adviser's Office may not directly serve the immediate goals of their clients. The State Department lawyer has "an obligation to consider a number of factors, including what international law says about an issue, what the concerned policy offices hope to achieve, what the past practice of the State Department has been, and what other agencies hope to accomplish."[16] Thus, the State Department lawyer cannot simply perform an advocacy role on behalf of policymakers.

To focus for a moment on one of these cross-cutting demands, the State Department must act consistently across practice areas and across time when representing the United States. A firm can take inconsistent positions with different clients. The State Department faces more scrutiny, both from the public and also from lawyers and diplomats from other countries, who may have long memories regarding inconsistent positions taken by the United States and its lawyers.[17] Thus, the Department must take care not to set a precedent that could undermine its positions in other areas or in the future. Policymakers and attorneys both mentioned the importance of taking consistent positions on behalf of the United States, asking whether others would think an action inconsistent. The attorney-advisers of L may be in a better position to spot these inconsistencies because their remit extends across the Department, compared with the narrower responsibilities of the bureaus, and because L personnel tend to have long tenure, contributing to a long institutional memory.[18]

As former Legal Adviser Harold Koh has stated, State Department lawyers serve not only as general counsel but also "act as a government wide contributor to and defender of international law."[19] The office of the Legal Adviser, in particular, is widely seen as the preeminent voice on international law matters, as discussed earlier. This view of State Department lawyers as defenders of international law may extend to the State Department as a whole, moreover. Joan Spero, Under Secretary of State for Foreign and Agricultural Affairs in the Clinton administration, for example, stated that the State Department was

[15] *See* Deeks, *supra* note 1, at 504–505.
[16] *See id.* at 505.
[17] *See, e.g.*, *id.* at 505.
[18] *See* Young, *supra* note 11, at 138.
[19] *See* Koh, *supra* note 6, at 1750–1751.

generally a keeper or advocate of international law, and that the State Department had an obligation in that regard.[20]

To what extent should L attorneys serve the interest of their immediate clients, like any other lawyer or general counsel, and to what extent should they operate as advocates of international law, in a sort of judicial role? This question has been the subject of much debate in the literature,[21] a debate that probably cannot be entirely resolved. Many of the former high-level officials and former L attorneys in this study readily identified these conflicting roles of State Department lawyers, either explicitly or implicitly. One former official, for example, explicitly described the two roles of State Department lawyers as advocates and judges, adding that he or she would have preferred that they take more of an advocate role.[22] While the lawyers might tell you how to do something you wanted to do, he or she said, they would also mention the constraints on that course of action. This tension between the lawyers' roles of judges and advocates is evident in much of the discussion that follows.

5.1.3 *The Clearance Process*

As noted earlier, the lawyers in L play a significant formal role in the State Department's decision-making process, adding to the influence, or at least visibility, of international law. Under the clearance process, also followed by other federal agencies,[23] the office responsible for proposing an action consults with any other offices or bureaus that have a substantial interest in that action by means of a memorandum or supporting documents.[24] Before the action memorandum is passed on to senior officials for a decision, it must

[20] Under Secretary Spero contrasted the State Department with the Office of the US Trade Representative, which she characterized as more political, more designed to be closer to the Hill, presumably meaning Congress. She said that the State Department would sometimes push back against USTR regarding international law. *See* Interview with Joan Spero, Under Secretary of State for Foreign and Agricultural Affairs, Clinton administration.

[21] *See* ASIL-ABILA Joint Committee Report, *supra* note 7, at 362–364; Koh, *supra* note 6, at 1755–1576; Deeks, *supra* note 1; John R. Crook, *Practicing International Law for the United States*, 6 J. TRANSNAT'L L. & POL'Y 1 (1996).

[22] *See* Interview 26, Former State Department Official.

[23] *See* MORTON H. HALPERIN AND PRISCILLA CLAPP, BUREAUCRATIC POLITICS AND FOREIGN POLICY 108 (2d ed., 2007).

[24] 2 Foreign Affairs Manual §1211.a (May 15, 2018), https://fam.state.gov/fam/02fam/02fam1210.html (last accessed May 28, 2020). "'Action' and 'clearance' are the processes by which the Department makes decisions. The processes place responsibility for action upon one office while ensuring that the information and opinions of other interested offices are brought to bear on the proposed action." Many of the former officials interviewed described this process in detail and the description here is drawn from those interviews as well as from the cited sourcs.

receive a clearance from all of the interested offices or bureaus,[25] usually including L. If a clearing office disagrees or dissents, attempts are made to resolve the disagreement.[26]

5.1.3.1 Formal Resolution of Conflicts

If the disagreement among bureaus cannot be resolved, it will be decided at a higher level.[27] In the formal process, the different views are captured in separate memos, or in a joint or split memorandum.[28] L plays the same role as any other bureau in the clearance process, and so can raise legal objections in this context.[29] Often, there is a meeting to resolve the dispute, based on these prepared memoranda.[30] The disputing bureaus are usually represented by their principals, such as an Assistant Secretary, or their designee. In the case of the Legal Adviser's Office, this is the Legal Adviser.[31] The discussion would take into account all the perspectives and there would be a give and take: Can the policy be accommodated to incorporate them?[32] Most disputes would be resolved at the Under Secretary or Deputy level. Sometimes the decision would go the Secretary, and in that case would involve two to three options and discussion of the legal considerations, as well.[33]

When disputes involved policymakers and L, both sides sometimes won and sometimes lost.[34] The Legal Adviser might have some advantage, in that he or she is trained to make convincing arguments in this kind of setting, but sometimes the decision would go against L's position. Nonetheless, Thomas Pickering asserted, he never saw a Secretary knowingly choose an option contrary to international law.[35]

[25] 2 Foreign Affairs Manual §1214 Clearance or Advice, *supra* note 24. *See also* 5 Foreign Affairs Handbook – 1 H-310, *Using Memoranda* (Mar. 15, 2016), https://fam.state.gov/fam/05fah01/05fah010310.html (last accessed Nov. 23, 2018).

[26] 2 Foreign Affairs Manual §1214 Clearance or Advice, *supra* note 24; *id.* at §1217, Resolving Clearance Differences.

[27] *Id.* at §1217, Resolving Clearance Differences.

[28] *Id.*

[29] *See* Lawyer Interview 1, Former State Department Lawyer.

[30] *See* Interview with Thomas Pickering, Under Secretary for Political Affairs, Clinton administration.

[31] *See* Lawyer Interview 1, *supra* note 29.

[32] *See* Pickering Interview, *supra* note 30; Interview 32, Assistant Secretary in the Obama administration.

[33] *See* Pickering Interview, *supra* note 30.

[34] *See, e.g.*, Interview 32, *supra* note 32.

[35] *See* Pickering Interview, *supra* note 30.

5.1.3.2 Informal Mechanisms

In addition to the formal clearance process, other mechanisms and avenues exist to resolve disputes between lawyers and clients, or among clients, over international law issues. Most disagreements are worked out between the parties. Negotiation is very important in the State Department because it consists of a matrix of functional and regional bureaus with different perceived interests. Since relevant bureaus must sign off on recommendations, there are negotiations all the way around.[36] Informal give and take between lawyers and policymakers is common, as discussed in more detail below. Where informal resolution is not possible, the parties or the lawyers may also appeal informally to a higher authority, as an alternative to formal mechanisms.[37]

The lawyers themselves may have various informal means to push back against policymakers who reject legal advice, at least in significant matters.[38] For example, the lawyer might take the matter up with the Legal Adviser.[39] If the Legal Adviser agreed with the lawyers' position, that view was determinative in one lawyer's experience, at least with respect to Assistant Secretaries[40] and lower-level officials. This approach ratcheted up the pressure on the Bureau or policymaker resisting legal advice.

A lawyer might also suggest to a trusted junior client that an issue is a close call and so, therefore, the official should make sure higher-level officials, such as the relevant Assistant Secretary or Under Secretary, are aware of it. The lawyer might even alert the higher official. The alert could simply consist of an informal word: Be aware that this is the advice L gave on the issue. These less formal, yet effective, mechanisms reflect the advantage of having a day-in, day-out working relationship with officials.[41] The lawyers' ability to pursue these informal mechanisms may depend on contextual factors, including seniority of the policymakers involved and the seriousness of the issue.[42]

Policymakers appeared to have close working relationships with the attorney-advisers assigned to work with the regional and functional bureaus. A number of former officials mentioned close or helpful relationships with attorney-advisers,

[36] *See* Interview with Phyllis Oakley, Assistant Secretary, Population, Refugees, and Migration, Clinton administration; Assistant Secretary, Intelligence and Research, Clinton administration.

[37] *See, e.g.*, Lawyer Interview 2, Former Senior Official in L.

[38] *See id.*

[39] *See id.*; Interview 9, Former Senior Obama Official.

[40] *See* Interview 9, *supra* note 39.

[41] *See* Lawyer Interview 2, *supra* note 37.

[42] *See* Lawyer Interview 1, *supra* note 29.

sometimes by name.[43] Some policymakers valued the contribution of the attorneys and welcomed their participation in decision-making because of their analytical and counselling skills.[44] One former attorney-adviser stated that one Assistant Secretary made it clear to staff not to even bring work product to him or her that the lawyers had not reviewed.[45] Many described the collaborative nature of the working relationship between lawyers and policymakers.[46]

The Legal Adviser may have personal influence with the Secretary of State, especially if the Secretary believes in the role of international institutions and norms.[47] Presumably, the Secretary has chosen the Legal Adviser precisely because the Secretary values his or her advice. Former officials mentioned the strong working relationships between, for example, John Bellinger and Secretary Rice,[48] and Will Taft and both Secretary Powell and his deputy, Richard Armitage.[49] In addition, as mentioned in Chapter 4, the stature and personality of the Legal Adviser may also make a difference in policy decisions – some former officials mentioned the forceful personality of Harold Koh, for instance.[50] Of course the existençe of a good relationship between a Secretary and a Legal Adviser could cut both ways, with the Secretary influencing the positions of the Legal Adviser.

As discussed below, policymakers in general viewed the decisions of the Legal Adviser's Office with some deference, based not only on their formal role in the process but also on their legal expertise. That is, the lawyers operate as a sort of epistemic community, leveraging their expertise for influence.[51] This deference may heighten the role of legal considerations in policymaking. In addition, the cultural norms regarding international law shared by policymakers, as described in Chapter 4, also play a role in shaping responses to international law concerns. Thus, the attitudes of policymakers toward the role and significance of international law in general affect their decisions.

43 *See, e.g.*, Interview 32, *supra* note 32; Interview 27, Former Senior Obama administration Official.

44 *See, e.g.*, Interview 32, *supra* note 32; Interview 8, *supra* note 4; Lawyer Interview 2, *supra* note 37.

45 *See* Lawyer Interview 2, *supra* note 37.

46 *See* discussion *infra* Section 5.3.1.

47 *See* Interview with J. Brian Atwood, Under Secretary of Management, USAID Administrator, Clinton administration.

48 *See e.g.*, Interview with James Glassman, Under Secretary for Public diplomacy and Public Affairs, George W. Bush administration.

49 *See, e.g.*, Interview with Arthur "Gene" Dewey, Assistant Secretary for Population, Refugees, & Migration, George W. Bush administration; Interview with Thomas Fingar, Assistant Secretary for Intelligence and Research, George W. Bush administration.

50 *See* discussion *supra* Chapter 4.

51 *See* discussion *supra* Chapter 2.

5.1.4 *Internal Politics: Between Individuals, Bureaus, and Administrations*

Some former officials stressed that decisions over policy involving legal issues could be contested among different bureaus or individuals within State and among agencies within the federal government.[52] These battles illustrate the role of bureaucratic politics in decision-making, as described in the bureaucratic politics literature discussed in Chapter 2. As noted previously, negotiation among bureaus is an essential aspect of policymaking. The perennial tension between functional and regional bureaus is a case in point.

Conflicts between the functional bureaus and the regional bureaus arise because of their different agendas, functions, and interlocutors. Functional bureaus may have an agenda that cuts across regions. Regional bureaus, in contrast, tend to take the position of the countries that they interact with, for various reasons.[53] Diplomats from the region may lobby their counterparts at State, for example, or, perhaps, bureau personnel tend to identify with the viewpoint of their particular region. One former official mentioned that they always "wore the hat" of their bureau's region.[54] Someone might say that the United States has to do something because it is important to the Saudis and Turks, for example. The former official would respond that the issue was not important to their region, which had more votes in the United Nations.

Two functional bureaus whose views might conflict with regional bureaus are Democracy, Human Rights, and Labor (DRL) and International Organizations (IO). DRL, said one former official, took an assertive position on human rights.[55] Regional bureaus, on the other hand, would take a minimalist position because they were dealing with host governments on a range of issues and, from their perspective, had other fish to fry. Interestingly, in this person's experience, DRL and the Legal Adviser's Office were on the same page more often than not. Other bureaus, such as Counterterrorism and the Ambassador for War Crimes might also be involved in discussions on issues and would have their own positions.

In the case of the Bureau for International Organizations, said a former Assistant Secretary for that bureau, there might be tension between obligations within the UN Treaty system and treaty obligations to a particular country, or obligations under a different treaty regime.[56] The tension had to be resolved

52 *See* discussion *supra* Chapter 3 and sources cited therein.

53 *See* Brimmer Interview, *supra* note 4; Interview with Kim Holmes, Assistant Secretary for International Organizations, George W. Bush administration; Interview 32, *supra* note 32.

54 *See* Interview 32, *supra* note 32.

55 *See* Interview 13, Assistant Secretary in the George W. Bush administration.

56 *See* Brimmer Interview, *supra* note 4.

and regional bureaus might be involved in that resolution. From the IO point of view, the most important factor was the systemic health of the UN since the United States is the anchor power of that organization.

Bureaucratic conflict could continue even after decisions were made and could extend through more than one administration. Thomas Shannon pointed to the drawn-out debates and relitigation of certain questions over the course of the George W. Bush administration.[57] One side might be driven from the field only to come back to fight another day. He recounted how John Bellinger, the Legal Adviser, engaged in single combat with the Vice President's office over prisoner interrogation, justification of war questions, and response to the International Criminal Court. By the end of Bush's second term, the Vice President had been driven from the field and many of Bellinger's positions had become accepted policy, Shannon stated.

Shannon and a former Assistant Secretary from a different administration recalled another ongoing dispute within the State Department and throughout the government that continued across administrations.[58] That dispute involved the Air Bridge Denial Program, which provided for assistance to the air forces of Peru and Columbia to intercept – and in some cases to shoot down – drug trafficking planes in their territories. The plan was controversial from its beginning in the Clinton administration, and the controversy extended at least into the George W. Bush administration. The plan was implemented initially in spite of concerns voiced by the Clinton administration Legal Adviser at the time, Conrad Harper. The controversy stemmed, in part, from international law concerns about whether US assistance could constitute extrajudicial execution.[59] The project came to a temporary halt when, in 2001, the Peruvian air force shot up and forced down a boat plane operated by an American missionary group, killing two people.

5.1.5 *External Politics: The Interagency Process*

This book focuses on internal State Department decision-making. For issues that do not extend beyond the State Department, its decisions are final. Other issues may be addressed and settled through direct discussions between interested agencies. For decisions that have wider ramifications, the State

57 *See* Interview with Thomas Shannon, Under Secretary of State, Obama and Trump administrations.

58 *See* Interview 7, Former Assistant Secretary.

59 For additional background information and an analysis of the legal issues, see Darren C. Huskisson, *The Air Bridge Denial Program and the Shootdown of Civil Aircraft under International Law*, 56 A.F. L. Rev. 109 (2005).

Department must vie with other agencies and, ultimately, the White House, in reaching decisions. This book focuses only tangentially on the interagency process, which other works already do a fine job of exploring.[60] Nevertheless, a brief outline of the interagency process will be helpful to place State Department policymaking in context.

Within the federal government, there are multiple potential sources of advice on international law. The Legal Adviser's Office is essentially the first among equals in providing that advice. Not surprisingly, conflicts arise between these sources regarding international law's scope and applicability, and there is no single, dominant mechanism to coordinate or resolve them into a singular state interest. There are, accordingly, many potential avenues for resolving legal issues and potential disputes about them, both formal and informal.[61]

This formal and informal process is collectively and loosely called the National Security Council system.[62] That system operates under the aegis of the National Security Council (NSC), a statutorily created meeting body consisting of the President, Vice President, and the heads of major cabinet agencies. The NSC itself meets seldom, but it need not convene in order to function.[63] The broader system includes the National Security Advisor, appointed by the President, the NSC staff, located in the White House and under the direction of the National Security Advisor, and the NSC's subsidiary decision-making bodies. These subsidiary bodies usually include some variation of a Principals Committee, a Deputies Committee, and Interagency Policy Committees, all consisting of representatives at different levels selected from among the relevant agencies.[64] The NSC staff generally handles

60 *See, e.g.*, Arturo Jimenez-Bacardi, Speaking Law to War: International Law, Legal Advisers, and Bureaucratic Contestation in U.S. Defense Policy (2015) (unpublished, Ph.D. dissertation, UCI) [hereinafter, Jimenez-Bacardi, Speaking Law]; HALPERIN & CLAPP, *supra* note 23; Rao, *supra* note 10; GABRIEL MARCELLA, AFFAIRS OF STATE: THE INTERAGENCY AND NATIONAL SECURITY, 8 (2008), https://press.armywarcollege.edu/cgi/viewcontent.cgi?article=1635&context=monographs.

61 Rao, *supra* note 10, at 229, 254.

62 Jimenez-Bacardi, *supra* note 60, at 71. When people refer to the NSC, they may be referring to the statutorily created National Security Council itself, the staff that supports it, or the processes used by the White House to discuss and adjudicate decisions across the agencies in the executive branch, or all of the above. *See* Congressional Research Service, *The National Security Council: Background and Issues for Congress*, at 7 (last updated June 3, 2021), https://crsreports.congress.gov/product/pdf/R/R44828 [hereinafter CRS, NSC Report].

63 *See* MARCELLA, *supra* note 60, at 108.

64 *See* CRS, NSC Report, *supra* note 62, at 8. The design of the committee structure is at the President's discretion, but has often resembled the following. The Principals Committee is a level below the NSC, convened by the National Security Adviser, and consists of the heads of departments or agencies involved with the subject at hand. The Deputies Committee generally includes the deputy heads of those agencies. The Interagency Policy Committees are

day-to-day political coordination and decision-making, along with the Interagency Policy Committees.[65] While the NSC itself is statutorily mandated, most of the NSC bodies and processes are not and depend on presidential directives, preferences and informal norms, groups, and processes.[66] Thus, the NSC system's structure and role varies to some extent from administration to administration, as it is reshaped to meet the policymaking preferences of each.[67]

Among the responsibilities of the NSC system are to make recommendations to the President and to coordinate and adjudicate the views of the departments and agencies of the government concerned with national security and international affairs.[68] The primary agencies in the system include the Departments of State and Defense, the intelligence community, and the Joint Chiefs of Staff.[69] Other agencies may take part depending on the issue at hand. These stakeholders are bound together by a functional interdependence because major national security and international affairs issues cannot be resolved by one agency alone.[70] Although the process is an interagency one, State has an opportunity to lead and shape decisions in the normal operating process.[71]

Legal issues can also percolate through the interagency process. Most legal issues in the federal government are handled by the agencies' general counsel offices.[72] Where there is a conflict between agencies, the matter would be elevated to the agencies' general counsels, who may be able to settle the matter among themselves.[73] At any point, the agencies could submit the issue to the Justice Department's Office of Legal Counsel (OLC) for a decision. Alternatively, the matter may be taken up by the NSC Legal Advisor, who plays a mediating role, and who has considerable independent authority.

established by the National Security Adviser in consultation with the Deputies Committee and are responsible for regular management of international and national security matters on a specific region or topic at the Assistant Secretary level.

65 *See* MARCELLA, *supra* note 60, at 8–9.

66 Jimenez-Bacardi, *supra* note 60, at 76–77.

67 *See* MARCELLA, *supra* note 60, at 8.

68 *See* CRS, NSC Report, *supra* note 62, at 7.

69 *See* MARCELLA, *supra* note 60, at 8. The statutory list of NSC members is longer and includes the President, Vice President, and the Secretaries of State, Defense, Treasury, and Energy. The Director of National Intelligence and the Chairman of the Joint Chiefs of Staff are advisors. CRS, NSC Report, *supra* note 62.

70 *See* MARCELLA, *supra* note 60, at 25.

71 Interview with Roberta Jacobsen, Assistant Secretary for Western Hemisphere Affairs, Obama administration; Ambassador to Mexico, 2016–2018.

72 Morrison, *Stare Decisis*, *supra* note 8, at 1461.

73 *See* Interview 9, *supra* note 39.

Although its emphasis may vary by administration, the main functions of the NSC Legal Advisor's Office include advising the NSC system and the president regarding national security law and coordinating the interagency legal process.[74] In all its roles, the NSC Legal Adviser serves the President's interests and mediates conflicts in light of those interests.[75] As part of the coordinating function, the NSC Legal Advisor "referees turf wars" between agencies, especially those between the State Department Legal Adviser and OLC.[76] In the view of one former official, in matters involving international law, there would be deference to the State Department Legal Adviser, although the extent of this deference is disputed.[77] Even so, OLC has the last word, that official said, presumably as a formal matter.

The NSC Legal Advisor may also convene an interagency Lawyers Group to subject issues and decisions to interagency legal review.[78] If time is of the essence, or the Lawyers' Group is at an impasse, the NSC Legal Adviser can refer a matter to OLC.[79] The White House and other policymakers, moreover, could bypass all of these mechanisms if they choose to do so.[80]

5.1.5.1 The Office of Legal Counsel

As discussed before, while the State Department Legal Adviser's Office is seen as the primary legal office on matters of international law and entitled to deference because of its specialized expertise, the Office of Legal Counsel generally has the final word within the executive branch, at least when it is consulted. OLC has a culture of, and a reputation for, providing impartial and high-quality legal analysis.[81] At the same time, OLC may be subject to some

74 *See* Jennifer N. Marett, *The National Security Council Legal Adviser: Crafting Legal Positions on Maters of War and Peace*, J. NAT'L SECURITY L. & POL'Y 153, 164–169 (2015).

75 *See* Rao, *supra* note 10 at 250–251.

76 *See Id.*

77 *See* Interview 9, *supra* note 39.

78 Its members generally include the top lawyers from the State Department, the CIA, the Defense Department, the Joint Chiefs of Staff, and the Department of Justice's Office of Legal Counsel. *See* Marett, *supra* note 74, at 168. The Lawyers' Group may address any national security legal issue that could go to the President for decision, may field legal questions related to both national security and foreign policy, and may consider issues pulled from the national security policymaking process. *See id.* at 168–169. The National Security Legal Adviser then conveys the consensus legal advice to the White House and presumably also to the principals.

79 *See id.* at 170.

80 *See* Rao, *supra* note 10, at 254.

81 *See id.* at 244–245.

political pressure from the administration, or, at the very least, "OLC is not entirely neutral to the President's agenda."[82]

On some occasions, administrations or agencies may seek to forum shop by referring international law-related matters to OLC, instead of to the Office of the Legal Adviser. Senior officials might consider resorting to OLC if L disagreed with an important policy objective. The White House may prefer OLC because OLC may be more responsive to the administration because of the level of political control over its work. The President appoints the head of the office and a number of its lawyers, and other young lawyers may be chosen by political appointees because of their legal philosophy.[83] Moreover, because OLC lawyers generally do not have international law expertise,[84] nor do they have the experience of career international lawyers at State, they may be less inclined to take international law and policy concerns into account. This may serve the interest of those less inclined to consider international law issues in the first place.

This type of forum shopping may have been at work regarding the infamous OLC memos regarding treatment of detainees in the war on terrorism. Figures in the George W. Bush administration allegedly froze out L and the State Department in favor of OLC in seeking favorable legal decisions on the treatment of detainees. They avoided consulting L in the first place and then OLC failed to circulate draft memos to other interested departments, including State and L, in direct contradiction to its normal practice of consulting other interested agencies before rendering an opinion.[85]

Thomas Pickering alluded to this conflict between L and OLC. Sometimes, he said, head-to-head conflicts interrupted the normal, calm decision-making process, pointing to the conflict between OLC and William Taft, then the Legal Adviser, regarding OLC opinions on detainees in the war on terror. He characterized the White House's view as saying "we win, we are not telling you why, but we have the right interpretation." OLC is important, he said, but there should be transparency, openness, and discussion to get the best legal advice.

Sometimes the game can be played the other way, however. From published reports at the time, it seemed to one commentator that the White

[82] *Id.*, quoting JACK GOLDSMITH, THE TERROR PRESIDENCY: LAW AND JUDGMENT INSIDE THE BUSH ADMINISTRATION 35 (2007).

[83] *See id.* at 244; Pillard, *supra* note 8, at 716 (OLC may be subject to political pressure because of the number of political appointees in the office).

[84] *See* Interview 9, *supra* note 39.

[85] *See generally*, Michael P. Scharf, *The Torture Lawyers*, 20 DUKE J. COMP. & INT'L L. 389 (2010). *See also* Pickering Interview, *supra* note 30.

House may have sought the advice of the Legal Adviser – as opposed to OLC – regarding the applicability of the War Powers Resolution to US involvement in the Libya military campaign in 2011.[86] Rather than submitting the question to OLC, the administration apparently instructed lawyers from key agencies to submit their views directly to the White House Counsel, who passed their views directly to the President. The President sided with the view presented by Harold Koh, the State Department Legal Adviser.[87]

5.2 INTERACTION BETWEEN "L" ATTORNEYS AND STATE DEPARTMENT POLICYMAKERS

Several dynamics affected the interaction between policymakers and legal advisers. First, the seniority of the policymaker affected the interaction. Senior officials, at the level of Under Secretary and above, were able to make decisions regarding legal issues, unless those needed to be cleared at even higher levels. Assistant Secretaries appeared to have significant decision-making authority, but the lawyers appeared to have some influence over them. Second, issues presented for decision did not fall into a simple dichotomy between legal concerns and policy concerns. There might be a range of options available to policymakers, some of which might be more or less in compliance, such that compliance may represent a choice among shades of gray. Finally, although policymakers may ultimately have final decision-making authority, the views of the lawyers in the Legal Adviser's Office were treated with a great deal of deference because of their official role in the decision-making process, their expertise, and the State Department's culture of respect for international law. Policymakers differed about the extent of that deference.

5.2.1 *Variations by Seniority in Authority and Attitudes Regarding International Law*

Authority to make decisions regarding international law varied by level and had an effect on interactions between lawyers and policymakers. Certainly, officials at the level of Under Secretary or above appeared to have greater discretion and authority to make those decisions. Some policymakers also

[86] *See* Morrison, *Libya*, *supra* note 8.

[87] *See* Michael Isikoff, *On Libya, President Obama Evaded Rules on Legal Disputes, Scholars Say*, msnbc.com (June 21, 2011), http://www.nbcnews.com/id/43474045/ns/politics-white_house/t/libya-president-obama-evaded-rules-legal-disputes-scholars-say/#.XiUbhchKhPY.

indicated that these senior officials take international law more seriously and are more attuned to the interplay between international law and state interests.

Numerous officials expressed the view that they were the decision-makers after considering legal advice.[88] Senior officials at the level of Under Secretary and above had more latitude to make decisions. One former official said that when talking about the most senior people, the lawyer is really an advisor.[89] If, for example, the Secretary wants to achieve X, they said, the lawyer's job is to go back and figure out a way to do that. Some of the lawyers interviewed supported this view. Even so, most issues would presumably first rise to the senior level through the clearance process and senior policymakers would have to elevate a decision to the Deputy, to the Secretary, or to the interagency process and the White House in sensitive or far-reaching matters.

The Assistant Secretary seemed to be the inflection point at which officials had more independence regarding international law matters than junior officials but were still subject to some institutional constraints. Former Assistant Secretary Esther Brimmer said that the views of the Legal Adviser's Office were significant, but not determinative because the policymakers, including Assistant Secretaries, are the decision-makers.[90] Brimmer justified this decision-making authority on the basis that the Assistant Secretary has a link to elected political authority because he or she is appointed by the President and the Senate, as opposed to the attorney-advisers.

One former Assistant Secretary, however, stated that even at that level, the lawyers would not give very much regarding their interpretation of the law, although there could be lots of discussion about alternative courses of action.[91] Interviews with former State Department lawyers supported this assessment.[92] In addition, as discussed before, the lawyers may be able to push back formally or informally against an Assistant Secretary who disregards serious international law ramifications. The lawyers indicated that Assistant Secretaries were the officials who most pushed back against legal interpretations.[93]

[88] *See, e.g.*, Brimmer Interview, *supra* note 4; Interview with Lincoln Bloomfield, Assistant Secretary for Political Military Affairs, George W. Bush administration; Interview with Timothy Wirth, Under Secretary for Democracy and Global Affairs, Clinton administration; Interview 35, Former State Department Official; Interview 5, Former Senior Trump administration Official; Interview 19, Former Trump administration Assistant Secretary; Interview 3, Former Trump administration Assistant Secretary. *See also* Interview with David Stillwell, Assistant Secretary for Political-Military Affairs, Trump administration.

[89] *See* Interview 26, *supra* note 22.

[90] *See* Brimmer Interview, *supra* note 4.

[91] *See* Interview 26, *supra* note 22.

[92] *See* Lawyer Interview 2, *supra* note 37.

[93] *See, e.g.*, Lawyer Interview 2, *supra* note 37.

Both perspectives about the authority of Assistant Secretaries contain some truth, and the reality in any given case may depend on various factors. These factors may include the nature and significance of the issues involved, the lawyers involved, and the personality, experience, and clout of the Assistant Secretary involved. All agreed that Assistant Secretaries could and did take issues to a higher level if they disagreed with a position taken by L, through the clearance process or otherwise.

A number of those interviewed believed that senior officials were more attentive to legal questions.[94] In addition, several former officials indicated that the more senior they were, the more they dealt with international law issues,[95] the more cognizant they were of the political implications of legal issues,[96] and the more flexible, or at least less formal, they could be in considering international law.[97] One former senior official said that at higher levels, getting legal advice and addressing the legal questions effectively becomes more important.[98] The issues become more challenging and harder to resolve. Failing to get legal advice in the early stages of considering an issue can lead to problems later on. The more senior the official, the more questions of the Constitution, morals, and law are part of the decision. At senior meetings in the White House, people debated these questions, there was always a lawyer in the room, and in the vast majority of meetings, these questions were on the table first. The more senior this official became, the more explicit the question of "right" was.[99]

As discussed in Chapter 4, legal considerations may not always be the determining factor and questions of national interest, political interest, morality, and other factors may play a role. The same senior former official put it this way: The higher someone in power is, the more challenging and harder it is to choose among many courses of action that may all reflect the "right" thing to do, as determined by Congress, law, or human rights, for example. All options may be horrible or sensible and the policymaker has to decide. At the presidential or Secretary of State level, it is constantly a balance of what is

94 *See id.*; Lawyer Interview 1, *supra* note 29; Interview 8, *supra* note 4; Interview 2, Former Senior Official.

95 *See* Interview with Melvyn Levitsky, Assistant Secretary for International Narcotics Matters, George H. W. Bush administration; Interview 2, *supra* note 94.

96 *See* Oakley Interview, *supra* note 36.

97 *See id.*; Interview 10, Former Assistant Secretary.

98 *See* Interview 8, *supra* note 4. This senior official was not a member of the Trump administration.

99 *See id.*

right, or legal.[100] Of course, the views of this senior official may reflect the administration they served in; they did not serve in the Trump administration.

5.2.2 *Overall Dynamic: Legal versus Policy Concerns*

Because other factors play a role in decision-making, several former officials said that an issue or situation would not be presented in a stark form opposing legal and policy concerns, as a question of complying or not complying.[101] Rather, said one former official, a situation would be presented in the following manner: these are the circumstances, these are the options, these are the legal implications.[102] Another former official[103] stated that law is not determinative because issues are not structured that way: There are lots of inputs and issues are not necessarily black and white because much international law is subject to interpretation.[104] Thus, there might be a range of options available to policymakers, some of which might be more or less in compliance: Compliance may represent a choice among shades of gray.[105]

Indeed, a number of policymakers confirmed that the lawyers would sometimes provide options, recommendations, and caveats about possible courses of action. A former senior career diplomat stated that the most valuable lawyers try to internalize the objective and come up with a sound legal strategy, caveated with downsides.[106] Or, said another, the attorney-adviser would say "here are the consequences of ABC options."[107] Phyllis Oakley said that the lawyers would never say this is what you have to do. Rather, they would recommend a course of action.[108] James Dobbins stated that the lawyers could be persuaded because it was their job to support policymakers, although they might clearly say, for example, that the courts might find against the decision, or that a certain decision might even be grounds for impeachment. But, he said, policymakers would make that decision.[109]

[100] *See id.*
[101] *See* Interview with Philip Zelikow, Counselor of the State Department, George W. Bush administration.
[102] *See* Interview 10, *supra* note 97.
[103] *See* Interview 28, Former Official.
[104] *See* discussion regarding ambiguity and interpretation *infra* Section 5.4.
[105] *See* Interview 36, Former Senior State Department Official.
[106] *See* Interview 31, *supra* note 4.
[107] Brimmer Interview, *supra* note 4.
[108] *See* Oakley Interview, *supra* note 36.
[109] *See* Interview with James Dobbins, Assistant Secretary for European Affairs, Clinton and George W. Bush administrations.

Two former attorneyadvisers confirmed this dynamic. One said that when putting forward a legally defensible, but tenuous position, the lawyer should describe the risks and, if appropriate, point out that the counter-argument is not trivial. For example, there might be a risk that a country could raise legal objections and there might be other consequences or countermeasures, such as sanctions under the GATT. Then it is up to the client to make the decision. The lawyer could also say that the question is a close call and, therefore, make sure the Assistant Secretary or Under Secretary are aware.[110] Another former lawyer said that when he or she might give in on an issue, it was his or her job to say what the consequences would be.[111] A former official with relevant experience said that where there was ambiguity and different possible interpretations, the best lawyers identify the ambiguity, stating that different countries view the issue in different ways and identifying the risks of taking a particular interpretation.[112]

5.2.3 *Deference to the Legal Adviser's Office*

Regardless of the locus of decision-making authority, former State Department officials clearly regarded the views of the Legal Adviser's Office on international law as highly influential. Former officials were asked a close-ended question regarding the weight that they gave the advice of the Legal Adviser's Office regarding US compliance with international law. Twenty-one percent of former officials said that the weight of L advice was determinative; 68 percent said it was significant, and 8 percent said it was of moderate weight.[113] Only one (1.6 percent) said that it had some significance and only one (1.6 percent) said it had little significance. Accordingly, most former officials (89 percent) stated that the advice of the Legal Adviser's Office was either determinative or significant on questions of international law. This is an extremely high percentage and reflects the influential role of State Department lawyers in decision-making. As discussed previously, that influence owes much to the formal role of the lawyers in decision-making, to the legitimacy provided by their expertise as members of an epistemic community, and to the overall cultural respect for international law within the Department.

An examination of former officials' specific, open-ended responses to the same question provides further insight and nuance into their views. These

110 *See* Lawyer Interview 2, *supra* note 37.

111 *See* Lawyer Interview 1, *supra* note 29.

112 *See* Interview 9, *supra* note 39.

113 Percentages of valid responses.

responses fell into three major clusters. The first group viewed the advice of the Legal Adviser's Office as essentially determinative, the second viewed legal advice as significant but not necessarily determinative, and the third group viewed it as of moderate importance, or less. In a related vein, in response to this and other questions, a number of other former officials expressed various views about the weight of L's advice but strongly asserted that legal advice was subordinate to policy concerns and to policymakers' judgment.

In a loose frequency count of the open-ended responses, about ten former officials fell into group one, in excess of forty into group two, and seven or so into group three. Some others fell between groups, or were difficult to differentiate. The distribution of responses broadly corresponds to the distribution of responses regarding the tension between international law and national interest discussed in Chapter 4. That discussion involved the question of policymakers' attitudes toward international law generally, while this discussion involves the dynamics of the interaction between policymakers and lawyers as a procedural and institutional matter.

The range of views reflected in the responses seems to reflect authentic differences of perspective. Nevertheless, some differences may derive from differences in nuance and semantics: Policymakers may couch their observations in different terms while describing essentially the same phenomenon. In addition, the distinctions among the categories are somewhat arbitrary, such that there is likely overlap in the views of many individuals. Differences in era or administration, differences in the seniority of participants, or differences in issue area of responsibility may also explain some variation of views.

5.2.3.1 The First Group: Deference to the Legal Advisors Office

Starting with the first category, some former officials indicated that with rare exceptions, L opinions regarding international law were determinative or extremely influential within the State Department and that they deferred to L on those questions.[114] Many former officials stated in no uncertain terms that if L held firm that a proposed course of action violated international law,

[114] *See, e.g.*, Interview 16, *supra* note 5; Interview 2, *supra* note 94; Interview with Karl Inderfurth, Assistant Secretary for South Asian Affairs, Clinton administration; Dewey Interview, *supra* note 49; Interview 34, Former Official; Interview with John Holum, Under Secretary for Arms Control and International Security, Clinton administration; Interview with Carl Ford, Assistant Secretary for Intelligence and Research, George W. Bush administration; Interview 22, Former Assistant Secretary in the George W. Bush administration.

then no meant no.[115] Another said that if the lawyers say no to something, their position is hard to fight.[116] Some former officials said that they never told L to come up with a justification that would violate international law, or never heard of that occurring.[117] Rather, policymakers might tell the lawyers to go back and find another way to accomplish the policy goal at hand, but not to find a means that would violate international law.

One former senior official stated that not being a lawyer, he or she had great dependence on the attorneys, so he or she often deferred to them.[118] The former official felt that they were always in accord with the lawyers. Where there was a gray area, this former official would always defer. If the lawyers said something was legal or not, the former official would always look through the issue but always felt that they should follow the lawyers' advice. Another former official said that people who do not listen to the lawyers are crazy.[119]

Several former officials expressed a qualified endorsement of the definitive nature of L opinions. While several former officials said that if L said no on a matter of national or international law, then it essentially had a veto, at least one former official said that the lawyers were rarely that unequivocal.[120] Several former officials expressed variations on the idea that the opinion of the lawyers on a pure question of law was definitive but less so when politics entered into the consideration.[121] Similarly, others said that the opinions of the lawyers were determinative in some cases, but not others.[122] Of course, a higher political authority outside the State Department could make a different final decision even then, perhaps based on the advice of legal counsel elsewhere in the executive branch.

Faith in L among the first group was not necessarily unquestioning. The same official who said they had great dependence on the attorneys noted that they would talk through issues with L and would sometimes ask questions about interpretations and other options.[123] But while the former official was

[115] *See, e.g.*, Interview with Richard Boucher, Assistant Secretary for South and Central Asian Affairs, Assistant Secretary for Public Affairs, Clinton administration; Interview 5, *supra* note 88; Interview with Ellen Tauscher, Under Secretary of State for Arms Control and International Security in the Obama administration.

[116] *See* Interview 16, *supra* note 5.

[117] *See e.g.*, Levitsky Interview, *supra* note 95.

[118] *See* Interview 2, *supra* note 94.

[119] *See* Tauscher Interview, *supra* note 115.

[120] *See* Boucher Interview, *supra* note 115.

[121] *See, e.g.*, Holmes Interview, *supra* note 53.

[122] *See, e.g.*, Interview with Anthony Quainton, Assistant Secretary for Diplomatic Security, George W. Bush administration.

[123] Interview 2, *supra* note 94.

sure it happened, they did not remember an instance of talking L out of its position. People respected L and it had a lot of influence. Other officials, however, were more than willing to push back against L, as discussed in the following section, especially when the nature of legal advice straddled the line between the legal and the political.

5.2.3.2 The Second Group: Lawyers' Views Are Significant, but Not Dispositive

The majority of former officials fell into the second category, viewing advice from the Legal Adviser's Office as significant, but not necessarily dispositive. Some former officials in this group noted that while legal recommendations might not always be followed, if L said you could not do something, that would certainly cause the policymakers to rethink.[124] Another former official, Richard Moose,[125] stated that if the Legal Adviser said that the United States could not do something, that would give pause to most Secretaries, who would feel bound to make arguments up the line. Another former official, Brian Atwood,[126] stated that while the views of the Legal Adviser were significant, L could still end up on the losing side in the decision-memo process. Sometimes, he said, efforts were made to find the gray zone and rationalize how to do something without violating international law.

The lawyers definitely played a significant role in decision-making and their opinions were often valued. One former official stated that policymakers would not do anything without the lawyers' opinion, to the extent of having the lawyers in the room when deciding or working on issues.[127] Policymakers do not always follow the letter of the law and would push back against them but wanted their opinion.

Many of these officials emphasized the collaborative nature of working with the lawyers to develop responses to foreign policy problems and viewed this process as a joint effort, as discussed in greater detail below.[128] This back and forth could be antagonistic, but many policymakers and lawyers found it to be collaborative and constructive. The lawyers, for example, were often willing to discuss alternative, legal means to address policy ends and that was helpful.[129]

[124] *See, e.g.*, Interview 15, Former Under Secretary.

[125] *See* Interview with Richard Moose, Undersecretary for Management, Clinton administration; Assistant Secretary for African Affairs, Carter administration.

[126] *See* Atwood Interview, *supra* note 47.

[127] *See* Interview 32, *supra* note 32.

[128] *See* discussion *infra* Section 5.3.1.

[129] *See* discussion *infra* Section 5.3.2.

5.2.3.3 The Third Group: The Lawyers' Views Carry Moderate Weight, or Less

The relatively small number of former officials in this group held nuanced views but generally gave less weight to L advice than those in other groups. One or two former officials discounted the weight of legal advice entirely. One former official in this group with a nuanced view stated that the weight given to advice from the Legal Adviser's Office was at least moderate, with some variation depending on the personalities and relationships involved.[130] On the one hand, if the Legal Adviser's Office said that we need to do X, the predisposition was to do X, or to find a way in which the Legal Adviser's Office can say we are in compliance. Rarely would the decision be made to take an action against international law. On the other hand, this former official could not recall any instance where policymakers decided not to do something because it would be a violation of international law.

Another former official concurred that the wight of L advice was significant to moderate, depending on the political issues involved.[131] David Stillwell, Assistant Secretary in the Trump administration said that the weight of L advice was moderate and would be considered in some way, but the ambiguity of international law provides for a band of freedom to maneuver, and L's job is to find opportunities within that band. Another former official stated that the weight of legal advice was not determinative or significant, but high. The President always wanted to hear the legal advice, and everyone wants or needs to know it.[132]

A number of former officials indicated that while L's view might be determinative on some issues, it would have minimal effect in matters of national security and perhaps other issues of compelling national interest.[133] Robert Gallucci, for example, stated that L's view might be determinative if it stated a straightforward application of the law in a non-security context, such as a matter of oceans law. But it would have little weight in the national security context.[134] This point is an application of a larger dynamic regarding the weight of policy compared to law, discussed at length in Chapter 4.[135]

[130] *See* Interview 31, *supra* note 4.
[131] *See* Interview 23, Former Official.
[132] *See* Interview 35, *supra* note 88.
[133] *See* discussion *supra* Chapter 4.
[134] Interview with Robert Gallucci, Assistant Secretary for Political-Military Affairs, Clinton administration.
[135] *See* discussion *supra* Chapter 4.

Several former officials said that they could not think of any situation where they could not do what they really wanted to do because of legal prohibition, although they might have had to pursue a different means of accomplishing their goal.[136] As discussed elsewhere, there may even be rare occasions when national interest is so compelling that the United States might act inconsistently with international law.[137] This would be a last resort, when other coping strategies are unavailable.

In a related vein, a number of former officials held varying views about the weight of legal advice, but for them, the essential dynamic between lawyers and policymakers followed a corporate counsel model, in which the lawyers' job was to facilitate the achievement of policy objectives.[138] These former officials have not been counted expressly in the third category of respondents. Nevertheless, policy goals came first and foremost for them. As discussed previously in Chapter 4, if the lawyers came up with an answer that did not serve those objectives, the policymakers would and could tell them to go back and reexamine their analysis, with at least the implicit expectation that the lawyers would come back with a supportive rationale.[139] In addition, Richard Boucher said, international law was often just not on the menu and legal rationales were developed after decisions were taken, at least in many cases.[140] (Nevertheless, Mr. Boucher acknowledged that legal considerations were taken into account in various ways and that, on the rare occasions the lawyers were adamant, their decision would be determinative.) At least two officials, moreover, stated that international law may influence how the United States does something, but not the decision about whether to do it in the first place.[141]

Former Under Secretary and Senator Tim Wirth, for example, said that the effect of the lawyers in L was anesthetizing because they were narrowly focused, by the book.[142] They did not always "get it," gave their own view of the world, and asserted that the law was paramount and clear. While L laid the

[136] *See, e.g.*, Interview 10, *supra* note 97; Interview 31, *supra* note 4; Gallucci Interview, *supra* note 134.

[137] *See* discussion *infra* Section 5.4.

[138] *See e.g.*, Dobbins Interview, *supra* note 109; Wirth Interview, *supra* note 88; Interview with Richard Solomon, Assistant Secretary for East Asian and Pacific Affairs George H. W. Bush administration; Boucher Interview, *supra* note 115; Gallucci Interview, *supra* note 134; Stillwell Interview, *supra* note 88; Interview 3, *supra* note 88; Interview 19, *supra* note 88.

[139] *See, e.g.*, Wirth Interview, *supra* note 88; Solomon Interview, *supra* note 138, Dobbins Interview, *supra* note 109; Boucher Interview, *supra* note 115.

[140] Boucher Interview, *supra* note 115.

[141] *See* Brimmer Interview, *supra* note 4, Interview 31, *supra* note 4.

[142] *See* Wirth Interview, *supra* note 88.

basis, the lawyers' views were not determinative, though significant. The political people would overrule them, he said.

The Trump political appointees interviewed, not including those who were originally career officials, strongly expressed their view regarding the primacy of political appointees in decision-making.[143] Admittedly, this group formed a small sample of four, but the similarity in their perspective was notable. In addition, as described more fully in Chapter 6, these former officials indicated the existence of tension between themselves and the lawyers. Three indicated their willingness not only to push back against the recommendations of bureau lawyers but also to take disputed issues to a higher level for resolution, either through a split memo or by informal means.[144] They claimed reasonable success in doing so. One argued that the lawyers had a tendency to exceed their role and offer policy recommendations, not just legal recommendations, which the policymakers regarded as beyond the lawyers' role.[145] Another asserted that the lawyers viewed issues from a narrow perspective of legality, without respect to policy.[146] While these complaints were not unique to Trump administration officials, those officials perhaps voiced them the loudest and most consistently.

5.2.3.4 Section Conclusion

To recap, 89 percent of former officials said the advice of the Legal Advisor's Office regarding US compliance with international law was determinative or significant. The qualitative comments reflect a range of views and more nuanced attitudes toward the role of advice from the Legal Adviser's Office. The majority of former officials and the handful of State Department lawyers interviewed characterized the second group's perspective as the predominant view, that the advice of the Legal Adviser's Office was highly influential but not necessarily determinative. Even those in the group that indicated that legal advice was determinative sometimes hedged their responses. Nonetheless, there seemed to be wide agreement that when L said no, that some course of action was definitely illegal, that was usually the final word. At least one pointed out, however, that such clear-cut cases were rare. Others pointed out that decisions at higher levels within the State Department and above might go against the advice of the Legal Adviser's Office. Thus, aside from comparatively clear areas

[143] *See* Interview 5, *supra* note 88; Interview 19, *supra* note 88; Interview 3, *supra* note 88. *See also* Stillwell Interview, *supra* note 88.

[144] *See* Interview 5, *supra* note 88; Interview 3, *supra* note 88; Stillwell Interview, *supra* note 88.

[145] *See* Interview 19, *supra* note 88.

[146] *See* Stillwell Interview, *supra* note 88.

of illegality, the weight of L's advice could vary, depending on the circumstances. The lawyers were part of the decision-making process and their views carried substantial weight with most policymakers.

5.3 NEGOTIATION AND FLEXIBILITY

As an additional route to assess the extent to which law and lawyers constrained policymakers in decision-making processes, policymakers were also asked whether there was an opportunity to negotiate with the lawyers on legal determinations and whether the lawyers were flexible in their opinions in light of US interests. The purpose of these questions was to assess the extent to which the lawyers were willing to adjust their view, or even subordinate their view, to the exigencies of policy. To what extent did the lawyers act as judges in defense of international law, or as advocates for their clients, the policymakers? To some extent, these questions sought similar information as the questions about the extent of deference to the lawyers. Nevertheless, the responses revealed different nuances.

Would the lawyers take legal positions that constrained US interests, and could they be moved from such a position? Again, policymakers' perspectives differed along familiar lines, ranging from a view that the lawyers were rather inflexible in their views about international law to a view that lawyers were malleable, or subject to policymaker direction. By far the majority of these characterizations fell in the middle of that range.

5.3.1 *Negotiation*

Former policymakers were asked whether they negotiated with the lawyers regarding the application of international law. Some former officials thought that the characterization of the process as a "negotiation" was too strong. Rather, one former official said, lawyers and policymakers would talk over issues and conclusions, exploring the parameters of the situation.[147] The policymaker might ask questions, for example about the legal interpretation – why interpret the matter this way or that? There might be some pressure regarding what constituted compliance and what did not. In short, lawyers and policymakers would engage in a discursive process. This policymaker never recalled an instance of talking the lawyers out of a position.[148] Many

[147] *See* Interview 2, *supra* note 94. *See also* Interview with Richard Armitage, Former Deputy Secretary of State, George W. Bush administration.

[148] *See also* Interview with Richard Schifter, Assistant Secretary for Human Rights and Humanitarian Affairs, Reagan administration and George H. W. Bush administration.

former officials indicated, however, that while the lawyers were usually unwilling to change an interpretation of the law, they were often willing to discuss alternative legal courses of action.

In the same vein, a number of former officials described the working relationship between policymakers and lawyers as a collaboration, rather than as a negotiation. Policymakers and lawyers would engage in discussion, asking questions in an iterative, nonantagonistic process. Perhaps this is not surprising, given the decision-making process in the State Department, under which L must sign off on recommendations involving international law in the clearance process. James Dobbins characterized State Department lawyers as stakeholders in decision-making.[149]

Thomas Pickering stated that most of the time, there was no irresolvable conflict between lawyers and policymakers. Rather, they wanted to get the job done and the question was how best to do that in the context of international law.[150] Pickering emphasized the role of process in State Department decision-making, in which the focus is on policy but under the assumption that the United States is going to comply with international law as it understands it. All perspectives would be taken into account, including the legal perspective. In a process of give and take, the question would be whether the policy can be accommodated to incorporate these other perspectives.

One former Assistant Secretary[151] explicitly described the decision-making process as collaborative. As the issue became more important, lawyers and policymakers worked to develop more options and explore the constraints or opportunities associated with them. Two of the lawyers interviewed also characterized the process as collaborative.[152] Richard Boucher suggested that because most of the lawyers also considered themselves policymakers, the approach was to accomplish particular goals in legal fashion, not for the lawyers to pass judgment.[153]

Another former Assistant Secretary, Esther Brimmer, gave a sense of the complicated nature of making decisions based on legal advice.[154] Sometimes there may be conflicting legal rules at issue, requiring navigation between, for example, obligations to the UN and treaty obligations to a particular country. In addition, different bureaus within State may take different positions or have

[149] *See* Dobbins Interview, *supra* note 109.
[150] *See* Pickering Interview, *supra* note 30.
[151] *See* Interview 10, *supra* note 97. *See also* Bloomfield Interview, *supra* note 88.
[152] *See* Lawyer Interview 1, *supra* note 29; Lawyer Interview 2, *supra* note 37.
[153] *See* Boucher Interview, *supra* note 115. *See also* Interview with Ivan Selin, Under Secretary for Management, George H. W. Bush administration.
[154] *See* Brimmer Interview, *supra* note 4.

different concerns, such as differences between the regional bureaus and her bureau, International Organization. Accordingly, the resolution of questions may not represent negotiation, so much as weighing, or threading the way through competing interests, and making a choice. Brimmer also asserted that the purpose of discussion was not to get a different legal opinion from the lawyers, because the legal opinion was not likely to change. She would take the legal determination, but that was inadequate to make a decision, as there were other considerations to take into account.[155]

Other former officials, however, were more than happy to characterize the process as a negotiation, indicating that they were willing to push back against legal advice.[156] Indeed, some suggested, there may be more room to push back because international law is often subject to interpretation, allowing for flexibility in application.[157] In spite of this more aggressive characterization, the description of the content of these negotiations was similar to the description of the collaborative approach, except in degree. For example, one former official said policymakers would sometimes push back against strict interpretations of the lawyers and argue about the application of the law.[158] They said that while policymakers cannot get the lawyers to change the law, they can get them to help in interpretation, to say what can and cannot be done. In that way, the lawyers can protect the policymaker from breaking the law. Another former senior career diplomat said that there would be negotiation and push-back and, as a result, the lawyers might moderate their views, or rethink them, or get the policymaker to think through his or her position.[159] In all, this group emphasized the back-and-forth nature of the discussion.

5.3.2 *Flexibility*

Former officials were also asked whether the lawyers were flexible in light of US interests. Some officials said they did not believe the lawyers were particularly flexible, whereas the majority indicated that they could be, though sometimes in different ways. That is, there seemed to be a consensus among former officials that many State Department lawyers were open and willing to discuss different courses of action, or options that would fall within the scope of the law, even if they were less flexible regarding the legal principle at issue.

[155] *See id.*
[156] *See, e.g.*, Interview 31, *supra* note 4; Interview 32, *supra* note 32; Interview 11, Retired Foreign Service Officer; Stillwell Interview, *supra* note 88; Interview 3, *supra* note 88.
[157] *See* discussion on interpretation, *infra* Section 5.4.
[158] *See* Interview 32, *supra* note 32.
[159] Interview 31, *supra* note 4.

They would bend but not break. Some policymakers, however, believed that the lawyers could sometimes be more flexible than that.

Some former officials indicated that the lawyers could be inflexible. John Holum, former Under Secretary for Arms Control and International Security in the George H. W. Bush administration, thought that the lawyers were not flexible but, rather, strict because they knew their stuff.[160] Arms control may be one of the areas of law that lends itself to strict interpretation, both because of the web of applicable treaties that constrain interpretation and also because of self-interest. As Holum seemed to suggest, strictness in the application of arms control treaties may be a good thing.

A few policymakers perceived the lawyers as inflexible and criticized them on that basis. David Stillwell, Assistant Secretary in the Trump administration, said that the lawyers were not flexible, that their idea was to execute the law as they saw it without respect to policy until the issue was forced.[161] This view was not limited to the Trump administration. Tim Wirth, Under Secretary of State for Democracy and Global Affairs in the Clinton administration, characterized the lawyers as narrowly focused, by the book.[162] They did not always get it, he said: They gave their own view of the world, and the law was paramount and clear in their view.

Another former official, an Assistant Secretary in the Obama administration, stated that characterizing the lawyers as flexible went too far.[163] Rather, the lawyers were helpful in understanding the intricacies of the law and how far a policy could go. Yet another former official provided a similar perspective: It was not so much getting the lawyers to change their view but in determining how to move forward within the requirements.[164] Officials who knew the law, this person said, could engage in constructive conversation about options and alternatives that the lawyers did not come up with.

Still, many former officials indicated that the lawyers could be flexible to some extent. That is, they said, the lawyers were usually unwilling to change an interpretation of the law but were often willing to discuss alternative legal courses of action within the confines of the law.[165] For example, Ellen Tauscher, Under Secretary of State for Arms Control and International

[160] *See* Holum Interview, *supra* note 114.
[161] *See* Stillwell Interview, *supra* note 88.
[162] *See* Wirth Interview, *supra* note 88.
[163] *See* Interview 32, *supra* note 32.
[164] *See* Interview 26, *supra* note 22.
[165] *See, e.g.*, Interview 11, *supra* note 156; Interview 26, *supra* note 22; Jacobsen Interview, *supra* note 71.

Security in the Obama administration[166] said that L was interested in keeping obligations but was creative about it and responsive to issues. The lawyers were tremendously helpful and skillful about moving forward, she said. When the lawyers said the United States could not do something, policymakers might respond by asking what could be done. The lawyers made every effort to explore alternatives that did not violate the tenor of an agreement and that kept the United States within boundaries agreed to. When crossing the water, she said, there are lots of ways to get across. But if the lawyers kept saying no, then the answer was no; her view, speaking for herself, was that policymakers could not go forward if L was adamant.

Some former officials thought that the lawyers could be even more flexible than that. Recall the discussion in Chapter 4 regarding those policymakers who believed that policy considerations took precedence, in varying degrees, over legal considerations.[167] In a similar vein, Robert Gallucci stated that the lawyers were infinitely flexible, at least on the national security side, where, he said, decisions simply were not going to be driven by international law. International law might have more weight where the issue was not so significant, he said.

Several other former officials indicated that they were sometimes able to shift the substantive positions of lawyers, although they indicated that was rare.[168] One former official said that the lawyers could sometimes be flexible on interpretation, and that their flexibility depended on the issue and the lawyer. If the issue was of such importance and had a positive impact, or a great deal of precedent, or where the legal interpretation was changing over time so that it was possible to push the envelope, then they could be more flexible. But that was extremely rare. Another former official answered their own rhetorical question: "Have we influenced legal positions? Absolutely."[169] The result might be a change in interpretation. The former official recounted an occasion in which they spent hours with the lawyers on an issue, exhausting options, asking questions, parsing the position.

Phyllis Oakley[170] indicated that the lawyers sometimes modified their advice, though generally they would go along on means as long as they were not giving in on principle. Sometimes there would be a negotiation, especially in murky areas. The lawyers could be flexible, and the degree of flexibility

[166] *See* Tauscher Interview, *supra* note 115.
[167] *See* discussion *supra* Chapter 4.
[168] *See, e.g.*, Interview 31, *supra* note 4 (the positions of the lawyers could be moved "some").
[169] *See* Bloomfield Interview, *supra* note 88.
[170] Assistant Secretary for Population, Refugees, and Migration, Clinton administration. *See* Oakley Interview, *supra* note 36.

depended on personality, issues involved, and how high the issue was taken. The higher up the issue went, officials were more flexible, because they were more cognizant of political implications. The lawyers could be moved, Oakley said. The lawyers were very creative, finding ways to do things. She never found them to be roadblocks.

Another former official stated that they would also press the lawyers in some cases.[171] On the Kosovo intervention, this former official said, the lawyers blanched. In that official's view, the status of Kosovo as an independent state was murky under international law at best. A cautious interpretation would have said no, regarding independence. Policymakers said that the United States was going ahead; can the lawyers make a case? The lawyers made the case. Nonetheless, this official said, if the lawyers had said absolutely not, that would have stopped it. In retrospect, the official said, the International Court of Justice determined that declaring independence was not illegal and so US recognition was the right thing to do. Failing independence, what would have happened? When would UN administration end? Kosovo would have been a troublesome province of Serbia.

Persuasion could go the other way, however, said Tom Shannon, former Under Secretary of State in the Obama and Trump administrations.[172] Sometimes the lawyers' views could be so strong that they could change the principals' minds, both within State and more broadly within government. The lawyers can suggest a third option that more completely reflects international law.

5.3.2.1 Two Kinds of Lawyers

A number of former officials – and former lawyers in L – described two kinds of lawyers and their different levels of flexibility. The first type of lawyer took a more circumscribed view of their role and was more apt to say that a proposed course of action violated the law. The second type saw themselves more as counselors, willing to be creative and to find alternative courses of action that might also comply. In other words, the first type saw themselves more as judges and the second more as advocates for their clients. A former Foreign Service Officer stated that some lawyers were not good because they took a superficial up or down view of the law – "no" was not helpful.[173] The most

[171] *See* Interview 6, Former Assistant Secretary. *See also* Interview 27, *supra* note 43; Interview 8, *supra* note 4.

[172] *See* Shannon Interview, *supra* note 57.

[173] *See* Interview 31, *supra* note 4.

valuable lawyers, this former official said, tried to internalize the policy objective and come up with a sound legal strategy, caveated with downsides. Melvyn Levitsky, Assistant Secretary for International Narcotics Matters in the George H. W. Bush administration, stated that the good lawyers would say how far you can go, providing a sense of the legal framework and red lines.

Another former official affirmed the overall characterization of lawyers playing dual roles as judges and advocates but asserted that the lawyers were not as aggressive as they could have been in advocating for policy outcomes.[174] If a policymaker asked the lawyers how to do something, they would tell you but would say that there are also constraints. This former official would have liked the lawyers to play more of an advocate role and not act as a judge.

The notion that some lawyers were more constructive than others was borne out by a former high-level State Department lawyer.[175] They said that State Department lawyers are trained not to just say no, although there were some lawyers who erred in that direction, just as there were some who were a little too client friendly. Simply saying no creates problems – for one thing, these lawyers might not have a great relationship with policymakers and might be avoided. Instead, the lawyers were trained to provide options for proceeding in a way consistent with international law. They were encouraged to go back with an answer. As discussed before, a number of policymakers and lawyers interviewed confirmed that the lawyers would sometimes provide options, recommendations, and caveats about possible courses of action.

5.4 RESOLVING CONFLICTS BETWEEN NATIONAL INTEREST AND INTERNATIONAL LAW

When significant national interest took priority over international law, former officials indicated that they sometimes followed several general strategies to minimize the conflict with international law. To be sure, international law considerations would still be a factor in decisions. Three strategies are discussed in descending order of preference. The first strategy was to attempt to determine whether alternative approaches were available that were colorably legal. The second strategy, if necessary, was to explore, together with the lawyers, alternative interpretations of the law that might frame US action in a more favorable light. On rare occasions, if the national interest was strong enough, policymakers could decide to proceed with a course of action that

[174] *See* Interview 26, *supra* note 22.
[175] *See* Lawyer Interview 2, *supra* note 37.

potentially violated international law. Two other strategies were mentioned by a few participants, but seem less likely options: Policymakers might engage in lawyer shopping to find a more amenable legal recommendation, or the United States might itself attempt to shift international law to suit its policies.

First, there could be a search for alternative approaches or alternative legal interpretations. As noted previously, many former officials emphasized the option of exploring alternative, legal means to accomplish policy goals when the initial approach created tensions with international law. A former senior Obama administration official stated that the first step in confronting a legal problem was to ask for an alternative that is compliant; reinterpretation was a last resort.[176] Another former official said that while he never recalled an attempt to "find a way around it," he or she did recall that sometimes policymakers said "come on guys," and asked the lawyers if there was another way to do something to achieve a policy goal.[177] Often, it was possible to find alternative means to comply after a first analysis, after looking back at the language or the facts. This did not happen when there was a clear legal or treaty obligation, however, he said: "there were no fancy rope tricks." Other former officials were less sanguine about the sticking power of international law, but the main point remains that a standard approach to conflicts was to explore alternative, legal means to achieve the same goal.

The inherent ambiguity of international law and its effects were discussed in Chapters 2 and 3. A number of former officials emphasized this ambiguity and the "wiggle room" it provides to identify an acceptable, compliant course of action that also serves US interests.[178] They stated that law has interpretive elements in general and that international law is not black and white because much is in a gray, interpretive zone.[179] Accordingly, people interpret international law as needed, to a degree.[180] One former official put it this way: The rules are elastic enough so it is not difficult to at least claim a wide umbrella.[181] Another said that although there is pressure to comply, if compliance is uncomfortable, interpretation can be helpful and there will be a huge effort to create a legal argument.[182]

[176] *See* Interview 27, *supra* note 43.

[177] Interview 34, *supra* note 114.

[178] *See, e.g.*, Interview 8, *supra* note 4; Interview 18, Former Obama administration Senior State Department Official; Pickering Interview, *supra* note 30; Interview 28, *supra* note 103; Interview 2, *supra* note 94; Interview 35, *supra* note 88.

[179] *See* Interview 28, *supra* note 103.

[180] *See* Interview 35, *supra* note 88.

[181] *See* Oakley Interview, *supra* note 36.

[182] *See* Interview with Alexander Watson, Assistant Secretary for Western Hemisphere Affairs, Clinton administration.

One former official put it a slightly different way. Because much international law is subject to interpretation, there might be a range of options available to policymakers, some of which might be more or less in compliance. Compliance may represent a choice among shades of gray.[183] As Philip Zelikow, former State Department Counselor put it, policymakers would not say that the United States is defying international law but would try to define that law in order to say that the United States is complying, to maintain at least a nominal compliance.[184]

Even so, Zelikow said, there are sometimes limits to the ability to interpret or reinterpret obligations. The issue is not "comply or do not comply," he said, but rather how strained a reading one is willing to adopt in order to say one is complying. An overly strained reading undermines a state's position and should be avoided. Another former official supported this view: People interpret international law as needed but only *to a degree*, because the interpretation cannot be outrageous or unbelievable.[185] As discussed in Chapter 4, greater precision of a legal obligation makes interpretive maneuvering less likely, because precise obligations are less subject to plausible, alternative interpretations that allow wiggle room.

From the weight of interviews with former officials, reinterpreting obligations in a calculated manner does not appear to be the norm. Of course, ambiguities may allow lawyers and policymakers options at the outset. The majority of the time, extreme tensions between policy goals and international obligations do not even arise. One former official, for example, stated that everyone follows international obligations 99 percent of the time, but in 1 percent of the time, it is necessary to have a reason to get out of a situation.[186]

One former official mentioned abrogation of the ABM Treaty[187] by the United States as an example, in their view, of lawyers in the Legal Adviser's Office coming up with an argument to justify getting around a legal obligation.[188] Another former official, Clinton administration Under Secretary for Arms Control and International Security John Holum,[189] argued that country-

183 *See* Interview 36, *supra* note 105.

184 *See* Zelikow Interview, *supra* note 101. *See also* Interview 28, *supra* note 103.

185 *See* Interview 35, *supra* note 88.

186 *See id.*

187 Treaty between the United States of America and the Union of Soviet Socialist Republics on the Limitation of Anti-Ballistic Missile Systems, May 26, 1972, 94 U.N.T.S. 13, 23 U.S.T. 3435.

188 *See* Interview 24, Former Official.

189 *See* Holum Interview, *supra* note 114. *See also* Abram Chayes, *Testing and Development of "Exotic" Systems under the ABM Treaty: The Great Reinterpretation Caper*, 99 Harv. L. Rev. 956 (1986).

specific political considerations won the day when the George W. Bush administration later decided to enter into the United States–India Civil Nuclear Agreement,[190] designed to lead toward civil nuclear cooperation with India, in spite of India's status as a nuclear weapons power that is not a party to the Non-Proliferation Treaty.[191] This example is discussed in Chapter 4 in greater detail.

One former official had a more positive spin, characterizing the willingness to interpret obligations favorably not as a way of evading compliance, but rather as a way to maintain the norm by applying it flexibly.[192] If US policy imperatives and international law are in tension, they said, the administration may square the circle by interpreting a norm in as flexible a way as possible to permit the action that is in tension, instead of saying that they do not care about the norm. This actually constitutes evidence that norms matter, rather than that they do not.

An example of creative interpretation mentioned by several former officials without prompting involved an interpretation of US law as applied to the military coup in Egypt in 2011, which illustrated for them the dynamic of reinterpretation more generally.[193] In that case, US law provided that the US must cut off aid to any country "whose duly elected head of government is deposed by military coup or decree."[194] The problem was that the United States did not want to cut off aid to the new Egyptian government at the time, because it was important for Egypt's economy and for the United States' close, long relationship with the Egyptian military.[195] The Obama administration ducked the question by saying that US law did not require a decision about the nature of the takeover, so that simply by not making a determination, the requirement would not be triggered.[196] This is not the only time the US government has taken a flexible view of this requirement of US law. [197]

[190] Agreement for Cooperation between the Government of the United States of America and the Government of India Concerning Peaceful Uses of Nuclear Energy (Oct. 10, 2008). *See also* Joint Statement between George W. Bush and Prime Minister Manmohan Singh, Office of the Press Secretary, White House (July 18, 2005), http://georgewbush-whitehouse.archives.gov/news/releases/2005/07/20050718-6.html.

[191] Treaty on the Non-Proliferation of Nuclear Weapons, July 1, 1968, 729 U.N.T.S. 161.

[192] *See* Interview 26, *supra* note 22.

[193] *See* Interview 35, *supra* note 88; Interview 27, *supra* note 43; Atwood Interview, *supra* note 47.

[194] *See* Consolidated Appropriations Act, Dec. 27, 2020, Pub. L. 116–260, 134 Stat. 1184.

[195] *See* Max Fisher, *U.S. Has Spotty Record on Law Requiring It to Cut Aid after Coups*, WASH. POST (July 5, 2013), https://www.washingtonpost.com/news/worldviews/wp/2013/07/05/u-s-has-spotty-record-on-law-requiring-it-to-cut-aid-after-coups/.

[196] *See* Atwood Interview, *supra* note 47.

[197] *See* David Francis, *When a Coup Is Not a Coup*, FOREIGN POL'Y (Jan. 21, 2015), https://foreignpolicy.com/2015/01/21/when-a-coup-is-not-a-coup/ (last accessed Oct. 12, 2018).

At least one former official remarked or suggested that the United States, because of its size and power, was in a position to change international law rules and goals to suit its policy. Smaller countries do not have this option. James Dobbins suggested that the Kosovo air war was a situation in which the United States could make international law, at least to the extent that the air war was legally controversial.[198] Presumably, he meant that the actions of the United States and its allies could provide state practice in support of a norm of humanitarian intervention. This does not seem like a viable strategy for many issues, particularly in the short term: The United States cannot act entirely on its own and it may take time to develop treaties or to generate significant state practice.

Several former officials suggested "lawyer shopping" as a mechanism for policymakers to shape legal recommendations to suit policy prerogatives. Lawyer shopping, in this context, might consist of hiring congenial lawyers in the first place, or seeking a second opinion when an initial one was not suitable. Thomas Pickering told the story of Henry Kissinger carefully selecting the lawyers around him to make sure they gave him the advice he wanted.[199] That strategy would seem difficult to implement on a broad basis in this day and age, especially at lower levels and for people who are not Henry Kissinger. One or two former officials suggested that seeking a second legal opinion was an ongoing, occasional practice.[200] Another senior former official, however, believed that practice occurred more frequently in the past. Now, there is more a foreign policy of laws than forty years ago, this official said.[201]

Several former officials said that where there was a compelling national interest, and where the aforementioned coping strategies described were unavailing, the United States might act contrary to international law. At that point, the United States would have to "take its lumps" in the best way possible.[202] As illustrated in the Chapter 4 discussion of examples of US compliance and noncompliance, the United States has certainly pushed the envelope in a number of cases.

Still, there was a sense among former officials that acting in a legally questionably manner was rare, and certainly not a first choice. One former official said that in their experience, which included experience in another government agency, no international law would actually be *broken* without

[198] *See* Dobbins Interview, *supra* note 109.
[199] *See* Pickering Interview, *supra* note 30.
[200] *See e.g.*, Interview 10, *supra* note 97.
[201] *See* Interview 8, *supra* note 4.
[202] *See, e.g.*, Oakley Interview, *supra* note 36; Watson Interview, *supra* note 182; Interview 17, Assistant Secretary, George H. W. Bush administration; Interview 15, *supra* note 124; Interview 31, *supra* note 4.

presidential involvement. Minimally contradictory positions might be taken at a lower level.[203] Another said that in their view, while the United States should stand from principles of law, there are cases when national interests prevail, but that the United States should never do wrong except with just cause.[204] At least two other former officials said that if the United States is considering a course of action that would not be consistent with international law, there must be a good argument and overriding national interest, or that the challenge would be to go and make the case for that inconsistent action.[205] In other cases, the United States might certainly decide to go ahead where legality was controversial, but where it could make a credible international law argument.[206]

5.5 CONCLUSION

To recap, 21 percent of former officials said the advice of the Legal Advisor's Office was determinative regarding US compliance with international law, 68 percent said it was significant, and 11 percent said it was of moderate weight or less. The qualitative comments reflect more nuanced attitudes toward the role of advice from the Legal Adviser's Office. Again, by far the majority of respondents said that legal advice was influential but not necessarily determinative. Even those in the group that indicated that legal advice was determinative sometimes hedged their responses. Nonetheless, there seemed to be wide agreement that when L said no, that some course of action was definitely illegal, that was the final word. One or two respondents said that this happened rarely, and it seems likely that a higher political authority outside the State Department could make a different decision even then.

Aside from those comparatively clear areas of illegality, however, the weight of L's advice varied, depending on the circumstances, according to policymakers. The lawyers were part of the decision-making process and their views carried substantial weight with most policymakers. Many policymakers viewed that process as collaborative, but some also viewed it as more of a negotiation and were willing to push back against the lawyers. The lawyers could be flexible: They were generally reluctant to back down on matters of legal interpretation but were willing to develop alternative, legal courses of action.

[203] *See* Interview 4, Former Senior Official.
[204] *See* Interview 17, *supra* note 202.
[205] *See* Oakley Interview, *supra* note 36; Gallucci Interview, *supra* note 134.
[206] *See* Dobbins Interview, *supra* note 109; Zelikow Interview, *supra* note 101.

Some policymakers asserted that the substantive position of the lawyers could sometimes be swayed.

Policymakers generally had the final say in implementing legal advice, depending on the nature of the issue at hand and on the seniority of the policymaker. Recall, however, the various channels the Legal Adviser's Office has for pressing its positions, particularly against Assistant Secretaries and lower-ranking officials. Policymakers could sometimes override the lawyers' advice as issues went up the decision-making chain.

Thus, when international law conflicted with significant policy or national interests, policymakers and lawyers might employ several strategies to get around the conflict. They might identify alternative, legal approaches to achieve the same result, or they might explore alternative interpretations of international law. On rare occasions, if the national interest was strong enough policymakers might decide to proceed with a course of action that pushed against the limits of international law. The first strategy appeared to be the most commonly accepted.

While the second was generally disfavored, the ambiguity of international law left a significant amount of room to maneuver. The lawyers, therefore, might from the outset be able to provide a range of legal options, though some might be heavily qualified with caveats. It appeared that at least sometimes, if the legal advice was not convivial, the lawyers would revisit the matter to come up with a more agreeable interpretation. Some former officials indicated that the lawyers resisted changing their interpretation after providing advice and that doing so was unusual. In extraordinary cases, policymakers at the highest levels might make a decision that violates international law or pushes its boundaries. Nevertheless, the predilection of most former officials was to follow international law. The views of the Legal Adviser's Office were taken seriously and played a significant role in policymaking in the State Department.

6

The Trump Administration and International Law in the State Department

As we have seen, the State Department's structure, procedures, and culture provide a role for international law in policymaking. What would it take to modify that normative culture, to revise it wholesale in a relatively short amount of time, beyond the accretion of normative change that would occur normally? The Trump administration attempted to do just that. The administration generally pursued strong unilateralist views and policies antagonistic to international institutions and promoted a narrow view of the scope of international law. The administration sought to impose these policy preferences on the State Department, like other administrations before it but did so to a greater degree. The administration installed political appointees who strongly adhered to the administration's views, discouraged dissent, removed dissenters, and took other steps to impose its will.

In a sense, the Trump administration experience provides a natural experiment in attempting to force cultural change within a bureaucratic organization. The normative theories in Chapter 2 focused on normative change in bureaucratic culture through contestation among bureaucratic actors arising from dispute about the application of norms to particular circumstances, a somewhat organic process. That mechanism may apply here, but there was also an inorganic, blunter strategy, an attempt to impose norms from above, including through replacement of personnel. As a senior former State Department Official in the Obama administration put it, speaking of international law and norms more generally, the whole system works if people decide that it should, implying that if people and states fail to follow norms, the normative system can fall apart.[1]

[1] Interview 18, Senior State Department Official, Obama administration.

Seven former officials who served during the Trump administration were interviewed, including former Under Secretary for Political Affairs Tom Shannon. In addition, former officials who served in other administrations were also asked about their understanding of the place of international law and institutions in the Trump State Department. This group consisted of some previously interviewed subjects who were reinterviewed for this purpose and some subjects who were interviewed for the first time after 2016. While the former officials from other administrations might not have had first-hand knowledge of developments, they were generally aware of news reports and may have been in touch with former colleagues.

One narrative that frames discussion of international relations, US foreign policy, and international law is the idea that the United States established and led a rule-based, liberal, multilateral international order following World War II. While the existence and nature of the liberal international order are contested, it is hard to deny the existence of the multilateral institutions that the United States created after the World War II and US leadership in maintaining and propagating those institutions for more than half a century. Many of the interview subjects in this study alluded to the liberal international order as a reason for the United States to comply with international law.

And, certainly, whatever we call it, the Trump administration demonstrated an antipathy to the existing international order. Instead of a multilateral approach, the Trump administration pursued a transactional, bilateral, case-by-case approach to relations with other states, dismissive of multilateralism and international institutions. The animating principle seemed to be an exclusive focus on the right of sovereign countries to act as they saw fit. The Trump assault on multilateralism also included, at best, a narrow application of international law and, at worst, some would say, violations of international law.

Various actions and statements by President Trump and his administration demonstrated antipathy to international institutions and international law. Former officials critical of President Trump cited, among other things, withdrawal from the Paris Climate Agreement, withdrawal from the Iran Nuclear Deal (JCPOA), and withdrawal from the Human Rights Council as examples of hostility to multilateralism. As actions that ventured into illegality, they cited the US airstrikes in Syria in response to chemical attacks, the treatment of asylum seekers, the travel bans on citizens of Muslim countries, and pushing the boundaries of trade law. The President and the administration, moreover, issued statements and took positions antagonistic to international institutions and international law.

Some commentators take the view that the Trump administration, through the actions described earlier, undermined international law and institutions in unprecedented ways. Others have taken a more sanguine view, arguing that the Trump onslaught on international law had a more limited effect. Nonetheless, a fair assessment of the Trump administration reveals some effect on international institutions and on the international legal order. Most importantly, it is fair to say that the Trump administration's America First rhetoric and its and isolationist policies damaged the standing and influence of the United States in that order. The absence of US leadership on international law and institutions created a void. For example, before and at the beginning of Russia's invasion of Ukraine, it was an open question whether and to what extent the United States would be able to lead NATO and others in opposition because of the state in which Trump had left transatlantic relations. President Trump's attacks on international institutions, moreover, undermined those institutions and their legitimacy. The Trump administration's disparagement of international law and the rule of law in general may have encouraged and provided cover for foreign leaders to take a similar stance and may have discouraged support for international law and institutions in other countries.

In order to pursue its policies, the Trump administration sought to force the foreign policy machinery of the United States government to do its bidding. Any administration, of course, would appoint its loyal followers to leadership positions and seek to make the bureaucracy implement its policies. The Trump administration pursued this goal in an extreme and unprecedented fashion.[2]

Indeed, the undermining of the State Department was part and parcel of President Trump's effort to bend the government and the civil service – the "Deep State" – to his will, to root out opposition to his policies throughout the government. The President sought to make political appointments primarily on the basis of loyalty to him. In order to hobble the bureaucracy further, he left numerous positions vacant, or appointed "acting" officials who did not require Senate approval and would be more directly under the administration's thumb. In the State Department specifically, appointments to the senior leadership were heavily skewed toward noncareer appointees, as opposed to career officials. The Trump administration also made notably more political appointments to ambassadorships than previous administrations.

The President's appointed officials, in turn, sometimes sought to enforce the administration's will and stifle debate and opposition within the government to administration policies. Not surprisingly, the atmosphere within the

2 *See generally*, Dem. Staff of S. Comm. on Foreign Relations, 117th Cong., *Diplomacy in Crisis: The Trump Administration's Decimation of the State Department* (July 28, 2020), https://www.foreign.senate.gov/imo/media/doc/Diplomacy%20in%20Crisis%20–%20SFRC%20Democratic%20Staff%20Report.pdf.

State Department became toxic. Many State Department employees felt they could not disclose wrongdoing without fear of reprisal and an increased number believed that senior leaders did not maintain high levels of honesty and integrity. In addition, it was clear from interview comments that there was no love lost on both sides between at least some Trump political appointees and at least some of the career officers in the State Department.

Several former officials noted a breakdown of the decision-making process in general. Decision-making was chaotic from the beginning, said one high-level former official. In particular, the interagency process broke down under John Bolton's tenure as National Security Adviser, depriving the State Department of an opportunity to provide broad input into government-wide decision-making. One former ambassador and former Assistant Secretary asserted that the process breakdown extended outside of Washington to operations of ambassadors.

The former officials differed regarding the extent to which the administration's position affected attitudes within the State Department. The majority believed that while some practices might change, underlying attitudes among the rank and file would not change substantially. The consensus view appeared to make a distinction between those at the policy decision level – high-level political appointees, with the potential exception of career officials and other technocrats appointed to those positions – and those at the policy development level – Foreign Service and Civil Service Officers. At the policy decision level, most political appointees adhered to administration policies and beliefs and, according to the aforementioned reports, attempted to impose their preferences on the Department as a whole. At the policy development level, the established culture prevailed, favoring multilateralism and respectful of international law. As a result, several former officials suggested that the overall culture and even the overall approach of the State Department likely did not shift very much.

Permanent change at the policy development level would have been more difficult because that would have entailed changing an established culture among a comparatively large number of career officials. One former official pointed out that the State Department could not bring in a whole cadre of new people willing to ignore international law and institutions.[3] Moreover, career Foreign Service Officers throughout the State Department may have been able to slow some administration policies by using the time-honored tactics of bureaucrats everywhere, expressing opposition, dragging their feet, and using other tactics. The consensus view among former officials in and

[3] *But see* discussion *infra* Section 6.4.

outside of the Trump administration was that the basic culture of the Department would not and did not change.

That is not to say, however, that attitudes from the top did not constrain action or shift attitudes at all. Over time, there was an exodus of senior officials from the State Department who might have been more likely to resist pressure. In addition, officials may have tried to use legal analysis but, when stymied, faced frustration and were less willing to go out on a limb or present a disfavored view. Perhaps Tom Shannon put it best when he said the following. The administration's views are expressed only on a case-by-case basis. No one stands up saying we are going to raspberry international law. But over time, people see what is going on. If an official is writing briefing memos and see things get struck by higher-ups, then if a memo is to go through, they stop raising the precipitating issues.

When asked whether views about international law and international institutions might swing back or change after the Trump administration, respondents said that it depended in large part on the presidential election in 2020. As one former official pointed out, the views of the State Department are likely to hew to the position of the President. If Mr. Trump had been reelected, then the views of his administration were likely to become more entrenched, making an eventual change in direction less likely.

Following the 2020 election, however, it seems that the State Department and its culture have snapped back, to a large extent. President Biden and his foreign policy team have made it clear in statements and actions that they intend to maintain traditional US support for the multilateral international order, while recognizing challenges from a rising China and a more multipolar world. There still may be a question of how much of a snapback there will be, however. Richard Armitage, former Deputy Secretary of State, said that he thought it was unlikely that respect for international law in the State Department would return to the *status quo ante*, that is, their level of prominence during the Obama administration.

If Mr. Trump, or someone else adhering to his views and tactics, is elected President in 2024, we could see further erosion of the traditional norms in the State Department. In that event, policy and cultural shifts in favor of unilateralism and control over the State Department bureaucracy are likely to resume. A second Trump administration or similar likely would implement the same approach to the bureaucracy as in the last Trump administration and could go even further.

6.1 THE LIBERAL INTERNATIONAL ORDER

One narrative that frames discussion of international relations, US foreign policy, and international law is the concept of the rule-based, liberal international order. According to this narrative, the United States established a multilateral system of institutions and alliances after World War II, within which member nations pursued security, free trade, and human rights, among other collective goals.[4] Many of the interview subjects in this study alluded to the liberal international order as a reference point, or cited the benefits of the liberal international order as a reason for the United States generally to comply with international law in order to maintain the system. Indeed, according to a former senior official, the State Department as an institution, while promoting and protecting US interests, does so with the belief that having more allies is better and that the United States should operate on a multilateral basis. This attitude is in sharp distinction to the attitude of the Trump administration.[5]

The very existence of the liberal international order has been subject to contestation, with realist critics in the forefront. Graham Allison dismisses the "myth of the liberal order," arguing that the long peace after 1945 was the result more of US power and the Cold War than of US support of, or adherence to, multilateralism and international law.[6] Other critics have argued that to the extent that a postwar order existed, it was neither liberal, international, nor orderly.[7] Nonetheless, it is hard to deny the existence of the multilateral institutions that the United States created after the World War II and its leadership role in maintaining and propagating those institutions, whatever its motivation in doing so.[8]

Beginning in the Obama administration and sharpening with the advent of the Trump and Biden administrations, scholars and policymakers have increasingly debated the status and relevance of the liberal international order.[9] Perhaps, they suggest, the decline of US hegemony and the

[4] *See* G. JOHN IKENBERRY, LIBERAL LEVIATHAN: THE ORIGINS, CRISIS, AND TRANSFORMATION OF THE AMERICAN WORLD ORDER xi (2011); Stewart M. Patrick, *Can Trump's Successor Save the Liberal International Order?* WORLD POL. REV. (Feb. 10, 2020), https://www.worldpoliticsreview.com/articles/28526/can-trump-s-successor-save-the-liberal-international-order. International relations scholar John Ikenberry has been perhaps the most visible proponent of the framework of the liberal international order in several books and in various articles in Foreign Affairs.

[5] See Interview 8, Former Senior State Department Official. The former official went on to say, however, that the State Department was disciplined and would figure it out and manage.

[6] See Graham Allison, *The Myth of the Liberal Order: From Historical Accident to Conventional Wisdom*, FOREIGN AFF. (July–Aug. 2018), at 124.

[7] *See* Patrick, *supra* note 4.

[8] *See id.*: "The broad thrust of U.S. policy, under 13 U.S. administrations before Donald Trump, was to support the gradual emergence of an open, rule-bound international system in which all sovereign states could ultimately pursue shared peace, prosperity and freedom."

[9] *See id.*

concurrent rise of other great and middle powers herald a shift to a different world order. And perhaps the Trump administration's policies and actions mark a rupture by the American electorate with past support of that order.

In any event, as discussed further below, the Trump administration demonstrated an antipathy to the existing international order, liberal or not.[10] Instead of a multilateral approach, it focused on a transactional, bilateral, case-by-case approach to relations with other states.[11] That transactional approach focused on zero-sum wins and losses in the context of each bilateral relationship, disavowing and disparaging multilateral organizations and systemic costs and benefits. Maintaining multilateral institutions, in this view, was not worth the cost. The Trump assault on multilateralism included an assault on international law as well.

6.2 THE TRUMP ADMINISTRATION'S APPROACH TO INTERNATIONAL INSTITUTIONS AND INTERNATIONAL LAW

In keeping with the Trump administration's view of foreign relations, the administration displayed a skeptical, if not hostile, view of international law, institutions, and agreements. Indeed, some commentators have variously labeled the administration's approach to international law as an "onslaught,"[12] or an "assault."[13] The administration's attitude reflected a new sovereigntist view of international law, according to which treaties give too much authority to international organizations and other states, stripping power from their rightful place in domestic political institutions.[14] Tom Shannon, former Under Secretary for Political Affairs in the Trump administration, confirmed that the Trump foreign policy had one salient quality: Sovereign nations are entitled to act in a sovereign fashion. That position only reluctantly admitted to any limits, including those imposed by treaty and international law.[15]

[10] *See* discussion *infra* Section 6.2.

[11] *See* Joseph S. Nye, Jr., *Will the Liberal Order Survive?*, FOREIGN AFF. (Jan–Feb. 2017), at 10.

[12] Jack Goldsmith, *The Trump Onslaught on International Law and Institutions*, LAWFARE (Mar. 17, 2017, 10:09 AM), https://www.lawfareblog.com/trump-onslaught-international-law-and-institutions.

[13] Oona Hathaway, *Reengaging on Treaties and Other International Agreements (Part 1): President Donald Trump's Rejection of International Law*, JUST SECURITY (Oct. 2, 2020), https://www.justsecurity.org/72656/reengaging-on-treaties-and-other-international-agreements-part-i-president-donald-trumps-rejection-of-international-law/.

[14] See *id.*

[15] *See* Interview with Thomas Shannon, Under Secretary of Political Affairs, Acting Secretary, Acting Deputy Secretary, Obama and Trump administrations. *See also* Interview 3, Former Assistant Secretary (Trump argument that sovereignty comes before all); Interview 33, Former Assistant Secretary with experience in the Trump administration.

Some commentators take the view that the Trump administration has undermined international law and institutions in unprecedented ways. Others have taken a more sanguine view, arguing that the Trump onslaught on international law had a more limited effect for various reasons. These include the broad scope of international law and limited bandwidth of any administration, as well as the limited time available to an administration in one term, and the inevitable swing away from many of the Trump administration's policies by the Biden administration. Nevertheless, a fair assessment of the Trump administration reveals effects on international institutions, on the international legal order, and on America's standing and influence on the world. The most important question is whether, and to what extent, those effects will continue.

6.2.1 *Withdrawal from International Institutions and Agreements*

The Trump administration withdrew, or took steps to withdraw, from various international organizations and nonbinding arrangements, executive agreements, and treaties. These include most notably:[16]

- The Joint Comprehensive Plan of Action with Iran
- The Paris Agreement on Climate Change
- The Intermediate-Range Nuclear Forces Treaty
- The Treaty on Open Skies
- The Trans-Pacific Partnership (not yet a party, the United States "unsigned," indicating its intent not to become a party)
- The Optional Protocol of the Vienna Convention on Diplomatic Relations
- The World Health Organization Constitution
- The UN Human Rights Council
- United Nations Education Scientific and Cultural Organization (UNESCO)
- The Global Compact for Safe, Orderly and Regular Migration (a non-legally binding process)
- The Global Compact on Refugees (a nonlegally binding process)
- The UN Relief and Works Agency (UNWRA) (withdrawing voluntary funding).

In addition, the Trump administration indicated that it did not intend to renew the START nuclear arms control treaty with Russia when it was set to

[16] *See* Hathaway, *supra* note 13.

expire in February 2021. The Biden administration, upon taking office, quickly reached agreement with the Russians to extend the treaty.[17]

In addition, the Trump administration threatened at times to withdraw from a number of other agreements, such as the Universal Postal Union and the Korea–United States Free Trade Agreement.[18] The president also made noises about leaving NATO and the WTO but did not follow through. Nonetheless, the administration took steps to undermine the WTO beyond the aggressive trade measures it adopted against China and even US allies. The administration effectively hobbled the WTO Dispute Settlement Appellate Body by vetoing the appointment of new members so that there were not enough judges to form three-judge panels, so that it could not hear new matters.[19] The administration also resisted joining new international agreements, submitting only five treaties for Senate consent, a significant drop compared to previous administrations.[20]

6.2.2 *Hostility and Rhetoric*

Beginning during the 2016 campaign and continuing into his administration, statements from President Trump and members of his administration regularly reflected hostility to international law.[21] Trump, for example, made no secret of his disdain for human rights norms. Candidate Trump promised to reinstate waterboarding and other coercive interrogation methods. After the election, his administration even attempted to reinstate interrogation of high-value alien terrorists outside of the United States. Fortunately, this attempt was effectively stymied by existing law and by internal opposition from military and national security officials.[22]

[17] *See* David E. Sanger & Anton Troianovski, *Biden and Putin Agree to Extend Nuclear Treaty*, N.Y. Times (Jan. 26, 2021), *available at* https://www.nytimes.com/2021/01/26/world/europe/biden-putin-nuclear-treaty.html (last accessed Mar. 18, 2021).

[18] See *id.*

[19] The Biden administration followed suit, also refusing to seat judges and continuing some of the Trump administration's other aggressive trade policies. *See* Bryce Baschuk, *Biden Picks Up Where Trump Left Off in Hard-Line Stances at WTO*, Bloomberg (Feb. 22, 2021), https://www.bloomberg.com/news/articles/2021-02-22/biden-picks-up-where-trump-left-off-in-hard-line-stances-at-wto.

[20] Hathaway, *supra* note 13.

[21] *See* John B. Bellinger III, *The Trump Administration's Approach to International Law and Courts: Are We Seeing a Turn for the Worse?*, 51 Case W. Res. J. Int'l L. 7, 10 (2019) (criticisms as a candidate).

[22] *See* Harold Hongju Koh, The Trump Administration and International Law 34–37 (2019).

In addition, he told the General Assembly in September, 2018 that "America will always choose independence and cooperation over global governance, control, and domination . . . ." Speaking of the ICC in particular, President Trump said "[w]e will never surrender American's sovereignty to an unelected, unaccountable, global bureaucracy."[23] Indeed, the ICC became a favorite whipping boy of the administration as a whole.

With the appointment of John Bolton as National Security Adviser in 2018, Bolton and the administration began an all-out campaign against the International Criminal Court. The ICC had been Bolton's *bête noir* since his tenure as Under Secretary of State in the George W. Bush administration, when he spear headed active steps to undermine it.[24] This time around, Bolton issued broadsides against the court and endorsed further steps against it.[25]

To be sure, some of the administration's reaction to the ICC was sparked by the ICC prosecutor's determination to investigate war crimes involving detainee treatment by the United States in Afghanistan and at CIA facilities in Europe.[26] Any administration, Democrat or Republican, would have opposed such an action. But the Trump administration's response was over the top. Even before the prosecutor received leave to proceed from the court, the administration seemed to have decided that the US would cease all cooperation with the ICC, reversing twelve years of cooperation dating back to the George W. Bush administration.[27] In response to the ICC investigation, the Trump administration first withdrew US visas for ICC officials and then froze US financial assets and restricted travel for individuals involved in the investigation and their families. These sanctions included the ICC Prosecutor.[28]

In particular, Trump's disdain for human rights weakened human rights norms. While the United States has practiced "exceptionalism," resisting some binding international human rights commitments, its constitutional and domestic law commitment to human rights has been strong. More

[23] Donald J. Trump, Remarks by President Trump to the 73rd Session of the United Nations General Assembly in New York, New York (Sept. 25, 2018), https://trumpwhitehouse.archives.gov/briefings-statements/remarks-president-trump-73rd-session-united-nations-general-assembly-new-york-ny/#:~:text=I%20honor%20the%20right%20of,honor%20our%20sovereignty%20in%20return.C.

[24] *See* Bellinger, *supra* note 21, at 11–16.

[25] *See id.*

[26] *See id.* at 13.

[27] *See id.* at 15.

[28] *See* Kyle Rapp & Kelebogile Zvobgo, *Biden Reversed Trump's Sanctions on International Criminal Court Officials. What Happens Now?*, Washington Post (Apr. 5, 2021), *available at* https://www.washingtonpost.com/politics/2021/04/05/biden-reversed-trumps-sanctions-international-criminal-court-officials-what-happens-now/.

importantly, the United States has long and consistently expressed a bipartisan "rhetorical commitment" to human rights as part of its foreign policy, central to which has been the human rights rhetoric of US presidents.[29] The Trump administration's abandonment of human rights talk not only weakened norms, it also undermined the ability of the United States to put pressure on human rights violations abroad.[30] Most importantly, Trump's disdainful rhetoric made the prospect of "snapping-back" to a pre-2017 world after the Trump administration that much more difficult.[31]

Some commentators have made related points about the damage done by the Trump administration's rhetoric to the discursive nature of law.[32] This is particularly true of Trump's explicit or implicit claim that international law does not matter, that only power matters. Monica Hakimi, for example, argues that the essential value of international law lies in the argumentative practice that is emblematic of law. That is, "law fosters the expectation that governance decisions must be rooted in authority; those who have the power to govern are expected to show . . . that they have the authority to do what they want to do."[33] Even though people inevitably will disagree about the existence or extent of authority, law structures a particular kind of argumentation. It requires participants to justify their decisions publicly and in ways that reflect not just their own preferences but the preferences of a broader group. Arguments are subject to scrutiny and debate; institutions and processes structure those arguments.

6.2.2.1 View of Former Officials

Most former officials seemed to agree that the Trump administration as a whole demonstrated skepticism, and even antipathy, toward international law

29 *See* Margaret E. McGuinness, *Presidential Human Rights Talk*, 56 WASHBURN L.J. 471, 473 (2017).

30 For discussion of the effects of presidential and US reticence damages the effectiveness of human rights norms, see *id.* at 481–485.

31 *See* Jack Goldsmith & Shannon Togawa Mercer, *International Law and Institutions in the Trump Era*, 61 GERMAN Y.B. INT'L L. 11, 37 (2019).

32 *See generally* Monica Hakimi, *Why Should We Care about International Law?*, 118 MICH. L. REV. 1283 (2020); Andrea Birdsall & Rebecca Sanders, *Trumping International Law?*, 21 INT'L STUD. PERSP. 275, 287 (2020). Birdsall and Sanders argue that law serves important political functions, helping states control each other and justifying their own actions. That is, states invoke legality to adjudicate legitimate conduct. Losing legitimacy means losing power and influence. States try to convince other states to accept their efforts to reinterpret or avoid the law. Even powerful states, against whom enforcement is difficult, may loses allies, social standing, and soft power, while at the same time initiating new rivalries. Birdsall & Sanders, *id.* at 279.

33 Hakimi, *supra* note 32, at 1300.

and international institutions. Even former Trump administration officials described the administration's views toward international institutions in similar, if more favorable fashion. Former noncareer Trump political appointees expressed the Trump administration's views about the US role in international affairs. They constituted a small sample of four, but their views generally corresponded with the characterization of other former officials and outside observers. They expressed sincere respect for international law, although they, like many from other administrations, did not see it as necessarily or always determinative. They saw law's ambit in narrow terms, however, limited almost exclusively to treaties, treaties from which the United States could and should legally withdraw if they were not in the perceived national interest. More broadly, these former officials viewed international affairs in essentially sovereigntist, unilateral terms, often expressing distrust of the United Nations and international organizations, as well as a strong aversion to internationalist views.

One former Trump Assistant Secretary stated that the administration was prepared to meet its international obligations but expected others to do so as well.[34] Mutuality of obligation was taken very seriously, they said. But the administration did not turn "internationalism" into a talisman. This official did not think that attitudes toward international law changed with the Trump administration. The difference, in their view, was in the role assigned by the Bush (41 and 43), Clinton, Obama, and Biden administrations to operations on an international, global, or regional stage. For example, the Biden administration supports centralism in governance, both domestically and internationally, when it would be better for states to operate independently.

Another former Trump Assistant Secretary put it in similar terms, saying they did not agree that the Trump administration interpretation of international obligations was more limited just because of disagreement about the appropriate role of the UN or its agencies.[35] The administration was truly guided by US law, using that to complement international agreements or well-established standards. The difference was in the packaging of the US role in the system. The Trump administration followed more of a classical appeal: Nation-states advance their own interest, but their interests are often parallel to the overarching goal of peace. Departing from international agreements did not reflect a different view of international law, but a difference on policy, on the substance of the agreements themselves. Even then, withdrawals from agreements were made within the terms of the agreements.

[34] *See* Interview 3, *supra* note 15.

[35] *See* Interview 19, Former Assistant Secretary, Trump administration.

Of course, not all former officials interviewed for this project disagreed with all international positions taken by the Trump administration. Former Trump noncareer officials were, not surprisingly, very supportive of administration policies. One or two other non-Trump former officials explicitly asserted that not all of the administration's actions have been questionable. Two expressed support for the US attack on Syria in response to use of chemical weapons, with one asserting that those attacks could have occurred under the Obama administration.[36] At least one former official expressed approval of the Trump administration's hard line on trade with China.[37]

6.2.3 *Illegality*

Administration actions went beyond rhetoric and retaliation and ventured into illegality, according to critics. The contest between the Trump administration and international law got off to a fast start shortly after the 2016 inauguration with a travel ban on entry into the United States by citizens of predominantly Muslim countries. The travel ban was actually a series of three executive orders, the first two struck down by the courts, but the third ultimately upheld by the Supreme Court.[38] The travel bans generated widespread criticism that they violated domestic and international law. Critics alleged that they discriminated against Muslims on the basis of religion, or at least were motivated by animus against Muslims and had a disparate impact on them.[39] As such, they potentially violated the International Covenant on Civil and Political Rights[40] and also the 1951 Refugee Convention.[41] Critics also claimed that

[36] *See* Interview 8, *supra* note 5; Interview 27, Senior State Department Official, Obama administration.

[37] *See* Interview 18, *supra* note 1.

[38] *See* Trump v. Hawaii, 138 S. Ct. 2392 (2018). The first two were the most problematic because they were directed against citizens of seven and then six predominantly Muslim countries and because they were accompanied by Trump statements highlighting their anti-Muslim purpose *See* KOH, *supra* note 22, at 23. The third executive order was more careful, targeting six majority-Muslim countries, plus Venezuela and North Korea (not majority-Muslim countries), and incorporating an extensive national security analysis. *See* Goldsmith & Mercer, *supra* note 31.

[39] *See* Goldsmith & Mercer, *supra* note 31, at 26–27.

[40] International Covenant on Civil and Political Rights, Dec. 9, 1966, 999 U.N.T.S. 171 (ratified June 8, 1992).

[41] Convention on the Status of Refugees, July 28, 1951, 189 U.N.T.S. 150. As Goldsmith and Mercer point out, the United States also could have been in violation of customary law rules regarding asylum and the non-refoulement principle, which prohibits states from forcefully repatriating refugees where that would expose them to danger. Goldsmith & Mercer, *supra* note 31, at 26, n. 78.

they violated domestic law that reflected the relevant international law norms.[42]

Even though a travel ban eventually survived Supreme Court scrutiny, the travel ban was seen widely as an attack on international human rights norms.[43] Other actions and statements by the Trump administration also seemed to take particular aim at human rights law and norms.[44] Sometimes, these attacks consisted of direct action and sometimes they were rhetorical. As mentioned earlier, the administration withdrew from UN human rights-related organizations and launched a vitriolic campaign against the ICC. The administration even halted cooperation with UN Special Rapporteurs regarding potential human rights violations in the United States[45]

On trade, the Trump administration initiated trade wars with China, Turkey, the European Union, and Canada by imposing tariffs based on various justifications under the WTO agreements.[46] Those countries replied with retaliatory tariffs and brought cases before the WTO dispute resolution body. For example, the Trump administration justified steel and aluminum tariffs on China, Canada, Mexico, and Europe by invoking the national security exception, allowed under domestic US law and under the WTO agreement.[47] The US claim was so broad, however, that if accepted, it would swallow the rule, opening the door for other countries to invoke the rule and undercutting the WTO regime.[48] The legality of this justification and others is in dispute.[49]

The US recognition of Jerusalem as the capital of Israel in late 2017 and the subsequent opening of the US embassy in Jerusalem in 2018 were also met with legal criticism. Palestine brought suit against the United States before the ICJ, arguing that that moving the embassy violated the Vienna Convention on

42 *See* KOH, *supra* note 22, at 23–25.

43 *See* Goldsmith & Mercer, *supra* note 31, at 27.

44 *See id.*; KOH, *supra* note 22, at 33–37.

45 Ed Pilkington, *US Halts Cooperation with UN on Potential Human Rights Violations*, THE GUARDIAN (Jan. 4, 2019), *available at* https://www.theguardian.com/law/2019/jan/04/trump-administration-un-human-rights-violations.

46 *See* Goldsmith & Mercer, *supra* note 31, at 12–15; Birdsall & Sanders, *supra* note 32, at 287.

47 *See* Section 232 of the Trade Expansion Act of 1962, 19 U.S.C. §1862; Article XXI General Agreement on Tariffs and Trade (GATT) 1947, 55 U.N.T.S. 194.

48 *See* Birdsall & Sanders, *supra* note 32, at 287. Other countries have followed suit, invoking the national security exception themselves. Even the Biden administration has taken the Trump administration's lead and invoked the exception in a case involving Hong Kong, asserting, moreover, that national security claims are non-justiciable by the WTO dispute resolution system because they fall within the discretion of states. *See* Baschuk, *supra* note 19.

49 *See* Goldsmith & Mercer, *supra* note 31, at 14–15 and sources cited therein.

Diplomatic Relations.[50] Commentators took a variety of positions on the legality of the US action.[51]

Regarding armed conflict, the most notable actions by the Trump administration were the two airstrikes against the Assad regime in Syria in response to the use of chemical weapons in 2017 and 2018. Many asserted that these strikes violated the United Nations Charter and international law prohibitions on the use of force, though some argued that the strikes might be permitted under the emerging doctrines of humanitarian intervention or responsibility to protect.[52] Harold Koh – no friend of the Trump administration's view toward international law, but a proponent of the legality of humanitarian intervention under specific circumstances – has argued that the strikes may have been lawful but criticized the Trump administration for not offering an explicit legal justification, as most administrations do.[53]

6.2.4 *Assessment: The Trump Effect in International Affairs*

The view among critical commentators is that the Trump administration, through the actions described above, significantly undermined international law and institutions in unprecedented ways.[54] The Trump administration also damaged the standing and influence of the United States. In the process, the administration hollowed out the United States' foreign policy apparatus in the State Department.

Nevertheless, some scholars and commentators have taken a more sanguine view, arguing that the Trump onslaught on international law has had a more limited effect on the international legal order. Thus, it makes sense to examine the countervailing forces that pressed back against the Trump administration, both externally and internally, and to assess the ultimate effect of the administration's efforts on the international legal order and on domestic foreign policymaking.

[50] ICJ, Application Institution Proceedings in the International Court of Justice, Relocation of the United States Embassy to Israel to Jerusalem (Palestine v. United States of America), Sept. 28, 2018. Vienna Convention on Diplomatic Relations 1961, 500 U.N.T.S. 95.

[51] *See* Goldsmith & Mercer, *supra* note 31, at 22–23 and sources cited therein.

[52] For contending views and citations, *see id.* at 24–25.

[53] *See* KOH, *supra* note 22, at 131–140.

[54] *See* Robert Jervis et al., *Introduction*, *in* CHAOS IN THE LIBERAL ORDER: THE TRUMP PRESIDENCY AND INTERNATIONAL POLITICS IN THE TWENTY-FIRST CENTURY ix–xv (Robert Jervis et al., eds., 2018). *See also, e.g.*, Bellinger, *supra* note 21; Hathaway, *supra* note 13; Karen J. Alter, *The Future of International law in an Age of Trump*, THE AMERICAN ACADEMY IN BERLIN, https://www.americanacademy.de/future-international-law-age-trump/ (last accessed June 24, 2021).

6.2.4.1 The Trump Effect on International Law and Institutions

It is fair to say that the Trump administration had a significant effect on international law and institutions, as well as on US leadership in the world. For example, before and at the beginning of Russia's invasion of Ukraine, it was an open question whether and to what extent the United States would be able to lead NATO and others in opposition because of the state in which Trump had left transatlantic relations. Indeed, it may not be too much of a stretch to suggest that transatlantic disarray played into Russia's calculation to invade Ukraine. As the NATO case illustrates, Trump's unilateralist disdain for allies reduced US influence and leverage. As one former senior official put it, this approach was antithetical to the ethos of the State Department. The State Department as an institution, while promoting and protecting US interests, does so with the belief that having more allies is better and that the United States should operate on a multilateral basis.[55]

The Trump administration's withdrawal from various treaties, moreover, also suggests that the Trump effect has been substantial, particularly the withdrawal from the JCPOA. These withdrawals may have been perfectly legal, but at least some are likely to have a continued effect. The Biden administration has faced challenges in its efforts to resuscitate the JCPOA and it may be a dead letter.[56] Whatever one's view of the merits of the JCPOA, this could be a lasting effect of Trump's policies and worldview.

Yet another example of a potentially permanent effect on a treaty relationship is the Trump administration's withdrawal from the Open Skies Agreement. The treaty provides for mutual reconnaissance flights by the thirty-four nations who are party to the agreement. Russia followed the Trump administration's withdrawal from the agreement with its own withdrawal. After an internal review, the Biden administration chose not to try to revive the agreement,[57] leaving the renewed START agreement as the only standing nuclear agreement between the two countries.[58]

[55] *See* Interview 8, *supra* note 5.

[56] *See* Matthew Lee, *U.S. Faces New Hurdles in Tantalizingly Close Iran Deal*, PBS News Hour (Aug. 19, 2022), https://www.pbs.org/newshour/world/us-faces-new-hurdles-in-tantalizingly-close-iran-deal.

[57] *See* Michael D. Shear, *U.S. Says It Will Not Rejoin Open Skies Treaty with Russia*, N.Y. Times (May 27, 2021), *available at* https://www.nytimes.com/2021/05/27/us/politics/us-russia-open-skies-treaty.html.

[58] The Trump administration previously also had left the Intermediate Nuclear Forces Agreement in 2019. *See* David E. Sanger & Edward Wong, *U.S. Ends Cold Wart Missile Treat, with Aim of Countering China*, N.Y. Times (Aug. 1, 2019), *available at* https://www.nytimes.com/2019/08/01/world/asia/inf-missile-treaty.html.

The Trump administration's rhetoric and attitude may have posed a more significant threat to international law and institutions than its specific actions, a threat that would have been even more serious had he been reelected.[59] The President's attacks on international institutions undermined those institutions and their legitimacy. Trump's disparagement of international law and the rule of law in general encouraged and provided cover for foreign leaders to take a similar stance and could have discouraged support for international law and institutions in other countries. The absence of US leadership on international law, moreover, created a void, one that could have been filled by other nationalist and authoritarian leaders.[60] In short, Trump undermined faith in international institutions and the rule of law more generally, just as he did in the domestic, American context.

Sanguine observers, however, have argued that Trump's bark has been worse than his bite, although they concede that his bark may have been consequential.[61] For example, even when the administration has sought to withdraw from treaties, it has done so following the terms of the treaties and their notification periods, demonstrating some respect for the structure of international law. In addition, while "Trump has attacked a handful of high-profile international laws and institutions . . . on the whole, international laws and institutions remain intact and are operating as they did before Trump became president."[62] The United States continued to participate in most international institutions and remained a party to the vast majority of treaties. The Trump administration was not able to achieve many of its most radical goals, perhaps due in part to push back from other countries and within the international legal system.[63] It is difficult for one state, and especially one presidential administration, to change the course of international law, suggesting the potential durability of the underlying legal order.[64]

Writing roughly half-way through the Trump administration's term, Harold Koh asserted that external and internal forces were able to blunt some of the Trump administration's agenda.[65] Under Koh's concept of transnational legal process, international law has developed into a mixture of international and

[59] *See* Goldsmith & Mercer, *supra* note 31, at 37–39; Birdsall & Sanders, *supra* note 32, at 291–292. *See generally* McGuinness, *supra* note 29.

[60] Birdsall & Sanders, *supra* note 32, at 291.

[61] *See* Goldsmith & Mercer, *supra* note 31, at 30.

[62] *Id.* at 31.

[63] *See* Birdsall & Sanders, *supra* note 32, at 278.

[64] *See* Goldsmith & Mercer, *supra* note 31, at 34.

[65] KOH, *supra* note 22, at 6–13, 148, 152–153. *See also* Birdsall & Sanders, *supra* note 32, at 277–278. Birdsall and Sanders place Koh's view squarely in the context of constructivist international relations and international law theory, which hold that the robustness of legal

domestic law created by a variety of public and private transnational actors.[66] External and internalized rules become routine and "sticky," and so difficult to ignore. Thus, it takes effort to change the rules and the attempt to change the rules can be opposed by other actors.

Specifically, Koh argued that resistance by officials from within the government, as well as external resistance from outside actors – states, NGOs, and others – may have reinforced preëxisting norms or other norms that are likely to counteract the Trump administration's approach. For example, in the domestic context, military officials and the weight of domestic law were able to thwart Trump's stated desire to reinstitute waterboarding and enhanced interrogation. In the international context, Trump's desire to leave the Paris Agreement on climate change was stymied by the built-in restrictions on treaty withdrawal, which provided that a state must wait for three years after the agreement goes into force for that state to submit notice of withdrawal and that withdrawal will only become effective one year after that.[67] That meant that Trump's withdrawal did not become effective until the day after the 2020 US election. President Biden, of course, immediately rejoined the Paris Agreement on his very first day in office.[68]

The effect of the Trump administration over time may be hard to assess.[69] For one thing, it may be challenging to disentangle the effects of the administration itself from the broader changes and forces in international affairs. The nationalist Trump approach reflects not a phenomenon unique to the United States, but a rise of nationalism and populism around the world. Perhaps the rise of nationalism more broadly, rather than the rise of Trump specifically, constitutes the real threat to the international liberal order.[70] In a related vein, popular support for Trump's policies may reflect the American US electorate's disenchantment with internationalism and the postwar bipartisan internationalist consensus following misadventure in Iraq, a long conflict in Afghanistan, and perceived negative effects from globalization.[71] Accordingly, it may be

norms is based on mutual interaction and so depends not only on US actions but also on the reactions of other states. Their findings also advance this theoretical view.

66 *See* discussion *supra*, Chapter 2.

67 Paris Agreement of the United National Framework Convention on Climate Change, Art. 28, Apr. 22, 2016, T.I.A.S. No. 16-1104.

68 Coral Davenport & Lisa Friedman, *Biden Cancels Keystone XL Pipeline and Rejoins Paris Climate Agreement*, N.Y. TIMES (Jan. 20, 2021), *available at* https://www.nytimes.com/2021/01/20/climate/biden-paris-climate-agreement.html.

69 Goldsmith & Mercer, *supra* note 31, at 33.

70 *See* Alter, *supra* note 54.

71 *See* Jonathan Kirshner, *Gone But Not Forgotten: Trump's Long Shadow and the End of American Credibility*, FOREIGN AFF. (Mar.–Apr. 2021), at 18, 22; Richard Haas, *Present at the*

that Trump was a symptom of other, larger forces, albeit forces that he and his movement may have accelerated.

In addition, changes in power relationships among states also threaten the continuation of the American-led, liberal international order. The unipolar moment of US dominance following the end of the Cold War could not last forever.[72] The decline of US hegemony and the concurrent rise of other great and middle powers may herald a shift to a different, multipolar order, regardless of the nature of US leadership. Still, it seemed at times as if the Trump administration actively sought to hasten US decline.

Another relevant question in assessing the effect of the Trump administration on US foreign policy and on the international legal order is whether the Trump administration marked a significant departure for the United States. Some commentators argue that the Trump administration's disregard for international law is not a marked shift for the United States, asserting that the United States has a strong tradition of exceptionalism, in the sense of standing apart from international law, and noting that other administrations pushed the boundaries of international law aggressively.[73] They highlight the actions of the George W. Bush and Ronald Reagan administrations, in particular but also some actions of the Obama administration.[74] After all, the George W. Bush administration was criticized for its unilateral approach to international affairs and its skepticism about international law, as was the Reagan administration before it. Perhaps the policies of the Trump administration mark simply a pendulum swing, if a large one, between, on the one hand, Democratic and moderate Republican administrations, and on the other, conservative Republican administrations. Perhaps we simply have been witnessing in the last forty years the periodic realization of American conservative disenchantment with the project of the liberal international order. In this view, the Trump administration has simply gone a little farther – the pendulum swing reaching its apogee.

The conclusions of sanguine observers, while representing a useful, calming corrective to some claims about the long-term effects of the Trump

Disruption: How Trump Unmade U.S. Foreign Policy, FOREIGN AFF. (Sept.–Oct. 2020), at 24, 27.

[72] *See, e.g.*, Alexander Cooley & Daniel H. Nexon *How Hegemony Ends: The Unraveling of American Power*, FOREIGN AFF. (July–Aug. 2020), at 143.

[73] *See* Birdsall & Sanders, *supra* note 32, at 278–279.

[74] *See* Goldsmith & Mercer, *supra* note 31, at 33; Birdsall & Sanders, *supra* note 32, at 278–279. On the Bush administration, *see also generally* Curtis A. Bradley, *The Bush Administration and International Law: Too Much Lawyering and Too Little Diplomacy*, 4 DUKE J. CONST. L. & PUB. POL'Y 57 (2009).

administration, seem a little too smug, a little too sanguine. The Trump administration's approach to international law and institutions differed in degree and in rhetoric from that of its predecessors. The George W. Bush administration, for example, more frequently used lawyers and legal arguments to support and rationalize their policies.[75] By so doing, the Bush administration acknowledged the legitimacy and role of law in international relations. The approach of the Trump administration to international law, in contrast, has been one of hostility and disinterest,[76] essentially of disengagement.

If the Biden administration had not followed the Trump administration, the Trump effect would have been much more pronounced. The Biden administration has simply reversed many of Trump's specific actions, seeking a return to multilateralism and the liberal international order. Before President Biden's inauguration, both Biden and his national security adviser, Jake Sullivan, essentially called for a return to an American-led international order, albeit a more cooperative one with clear priorities and limits.[77] The administration's record through the first months of 2022 suggests that it has carried through on that prescription,[78] especially in its leadership of the NATO alliance over the war in Ukraine.

In addition, the Biden administration quickly returned to the Paris Agreement and initially sought to rejoin the JCPOA with Iran, for example.[79] Such a recalibration in American policy with the change of administrations is hardly unusual and represents the norm, rather than the exception. The Obama administration recalibrated US foreign policy following the Bush administration, just as the Biden administration has recalibrated. Moreover, while the United States in the last eighty years has either been the dominant global power, or during the Cold War one of two dominant powers, there may

75 *See* Birdsall & Sanders, *supra* note 32, at 279; Alter, *supra* note 54.

76 *See* Birdsall & Sanders, *supra* note 32, at 276–277.

77 *See* Joseph R. Biden, Jr., *Why America Must Lead Again: Rescuing U.S. Foreign Policy after Trump*, FOREIGN AFF. (Mar.–Apr. 2020), at 64; Jake Sullivan, *Yes America Can Still Lead the World*, THE ATLANTIC (Jan.–Feb. 2019), at 77.

78 *See G7 Summit: Biden Says America Is Back at the Table*, BBC NEWS (June 14, 2021), https://www.bbc.com/news/world-us-canada-57462047. *But see* Trish Bendix, *Best of Late Night: Seth Meyers Sums Up Biden's Time at G7*, N.Y. TIMES (June 15, 2021), https://www.nytimes.com/2021/06/15/arts/television/seth-meyers-biden-g7.html ("Biden's message at these meetings has been simple: America is back. You know, like the McRib, America's back for a limited time only, offer not valid in Florida.").

79 Steven Erlanger, *Biden Wants to Rejoin Iran Nuclear Deal, But It Won't be Easy*, N.Y. TIMES (Nov. 17, 2020), https://www.nytimes.com/2020/11/17/world/middleeast/iran-biden-trump-nuclear-sanctions.html.

be limits to its effect on the international legal order, especially in the short-term of one presidential administration.[80]

Nevertheless, the Biden administration, like other successor administrations, may find it difficult to retrench entirely from the policies of previous administrations because of the legal and political difficulties in doing so.[81] The Obama administration could not entirely close Guantanamo and continued the Bush administration's drone war against terrorists, albeit with modifications. Similarly, the Biden administration has continued some of the Trump administration's strategies on trade, on withdrawal from Afghanistan, and on leaving the Open Skies Agreement.

There are other reasons why a complete "snap-back" may be difficult. The Trump administration's actions and rhetoric may have undermined the faith of other countries' leaders in America's propensity to comply with agreements and to support the international legal order. Other countries may fear that the United States will renege on hard-won agreements, like the Paris Agreement or the JCPOA, when the executive changes parties and the winds shift. Their best bet may be to hedge and avoid major commitments.[82] With the United States' reputation for reliability and for international leadership tarnished, Washington's power to persuade other countries through the force of its example may be diminished. Thus, it may not be so easy for the United States to resume its leadership role in the international community.[83]

6.3 UNDERMINING THE STATE DEPARTMENT

The level of damage to the United States' foreign policy apparatus during the Trump administration, especially within the State Department, was extensive. Just as Trump's ability to change the international legal order was limited, his ability to undermine and hobble the State Department was more directly under his control and more achievable. Thus, although Foreign Service Officers in the State Department and others were able to push back sometimes in the domestic context, they were ultimately swamped by the political control over the State Department exerted by the White House and by Trump's appointed allies. Nevertheless, underlying attitudes of career officials below the political level probably were not permanently altered. The return of a more

[80] *See* Birdsall & Sanders, *supra* note 32, at 277–278.

[81] *See* Goldsmith & Mercer, *supra* note 31, at 34.

[82] *See* Jessica T. Mathews, *Present at the Re-creation? U.S. Foreign Policy Must Be Remade, Not Restored*, FOREIGN AFF. (Mar.–Apr. 2021), at 12. *See also* Kirshner, *supra* note 71.

[83] *See* Matthews, *supra* note 82, at 10.

internationalist foreign policy with the Biden administration has allowed for some institutional recovery.

Normally, any administration would seek to have the bureaucracy serve its ends and would also seek to embed its preferences in the bureaucracy to preserve them after it left office. But, in this case the populist and nationalist norms and policies motivating the Trump administration contrasted sharply with those of foreign policy bureaucrats, who essentially reflected an internationalist set of norms and preferences not only on big issues but also in regular operations. The administration could not successfully embed its preferences, by, for example, creating new institutions or reorganizing existing ones, so instead proceeded to undermine the existing bureaucracy.[84]

To understand fully the fate of the Trump State Department and, hence, the role of international law within it, it is crucial to understand President Trump's approach toward the government as a whole. The undermining of the State Department was part and parcel of President Trump's effort to bend the government and the civil service – the "Deep State" – to his will, to root out opposition to him and his policies. The President and the administration employed various means to exercise this control.[85]

By the end of Trump's term, the result of these efforts was "a thin layer of political loyalists on top of a cowed bureaucracy."[86] The President sought to make political appointments primarily on the basis of loyalty to him. In order to hobble the bureaucracy further, he left numerous positions vacant, or appointed "acting" officials who did not require Senate approval[87] and could be more directly under the administration's thumb.[88] The President's appointed officials, in turn, sometimes sought to enforce the administration's will and stifle debate and opposition within the government to administration policies. Those independent-minded officials they did not drive out or co-opt, they sought to cow. President Trump and his appointees retaliated against and

84 *See* Daniel W. Drezner, *Present at the Destruction: The Trump Administration and the Foreign Policy Bureaucracy*, 81(2) J. Pol. 723, 724 (2019).

85 *See generally*, George Packer, *The President Is Winning His War on American Institutions: How Trump Is Destroying the Civil Service and Bending the Government to His Will*, The Atlantic (Apr. 2020), *available at* https://www.theatlantic.com/magazine/archive/2020/04/how-to-destroy-a-government/606793/.

86 *Id.*

87 *See* Danielle Schulkin & Julia Brooks, *Loyalty Above All: The "Shallow State" of the Trump Administration*, Just Security (Nov. 2, 2020), https://www.justsecurity.org/73226/loyalty-above-all-the-shallow-state-of-the-trump-administration/ [hereinafter, *Loyalty*].

88 *See* Carrie Cordero & Joshua Geltzer, *Trump's Preference for Acting Officials Puts National Security at Risk*, Just Security (May 20, 2019), https://www.justsecurity.org/64197/trumps-preference-for-acting-officials-puts-national-security-at-risk/.

made examples of those who opposed, or who they perceived to oppose, the President or the administration's policies, *pour encourager les autres.*[89]

Although the administration undermined the federal bureaucracy as a whole, it seemed to target the Justice Department and the State Department in particular.[90] The rationale for undermining the Justice Department was self-evident, to control investigations against Trump and his allies, to weaponize the DOJ against his enemies and in favor of his friends, and to support his policy choices.[91] As indicated earlier, undermining the State Department was one way to bring the foreign policy bureaucracy under the administration's control and to further its foreign policy aims. It may also be that the State Department's predominantly internationalist ethos simply antagonized an administration whose policies and priorities were so completely different. In any event, the hostility of the administration toward the State Department was clear. President Trump publicly referred to the "the Deep State Department," suggesting it was out to sabotage him.[92] One former ambassador went so far as to say that diplomacy was not valued in a foreign policy focused mostly on threats.[93]

Even before the Trump administration came into power, the State Department was in a precarious condition.[94] A series of budget cuts since

89 Merriam-Webster translates and defines the phrase: "in order to encourage the others – said ironically of an action (such as an execution) carried out as a warning to others." *Merriam-Webster.com Dictionary*, Merriam-Webster, https://www.merriam-webster.com/dictionary/pour%20encourager%20les%20autres (last accessed Jan. 23, 2021). The phrase comes from Voltaire's Candide and refers to a historical incident. In 1756, the British Admiral John Byng failed to break a French blockade and did not actively engage the enemy. He was court-martialed for neglect of duty and executed. In Candide, one of Voltaire's characters remarked, "[I]n this country [England] we find it pays to shoot an admiral from time to time to encourage the others." Frank O. Bowman III, *Pour Encourager Les Autres? The Curious History and Distressing Implications of the Criminal Provisions of the Sarbanes-Oxley Act and the Sentencing Guidelines Amendments That Followed*, 1 Ohio St. J. Crim. L. 373, 373–374 (2004). Packer points out that every member of the FBI leadership that investigated Trump was forced out of government service and vilified, along with Justice Department officials. In illustrating the administration's targeting, Packer points to the humiliation and firing, shortly before his pension vested, of the Former Deputy Director of the FBI, Andrew McCabe. While McCabe may not have acted entirely without fault, it is hard to avoid the conclusion that Trump sought to make an example out of him. Packer, *supra* note 85.

90 *See* Packer, *supra* note 85.

91 *See* Benjamin Wittes, *Trump and the Powers of the American Presidency*, Brookings (Nov.14, 2016), https://www.brookings.edu/blog/up-front/2016/11/14/trump-and-the-powers-of-the-american-presidency/.

92 See *id.*

93 *Facing the World, Blindfolded: The Dereliction of American Diplomacy*, The Economist (Aug. 15, 2020), https://www.economist.com/international/2020/08/13/the-dereliction-of-american-diplomacy, citing Roberta Jacobsen, former Ambassador to Mexico.

94 *See id.*

the end of the Cold War in the 1990s had reduced the Department's capacity significantly. For example, spending on core diplomatic capability declined by nearly a quarter between 2008 and 2016.[95]

Trump's first Secretary of State, Rex Tillerson, sought to reorganize the Department but further weakened it in the process. He introduced a hiring freeze, which meant, among other things, that crucial political appointments, especially at the Assistant Secretary level, remained unfilled for months. At the same time, an exodus of experienced senior officials began that continued through the rest of Trump's term. Hundreds of career diplomats retired or resigned,[96] as discussed more extensively below. Trump's second Secretary, Mike Pompeo, ended the hiring freeze and pledged to fill empty senior positions. His record on hiring was mixed, at best, however.

In addition, as related in a 2020 report by the Senate Foreign Relations Committee's Democratic staff, many senior positions and ambassadorships remained vacant or were filled by acting officials, including eleven Assistant Secretary or Under Secretary positions.[97] The administration never confirmed an Assistant Secretary for South Asia, and the Assistant Secretary post for Europe and Eurasia had been vacant since February 2019, with no nominee submitted at the time of the report.[98] Failing to fill positions with Senate-confirmed officials bypasses the Senate's role to approve key positions within the executive branch.[99] Appointing officials to acting positions, moreover, eliminated guard rails that constrain the administration. As President Trump himself said, "Acting [officials] give you much greater flexibility. A lot easier to do things."[100] In short, acting officials are much more subject to presidential whim and hence, control.

Furthermore, the appointments the Trump administration made to the senior leadership were heavily skewed toward political appointments, as opposed to career officials, further contributing to the politicization of diplomacy.

[95] *See id.*, citing Barbara Stephenson, then head of the American Foreign Service Association (AFSA).

[96] Editorial Board, *Trump and Pompeo Have Overseen the Degradation of the State Department*, Washington Post (Aug. 15, 2020), https://www.washingtonpost.com/opinions/global-opinions/trump-and-pompeo-have-overseen-the-degradation-of-the-state-department/2020/08/14/7aaa1bca-d34e-11ea-9038-af089b63ac21_story.html [hereinafter, Post Editorial Board].

[97] Democratic Staff, United States Senate Committee on Foreign Relations, *Diplomacy in Crisis: The Trump Administration's Decimation of the State Department* (July 28, 2020) [hereinafter, Democratic Staff Report], at 12–13, https://www.foreign.senate.gov/imo/media/doc/Diplomacy%20in%20Crisis%20-%20SFRC%20Democratic%20Staff%20Report.pdf

[98] *See id.*

[99] *See* Schulkin & Brooks, *Loyalty*, *supra* note 87, at 2.

[100] *See id. See also* Cordero & Geltzer, *supra* note 88.

Between 1975 and 2014, the share of career diplomats in senior positions at the Assistant Secretary level and above had already shrunk from 60 percent to 30 percent. In the Trump administration, that figure was 8 percent, as of summer 2020.[101] At that time, no career officer occupied a Senate-confirmed Assistant Secretary position, which had never happened before.[102] The Trump administration also made significantly more political appointments to ambassadorships than previous administrations. Historically, between a quarter and a third of ambassadors have been political appointees, whereas 43 percent of the Trump administration's ambassadors were political.[103]

The level of expertise in the State Department suffered as experienced senior and mid-level diplomats left.[104] By the end of 2017, 60 percent of the Department's Career Ambassadors, its most experienced officers, had departed.[105] According to two well-respected former officials, these losses represented the "most significant departure of diplomatic talent in generations."[106] As a result, the State Department was essentially hollowed out, reducing US effectiveness in diplomacy and degrading US global leadership. Other countries noticed. Columbia's Foreign Minister was caught on tape telling a fellow diplomat that "The US State Department, which used to be important, is destroyed, it does not exist."[107]

At least two former officials interviewed for this project noted the "hollowing out" of the State Department. Former Deputy Secretary Richard Armitage stated that even during his tenure, there appeared to be a growing dearth of quality, experienced people available to post abroad and that was exacerbated by the small number of people in incoming classes. Roberta Jacobsen cited the hollowing out at all levels, not just at the senior level, but most importantly at the midgrade level, of Foreign Service Officers with five to fifteen years' service, consisting of senior desk officers and deputy directors.[108] The loss at this level was the most damaging, she said.

[101] *See* ECONOMIST, *supra* note 93, citing Ronald Neumann, president of the American Academy of Diplomacy.

[102] See *id.*

[103] *See* ECONOMIST, *supra* note 93.

[104] Democratic Staff Report, *supra* note 97, at 17–19.

[105] *Id.* at 18.

[106] *Id.* at 17, citing Nicholas Burns & Ryan C. Crocker, *Opinion, Dismantling the Foreign Service*, N.Y. TIMES (Nov. 27, 2017), *available at* https://www.nytimes.com/2017/11/27/opinion/dismantling-foreign-service-budget.html.

[107] Democratic Staff Report, *supra* note 97, at 19, quoting Jim Wyss, *Colombian Diplomats Spill the Beans on "Destroyed" US State Department in Secret Recording*, MIAMI HERALD (Nov. 21, 2019).

[108] *See* Interview with Roberta Jacobsen, Assistant Secretary for Western Hemisphere Affairs, Obama administration; US Ambassador to Mexico, Trump administration.

Officials left the Trump administration State Department for various reasons,[109] but numerous senior officials, especially early in the administration, were pushed out,[110] some apparently for partisan reasons. Other senior officials were simply sidelined and not offered other senior roles. Still other officials left because they could not support the Trump approach to foreign policy, several submitting stinging resignation letters or public statements on their way out.[111]

According to the Democratic Staff Report and other sources, Trump appointees targeted and retaliated against a number of career officials deemed insufficiently loyal.[112] These practices helped to drive the exodus of career employees from the Department and caused others to hide out in lower-profile jobs where they could avoid fights and the attention of political appointees.[113] For example, by early 2017, State Department documents show that senior White house and State Department officials had labeled some employees as "leaker," "troublemaker," and "turncoat."[114] An investigation by the State Department Inspector General found that two senior political appointees had regularly accused several career officials of being "Obama holdovers," or as disloyal based on their political views, and had engaged in retaliation against them.[115] Another Inspector General's investigation found that senior political appointees had truncated the assignment of a career official after significant discussion about the employee's political views and ethnic origin.[116] Such practices may have been more widespread. The Inspector General, Steve Linick, was later fired by Pompeo while he was conducting an investigation into inappropriate use of staff for personal errands by Pompeo and his wife.

[109] *See* Democratic Staff Report, *supra* note 97, at 18. These may have included a lack of opportunity to advance and up or out promotion system. *See* ECONOMIST, *supra* note 93.

[110] *See* Democratic Staff Report, *supra* note 97, at 17, citing Gardiner Harris, *Diplomats Sound the Alarm as They Are Pushed Out in Droves*, N.Y. TIMES (Nov. 24, 2017), *available at* https://www.nytimes.com/2017/11/24/us/politics/state-department-tillerson.html.

[111] Democratic Staff Report, *supra* note 97, at 17–18.

[112] *See id.* at 26.

[113] *See id.*

[114] *See id.*, citing Nahal Toosi, *Emails Reveal Conservative Alarm over "Obama Holdovers in Trump Administration*, POLITICO (Mar. 5, 2018), https://www.politico.com/story/2018/03/15/emails-trump-administration-alarm-over-obama-holdovers-465528.

[115] *See* US Department of State, Office of Inspector General, *Review of Allegations of Politicized and Other Improper Personnel Practices in the Bureau of International Organization Affairs*, at 1 (Aug. 2019), https://www.stateoig.gov/report/esp-19-05; Democratic Staff Report, *supra* note 97, at 26.

[116] *See* US Department of State, Office of Inspector General, *Review of Allegations of Politicized and Other Improper Personnel Practices Involving the Office of the Secretary*, at 1 (Nov. 2019), https://www.stateoig.gov/report/esp-20-01; Democratic Staff Report, *supra* note 97, at 26.

Accordingly, the Democratic Staff Report stated, annual employee surveys revealed "serious concerns that coercive partisanship and prohibited personal practices have run amok, coupled with a starkly declining confidence in senior leadership ...."[117] These tactics were all the more disturbing in the context of the State Department, where officials have long prided themselves on their nonpartisanship and their ability to work with administrations of either party. Pompeo's dismissal of the Inspector General and failure to support officials caught up in President Trump's effort to pressure the Ukrainian government into investigating the son of the likely Democratic presidential nominee could not have helped to dispel these concerns.

Not surprisingly, the atmosphere within the Department became toxic. Annual employee surveys revealed a "steady and significant deterioration of morale, effectiveness and leadership from 2017–2020, with particularly precipitous declines in several offices and bureaus."[118] It was clear from interview comments that there was no love lost between some Trump political appointees and at least some of the career officers in the State Department. One former noncareer political appointee stated that the State Department was not a hospitable environment for appointees, and this surprised them because of prior dealings with the State Department. This former official took pains, however, to emphasize that any antipathy was displayed by a minority of career employees and that most were driven by public service.[119] Another indicated that there seemed to be a whole cohort who did anything to undermine the President, including some of the lawyers in L.[120] That official found the use of the Dissent Channel disturbing, on the grounds that officials should either support the President or resign. One former official, however, said that he or she found the tension between political appointees and career officials higher in the George W. Bush administration and that he or she found a more civil relationship and willingness to compromise during his service in the Trump administration.[121]

In any event, the lack of love was returned by some career officials. One former career official said that there were lots of toxic political appointees, many of whom were also proselytizers for the Trump line.[122] The campaign, not policy, was the substantive driver and loyalty was the key attribute, they

[117] *See* Democratic Staff Report, *supra* note 97, at 34.
[118] *See id.*
[119] *See* Interview 19, *supra* note 35.
[120] *See* Interview with David Stillwell, Assistant Secretary for East Asian and Pacific Affairs, Trump administration.
[121] *See* Interview 5, Former Senior Official, Trump administration.
[122] *See* Interview 33, *supra* note 15.

said. Roberta Jacobsen stated that her impression was that the Dissent Channel was employed more often than previously: She did not know how many times, but even the incidents that she knew about were more than when she was Assistant Secretary for five years in the Obama administration.[123] Nevertheless, Tom Shannon said that Foreign Service Officers can say they do not like new policies, but cannot stop them, cannot be saboteurs. They are under a professional requirement to get stuff done or get out of the way.[124]

The tension was clear when the noncareer officials discussed their relationship with State Department lawyers. As discussed in Chapter 4, Trump noncareer political appointees often had an antagonistic relationship with the lawyers. One former official stated that when they faced opposition from the legal action officers in their bureau, they would go over their heads to discuss the issue with the Legal Adviser himself, or submit a split memo to Secretary Pompeo. The Legal Adviser agreed with him every time and Pompeo supported him or her much of the time.[125]

Several former officials noted the breakdown in the interagency policy coordination process under Trump, and especially under National Security Adviser John Bolton, as a factor that diminished the role of the State Department and international law in policy formation. The policy coordination process takes places under the leadership of the National Security Council (NSC), and involves the National Security Adviser, the NSC's subsidiary bodies, and the NSC staff.[126] Although the process was an interagency one, State has an opportunity to lead and shape decisions in the normally operating process.[127]

The constant turnover of the National Security Advisor and of the NSC staff hobbled the functions of the National Security Council Staff in general. President Trump appointed four National Security Advisors, each of whom replaced other officials with their own people. This churn occurred on top of already high turnover rates among NSC staff. Robert O'Brien, Trumps' fourth and final National Security Adviser, sought to cut NSC staff, ostensibly in an effort to make it more efficient, not an unreasonable goal in and of itself. At a time when there was already high turnover and a lack of foreign policy coherence, however, that also seemingly would have hampered the NSC's

[123] *See* Jacobsen Interview, *supra* note 108.
[124] *See* Shannon Interview, *supra* note 15.
[125] *See* Stillwell Interview, *supra* note 120.
[126] *See* discussion of the NSC and its process, *supra* Chapter 5. *See also* Congressional Research Service, *The National Security Council: Background and Issues for Congress* (last updated June 3, 2021), *available at* https://crsreports.congress.gov/product/pdf/R/R44828.
[127] *See* Jacobsen Interview, *supra* note 108.

effectiveness.[128] Speculation persisted that O'Brien's real goal was to further hobble Trump's perceived enemies in the bureaucracy, or to enact retribution for the role of some NSC staffers as impeachment witnesses or whistleblowers related to President's Trump's efforts to pressure the Ukrainian government to investigate opposition presidential candidate Joe Biden and his son.[129]

In addition, the policy process changed during the Trump administration. First, policymaking was often chaotic and dominated by the White House, rather than going through the normal interagency or policy coordination process.[130] This was one way that the State Department as a whole was cut out of decision-making. As noted previously, "The Trump administration was process challenged from the beginning," according to Tom Shannon, Under Secretary of Political Affairs in the early Trump administration. "There was a lot of stuff that was done on the fly."[131] On some occasions, the President would make foreign policy decisions essentially by himself, or after discussion with a limited number of people – the result was often chaos or consternation as the administration scrambled to back-fill the President's position.[132] At other times, decisions were taken by small groups of people, primarily in the White House, without consultation or even dissemination of decisions.[133]

Second, the interagency policy coordination process itself broke down during John Bolton's term as National Security Adviser, when he called only occasional meetings and did not seek regular input from cabinet agencies as a whole.[134] "The rest of the government does not really know what the policy is. There's no record, there's no decision form. There's nothing out there to fall back on. Countries that we deal with do not really know what our policy is because people in the government do not know."[135] Under Bolton, meetings of the Principals Committee were rare and even meetings of the Deputies

[128] *See* Kathryn Dunn Tenpas, *Crippling the Capacity of the National Security Council*, BROOKINGS (Jan. 21, 2020), https://www.brookings.edu/blog/fixgov/2020/01/21/crippling-the-capacity-of-the-national-security-council/.

[129] *See* John Gans, *Enacting Trump's Revenge Campaign*, ATLANTIC (Feb. 27, 2020), *available at* https://www.theatlantic.com/ideas/archive/2020/02/cuts-nsc-are-not-about-number-staffers/607144/.

[130] *See* Jacobsen Interview, *supra* note 108.

[131] Thomas Shannon, *quoted in* Alex Ward, *Biden Wants American to Trust the Process Again*, VOX (Feb. 10, 2021), https://www.vox.com/22272240/biden-trump-national-security-council-yemen-myanmar.

[132] See *id.*

[133] *See* Jacobsen Interview, *supra* note 108.

[134] *See id.*

[135] Ivo Dalder, *quoted in* Nahal Toosi et al., *Cabinet Chiefs Feel Shut Out of Bolton's "Efficient" Policy Process*, POLITICO (July 25, 2018) (Ivo Dalder is a former US Ambassador to NATO and President of the Chicago Council on Global Affairs).

Committee declined in number. The only continuing meetings were the third-tier interagency policy committees at the Assistant Secretary level.[136] By contrast, both H. R. McMaster, who preceded Bolton, and Robert O'Brien, who succeeded him, employed standard national security processes, at least to the extent possible in the Trump administration.[137]

In lieu of the standard process, Bolton relied on smaller informal meetings with senior officials, such as the Secretaries of State and Defense, on the rationale that this approach saved time and cut through bureaucratic red tape. To be sure, the "regular" national security process, especially during the Obama administration, was criticized for delaying the decision-making process, holding too many meetings, and micromanaging agencies.[138] Bolton's informal meetings, however, did not produce a record that could inform those at lower levels of policy decisions.[139] In addition, these high-level, informal meetings were disconnected from lower-level meetings and the President's sometimes mercurial thinking.[140] Principals' meetings in the regular process allow each department head to bring their department's specialized knowledge to bear, explore the trade-offs of each option, and present how their team can help execute it.[141]

As a result, said Jacobsen and others, there was little way for policymakers or lawyers at State to participate in government decisions generally, including decisions that could have had legal repercussions.[142] This created the impression that options were not presented, or violations not adequately considered. Input was not heard, or more importantly, not sought because the administration did not want to hear it, since input could present greater obstacles.[143]

This failure of process and lack of coordination extended beyond Washington.[144] In what she characterized as an extreme example, Roberta Jacobsen, as Ambassador to Mexico from 2016–2018, reported that she was

[136] *See id.*.

[137] *See* Jacqueline Feldscher, *After Trump "Chaos," National Security Council Seeks a Return to "Regular Order,"* DEFENSE ONE (June 14, 2021), https://www.defenseone.com/policy/2021/06/after-trump-chaos-national-security-seeks-return-regular-order/174722/.

[138] *See, e.g., id.*

[139] *See* Toosi et al., *supra* note 135.

[140] *See* Karen DeYoung et al., *John Bolton Puts His Singular Stamp on Trump's National Security Council,* WASHINGTON POST (Mar. 4, 2019), *available at* https://www.washingtonpost.com/world/national-security/john-bolton-single-minded-advocate-puts-his-stamp-on-the-national-security-council/2019/03/04/5c59517e-3609-11e9-854a-7a14d7fec96a_story.html.

[141] *See* Toosi et al., *supra* note 135. As one former official put it, State would have a say in a normal administrations. Interview 11, Assistant Secretary in the George W. Bush administration.

[142] *See* Jacobsen Interview, *supra* note 108; Interview 33, *supra* note 15.

[143] *See* Jacobsen Interview, *supra* note 108.

[144] *See supra* text accompanying note 135.

not adequately briefed about developments at home that were relevant to her job.[145] The Mexican Foreign Minister often knew more about meetings that had taken place in her own government than she did and took glee in briefing her about them. Needless to say, that undercut her position with the Mexican government.

6.3.1 *The Long-Term Effect on the State Department*

The majority of former officials who addressed the matter believed that while some practices might change, underlying attitudes about international law and institutions among career officials during the Trump administration did not change substantially.[146] Changes that did occur in attitude occurred at the policy decision level, rather than at the lower, policy development level. The policy decision level consists primarily of political appointees, some of whom may be career Foreign Service Officers, but many of whom come from outside the State Department. For obvious reasons, noncareer political appointees at the policy decision level shared the administration's viewpoint about international law and institutions and pushed that view more vigorously.

At the policy development level, in contrast, most former officials thought that attitudes toward international law and institutions would not and did not change. Roberta Jacobsen, former Assistant Secretary for Western Hemisphere Affairs and Ambassador to Mexico, for example, stated that attitudes toward international law and international institutions shifted at the top, but not within the core of the Department.[147] Jacobsen stated that the vast majority of career officials believed in international law, for example. Another former official added that the attitudes of career officers likely would not change because the nationalist argument is not strong below the first level.[148] One former official pointed out that the State Department is not likely to bring in a whole cadre of new people willing to ignore international law and that while the parameters between left and right in the Department might shift a little, they are not going to change precipitously.[149]

[145] *See* Jacobsen Interview, *supra* note 108.

[146] *See, e.g.*, Shannon Interview, *supra* note 15; Interview 5, *supra* note 121; Interview 33, *supra* note 15; Jacobsen Interview, *supra* note 108; Stillwell Interview, *supra* note 120; Interview 11, *supra* note 141; Interview with James Dobbins, Assistant Secretary for European Affairs, Clinton and George W. Bush administrations.

[147] *See* Jacobsen Interview, *supra* note 108.

[148] *See* Interview 5, *supra* note 121.

[149] *See* Interview 12, Assistant Secretary in the George W. Bush administration.

Several former officials noted that career Foreign Service Officers in political appointments were more likely to take a traditional view more favorable to international law and institutions. Not only are they acculturated to this view, they also have a primary loyalty to the institution and have to think about their long-term future in the next administration, and so are less susceptible to the preferences of the current administration.[150] This is not to say that these officials can or do ignore the administration's policies.

In addition, many policy decisions are made below the radar in the ordinary course of business and are less likely to attract political attention. Many issues do not rise to political levels at all because they are not as politically salient or because they are complicated and technical. The topic of riparian rights is an example of this kind of technical issue, and, in such a case, the lawyers would likely hold sway.[151] Even in cases that rose to a political level, there would be some issues where a political appointee would not act much differently than a career appointee.[152]

Nonetheless, the administration's views could filter down or affect career officers and staff in the following ways. Perhaps Tom Shannon put it best when he said that the administration's views are expressed only in a case-by-case basis.[153] No one stands up saying we are going to raspberry international law, he said. But over time, people see what is going on. If an official is writing briefing memos and sees things get struck by higher-ups, then if a memo is to go through, they stop raising the precipitating issues. For example, if an official is writing a memo to their principal regarding a meeting about reproductive rights, they might want to make sure that the memo does not indicate respect for international law that would limit the US approach. Roberta Jacobsen made essentially the same point: Officials try to use legal analysis but, when stymied, face frustration and are less willing to go out on a limb or present a disfavored view.[154] In contrast, an attitude from above that disfavors international law and institutions could potentially give license to take actions that reflect that attitude, said a former Republican official from another administration.[155]

Some former officials suggested that career Foreign Service Officers in these positions might have been able to push back on some administration policies. Indeed, the comments from noncareer political appointees quoted here

[150] *See id.*; Interview 11, *supra* note 141.

[151] *See* Interview 11, *supra* note 141.

[152] *See, e.g.*, Interview 33, *supra* note 15.

[153] *See* Shannon Interview, *supra* note 15.

[154] *See* Jacobsen Interview, *supra* note 108.

[155] *See* Interview 13, Former Assistant Secretary, George W. Bush administration.

suggest that career bureaucrats did push back by raising concerns and making objections. Pushing back may have been difficult, however, for the same reasons that it was hard for career bureaucrats to raise issues in the first place. In addition, as noted earlier, there was an exodus from the State Department of officials who might have resisted pressures against international law and institutions.

In addition to raising concerns and objecting, career bureaucrats might have been able to use the time-honored tactics of bureaucrats: dragging their feet, seeking political support in Congress, leaking to the press, use of the Dissent Channel, and other tactics.[156] Seeking support in Congress was less likely to be successful during the Trump administration, with Republicans in charge of at least one house of Congress.[157] Republicans in Congress were not keen on pursuing Congress' oversight functions in a Republican Trump administration. Roberta Jacobsen pointed out two inhibitions in trying to go to Congress: fear that people on the Hill will use issues politically, rather than for policy reasons, and the fact that there were fewer appearances by appointees to give testimony due to administration recalcitrance, and hence fewer opportunities for Congress to insert itself into the process.[158] The risk-averse approach is for people not to talk to Congress or the Press: They cannot get in trouble for keeping quiet, she said.

While it is possible that dissatisfied officials could have employed the Dissent Channel more often to register their disagreement with administration policy, experience suggested that was not likely to have much effect. The Dissent Channel is an officially sanctioned mechanism through which State Department employees can register their objection to senior officials regarding a substantive foreign policy matter without fear of penalty.[159] It provides the opportunity to let people feel they say their piece for the record and their conscience. But use of the Channel is unlikely to affect the policies at issue.[160] One former official pointed out that the Dissent Channel objection to the Muslim ban on immigration at the beginning of the Trump administration went nowhere and generated antagonism toward the State Department within the administration.[161]

[156] *See* Jacobsen Interview, *supra* note 108; Interview 12, *supra* note 149.
[157] *See* Interview with Richard Armitage, Deputy Secretary of State, George W. Bush administration; Jacobsen Interview, *supra* note 108.
[158] *See* Jacobsen Interview, *supra* note 108.
[159] *See* 2 Foreign Affairs Manual 070.1.b., Dissent Channel; Policy Statement (Sept. 11, 2018), https://fam.state.gov/fam/02fam/02fam0070.html.
[160] *See* Jacobsen Interview, *supra* note 108.
[161] *See also* Michele Kelemen, *At State Department, "Dissent Channel" in High Gear with Refugee Ban Protests*, N.P.R. (Jan. 30, 2017), https://www.npr.org/sections/parallels/2017/01/30/512494230/at-state-department-dissent-channel-in-high-gear-with-refugee-ban-protests.

6.3.2 *Repairing the State Department*

Toward the end of the Trump administration in 2020, proposals from several sources called for revitalizing the State Department. Among other groups, the Council on Foreign Relations issued a set of recommendations, as did the American Diplomacy Project, a group of former high-level diplomats based at Harvard's Kennedy School.[162] Many of the recommendations clearly grew out of the Department's experience during the Trump administration, when it reached a nadir in terms of personnel, influence, and morale. But many of the deficiencies identified in these recommendations reflected long-standing trends and problems that had been brewing long before 2016, such as woefully inadequate funding, a stifling bureaucracy, a risk-averse culture, a discouraging personnel system, and a lack of diversity.

The recommendations offered by these groups are similar and overlap to a great extent. The major recommendations include increasing funding for the State Department, which has languished for many years; increasing the size of the Foreign Service, which was in decline even before the Trump administration; overhauling the personnel system to, among other things, reward competence and expertise, remove disincentives, provide flexibility for families, and improve opportunities for advancement; increasing the diversity of the Foreign Service; increasing the percentage of career professionals in ambassadorial and senior positions, avoiding politicization of the State Department and professionalizing its upper ranks; changing the internal culture of the State Department to promote innovation and risk-taking, accountability, inclusive management, and leadership; and improving decision-making processes.

[162] *See* Uzra S. Zeya & Jon Finer, Council on Foreign Relations, Revitalizing the State Department and American Diplomacy (Nov. 2020) (Council Special Report No. 89) [hereinafter CFR Report]; Nicholas Burns et al., American Diplomacy Project, *A U.S. Diplomatic Service for the 21st Century* (Nov. 2020), https://www.belfercenter.org/sites/default/files/2020-11/DiplomaticService.pdf. Another set of recommendations was developed by the Truman Center for National Policy. *See* Truman Center, *Transforming State: Pathways to a More Just, Equitable, and Innovative Institutions* (Mar. 2021), https://assets-global.website-files.com/60b7dbd50474252e6c8c4fc5/60f5acf9dcd30575c7386ab1_Truman-Center-Task-Force-Transforming-State-Final.pdf. Finally, Former Deputy Secretary of State and current head of the CIA William Burns wrote a series of articles on the topic, one in conjunction with Linda Thomas-Greenfield, now Ambassador to the United Nations. *See* William J. Burns & Linda Thomas-Greenfield, *The Transformation of Diplomacy: How to Save the State Department*, 99 FOREIGN AFF. (Nov./Dec. 2020) at 100; William J. Burns, *The Damage at the State Department Is Worse Than You Can Imagine; But It's Also More Reparable*, THE ATLANTIC (Mar. 12, 2020), *available at* https://www.theatlantic.com/ideas/archive/2020/03/how-rebuild-state-department/607837/.

The Biden administration and Congress have taken steps to address these issues. The Biden administration has asked for increased spending on the State Department in budget requests and spending has gone up compared to the Trump years.[163] In 2021, Congress passed the first State Department authorization act in twenty years, which, however, was somewhat limited in its reach, dropping some provisions on diversity and management reforms.[164] The State Department has also taken action on its own. As of spring, 2022, the Department had hired additional Foreign Service Officers, was on pace to hire more, and had overhauled its hiring process.[165] The Department has also revived the Dissent Channel and added a new Policy Ideas Channel, taken steps to enhance diversity, modified some work restrictions, and moved to enhance technology.[166]

6.4 WILL STATE DEPARTMENT CULTURE SNAP BACK?

When asked whether views about international law and international institutions might snap back or change after the Trump administration, former officials generally responded yes. Much depended on the 2020 election and would also depend on future elections, since the formal positions of the State Department would hew closely to that of the President,[167] and the President's appointees have the opportunity to influence procedures and policies. If President Trump had been reelected in 2020, then the views of his administration would likely have become more entrenched. Even with the results of the 2020 election, Richard Armitage, former Deputy Secretary of State, thought it was unlikely that respect for international law in the State Department would return to the *status quo ante*, that is, to their level of prominence during the Obama administration.[168]

[163] See Congressional Research Service, *Department of State, Foreign Operations, and Related Programs: FY 2023 Budget and Appropriations* (Apr. 18, 2022), *available at* https://crsreports.congress.gov/product/pdf/R/R47070/2.

[164] *See* Rachel Oswald, *Vehicle for State Reauthorization Leaves Some Policy Goals Behind*, RollCall (Dec. 2021), https://rollcall.com/2021/12/20/vehicle-for-state-reauthorization-leaves-some-policy-goals-behind/.

[165] *See* Eric Katz, *State Department Says It's Rebuilding after Trump "Decimated" It, but Will Still Fall Short on Some Key Biden Goals*, Gov't Executive (May 3, 2022), https://www.govexec.com/workforce/2022/05/state-rebuilding-department-after-trump-decimated-will-still-fall-short-key-biden-goals/366461/.

[166] *See* US State Department, *Secretary Anthony J. Blinken on the Modernization of American Diplomacy: Remarks* (Oct. 27, 2021), https://www.state.gov/secretary-antony-j-blinken-on-the-modernization-of-american-diplomacy/.

[167] *See* Interview 12, *supra* note 149.

[168] Armitage Interview, *supra* note 157.

Transitions and changes in direction between administrations take time and are never total. As Tom Shannon pointed out, there was a big, dramatic transition between Obama and Bush, just as there has been between the Trump and Biden administrations. The Obama administration could not reverse everything the Bush administration had done; Obama could not completely close Guantanamo, or prosecute those who had run enhanced interrogation. For that reason, Shannon suggested that it would be difficult for the Biden administration to snap back completely to the *status quo ante*. But, Shannon asserted, the Biden administration should have it easier in one respect. Because the Trump administration moved so slowly to appoint officials, it exerted weaker control over the bureaucracy compared to the Obama administration, which moved quickly to put people in place. Accordingly, the snap back will be easier for the Biden administration because it will not be dealing with such engrained behavior, Shannon said. The Trump administration also had only one term to inculcate its procedures and policies into the State Department, whereas the Bush and Obama administrations had two terms each. An additional impediment to snapping back identified by at least two former officials was the hollowing out of the State Department not only during the Trump administration but previously, as discussed earlier.

The Biden administration, however, has reversed many Trump administration policies, and has reasserted America's leadership role in international society, while pursuing a multilateral approach. The administration and Congress have also taken tentative steps to rebuild and reform the State Department. As indicated earlier, moreover, many former officials believed that underlying attitudes toward international institutions and international law among career staff did not change during the Trump administration. Tom Shannon stated that if you had penetrated the hearts and minds of career officials and staff, there would still be a profound commitment to international law.[169] Accordingly, many expected those attitudes to resurface.[170] One former official stated that they knew people in L and in the bureaus, and they had seen how the damaging turn away from international engagement had hurt the United States.[171]

If Mr. Trump, or someone else adhering to his views and tactics, is elected in 2024, we could see a return to further erosion of the traditional norms in the State Department, especially if that President served two full terms in office. In that event, cultural and policy change at the State Department is

[169] Shannon Interview, *supra* note 15.

[170] *See, e.g., id.*; Interview 33, *supra* note 15; Jacobsen Interview, *supra* note 108.

[171] *See* Interview 33, *supra* note 15.

likely to escalate. A Trump administration or similar likely would implement the same policies used in the last Trump administration. In addition, such an administration could even implement plans to revamp the civil service, likely including the Foreign Service, to undermine civil service protections in order to subject officials to political pressure. Indeed, in October 2020, the Trump administration proposed an executive order that would have exempted policy-oriented positions from civil service hiring rules and protections. It was never implemented, but news stories in the summer of 2022 reported that the plan has become a part of the plan for a Trump second term and has support among other Republican presidential hopefuls.[172] Trump, himself, has pledged to follow through on that plan and to fire bureaucrats.[173] So, contrary to the seemingly far-fetched hypothetical of the former official mentioned earlier, a new administration conceivably could bring in an entirely new cadre of lower-level officials into the State Department.

In that case, we could see a change in the culture of the State Department, which, with some variation from party to party, has generally remained consistent over decades. We could even see a change in State Department processes to downgrade the role of international law in decision-making. In that case, this book would constitute not a description of a living culture and a living process but a historical record of a vanished culture, of a lost tribe.

[172] *See* Loren DeJonge Schulman, *Schedule F: An Unwelcome Resurgence*, LAWFARE (Aug. 12, 2022), https://www.lawfareblog.com/schedule-f-unwelcome-resurgence. *See also*, Jonathan Rauch, *Trump's Second Term Would Look Like This*, THE ATLANTIC (Aug. 29, 2022), https://www.theatlantic.com/ideas/archive/2022/08/trump-2024-reelection-viktor-orban-hungary/671264/.

[173] *See* Maggie Haberman & Shane Goldmacher, Political Memo: *Trump, Vowing "Retribution," Foretells a Second Term of Spite*, N.Y. TIMES (Mar. 7, 2023), https://www.nytimes.com/2023/03/07/us/politics/trump-2024-president.html.

7

Conclusion

This book is about three things. First, it explores whether, why, and how states comply with international law, focusing on the United States and the factors that affect state calculations. Second, it examines the culture, structure, and processes of the State Department and their effect on the role of international law considerations in shaping State Department decision-making. Finally, it investigates the effect of the Trump administration and its views about international law on the culture and processes of the State Department, as well as the likely effect of a similar administration in the future. To help address these questions, seventy-seven high-level former State Department officials were interviewed, as well as a handful of former high-level attorneys in the Office of the Legal Adviser.

The project's first focus is on state compliance with international law and reasons for that compliance. The observations, perceptions, and attitudes of former officials are relevant here for two reasons: They may provide insight into the behavior and motivations of states in response to international law, and they also reveal the attitudes of State Department elites, attitudes that are likely to shape their behavior and decision-making.

In examining policymakers' views of state compliance, the study takes into consideration various theories of compliance in the international relations and international law literature. While the study may confirm or illustrate the applicability of these theories, that is not its purpose nor is that necessary for the study to be valuable in illuminating the motivations that affect policymakers and states. Instead, consulting theory provides a context for the study and a conceptual set of tools for understanding.

Most former officials expressed the opinion that international law constrains state behavior and that states generally comply with international law. To the extent that this observation reflects actual state behavior, it supports the proposition that international law plays a role in international affairs. The former officials collectively identified various factors that encouraged or discouraged states to comply with international law. The top positive factors, in order of the frequency cited, were reputational concerns, state interest in a stable legal and institutional system; reciprocity, or the prospect of retaliation; ethical considerations, including ethical values underlying international law rules and respect for the rule of law; idiosyncratic factors, including the political culture of states and their adherence to the rule of law; and benefits flowing from participation in specific regimes. Among the factors militating against compliance by states, state interest was the most significant factor, followed by the ambiguity of international law; the notion that some rogue states do not comply; the perception that compliance by some states is shallow; the role of domestic politics; and sovereignty concerns.

Two aspects of these results are especially significant. The salience of ethical factors supports normative theories about compliance. The normative factors mentioned included not only the ethical values underlying legal rules, such as human rights, but also respect for the rule of law. In a related vein, a number of officials asserted that countries with a history or culture of respecting the rule of law domestically were more likely to respect the rule of law in international affairs as well.

A large proportion of former officials, moreover, emphasized the value of the international legal system and the utility of maintaining it. The interest in maintaining a stable international system serves the interests of all states, particularly powerful states. Accordingly, it seems safe to say that the worldview of most former officials was multilateralist, institutionalist, and rule of law-oriented.

Nevertheless, many former officials explicitly suggested that decisions about compliance with international law involved a cost–benefit calculation. This calculation involved a balance of many of the considerations discussed above, along with legal considerations. Though the predilection of most policymakers was to follow international law, legal considerations might not always prevail in that calculation.

The perception of many former US officials was that other states were concerned primarily with hard befits and costs, especially carrots and sticks offered by the international community, as opposed to systemic or altruistic concerns. The United States, in contrast, was motivated in part by systemic and altruistic concerns. This perception is in line with realist notions regarding the effect of direct incentives to comply provided by powerful states. One can speculate that it betrays some chauvinism, as well. After all, former officials also suggested, smaller countries do have a stake in the international legal order to the extent that it can constrain larger states.

Former officials also expressed a belief that the United States complied with international law most of the time. This subjective assessment may be disputed and may indicate an idealized self-image. But it also suggests the importance of international law in the calculations of American policymakers.

In making decisions about compliance, the United States was motivated by considerations similar to those of other states in complying with international law, with some nuances and divergences. Ethical considerations were the most frequently cited factor favoring compliance by the United States. Ethical considerations were also reflected in two other frequently cited factors: US exceptionalism in the sense of moral leadership, and a belief in the sanctity of treaty obligations. Policymakers also cited the US interest as a conservative *status quo* power in maintaining the international order. The view of allies can also play a role in US decision-making, both for and against compliance. The factors that former officials cited that militate against compliance by the United States included national interest, ambiguity of legal obligations, sovereignty concerns, and various domestic political and bureaucratic impediments.

The project assessed tensions in US decision-making between the requirements of international law, on the one hand, and policy concerns or national interest, on the other. While the predilection of former officials may have been to follow international law, that was not always determinative. As indicated earlier, legal issues were considered as one factor among a variety of factors, essentially involving a cost–benefit analysis. The most significant factors appeared to be the nature of the national interest or policy at stake, the nature and importance of the international legal rule involved, the ethical considerations involved, the views of allies, the ambiguity or precision of the legal obligation, the weight of domestic political and bureaucratic concerns, and the effect of the policymaking process.

In response to specific questions, former officials provided examples of instances where the United States may have violated or bent international law and examples where the United States acted scrupulously in complying with international law. To a large extent, these examples were similar to the description by former officials of areas involving greater or lesser compliance of states overall. That is, compliance was less likely in areas of high politics and more likely in areas of low politics, supporting an instrumentalist view of compliance. In addition, reciprocity bolstered compliance in several cases, and compliance was more evident in coordination situations, such as postal unions, as predicted by instrumentalists. Nevertheless, other results from this study highlight the role of ethical and normative considerations in compliance decisions, as reported by former officials.

The project's second focus was to explore the role of international law in State Department decision-making. The structure of the Department, the explicit role of lawyers in decision-making, and its culture and organizational norms all ensure that international law considerations play a role, both informally and informally. State Department lawyers may constitute an "epistemic community" and so may be able to leverage their expertise and legitimacy to influence policymaking.

The analysis incorporated two normative, process-oriented approaches, the international legal process approach and the Sandholtz and Whytock approach. Both of these frameworks are particularly helpful in understanding this study's findings regarding the operation and effect of international law within the State Department and the United States government. They emphasize the role of internalized norms and recognize the importance of process and organizational structure in guiding political decision-making. They also recognize that the ambiguity of much international law can create challenges for compliance because it can allow states considerable discretion in applying the rules. Nevertheless, neither approach asserts that law or institutions control the exercise of state power, and both admit that national interest is influential and even decisive.

Rebecca Sanders takes a related, somewhat more skeptical approach, which illustrates explicitly the tension between state power and law.[1] She argues that realists, on the one hand, emphasize the supremacy of state authority over law, or *law as permit*, while liberals and constructivists, on the other hand, emphasize the rationalist and normative forces that shape state action, or *law as constraint*. Sanders argues, instead, for a model of *permissive constraint*, that law is permissive in that it can be manipulated to justify legal abuses through plausible legality, but constraining because law also provides an influential standard of appropriate conduct. These three approaches sit adjacent to each other on a spectrum regarding accommodation between law and state interest, or power.

The majority view of former officials in this study corresponds roughly to the views presented by these three approaches. That is, law, process, and institutions may constrain or channel the policy of the United States, but not always. Policymakers have a preference to comply with international law, but their job is to pursue the interest of the United States.

Policymakers generally had decision-making authority on the legal advice present to them, depending on the seniority of the policymaker and the nature of the issue. Significant matters would be decided at upper levels, and really significant matters would be decided through the interagency process and the White House. Nevertheless, almost 90 percent of former officials regarded the views of the Legal Adviser's Office as highly influential. Qualitative comments were more nuanced but indicated that legal advice was influential, if not necessarily determinative. There seemed to be widespread agreement that

[1] *See* Rebecca Sanders, Plausible Legality: Legal Culture and Political Imperative in the Global War on Terror 3 (2018).

when the lawyers said no, that a course of action violated international law, that that was the final word. Otherwise, the weight given to L's advice varied, depending on the circumstances.

The relationship between policymakers and lawyers involved some contestation, as described by Whytock and Sanders and the international legal process school. While many former officials indicated that the development of policy was a collaborative and constructive process, a significant number were willing to push back against the lawyers regarding the interpretation or application of the law. Policymakers could sometimes change the lawyers' minds or, at senior levels, could override legal advice. For this group, the interaction between policymakers and lawyers resembled more of a negotiation.

When significant national interest took priority over international law, numerous former officials mentioned three possible strategies to accommodate policy interests in a descending order of preference. First, the lawyers might try to identify alternative legal means to achieve the objective. Second, the lawyers and the policymakers might explore alternative interpretations of the law that could justify a proposed course of action. Officials emphasized the inherent ambiguity of much international law and the resulting opportunity for interpretation, which could provide "wiggle room." From the weight of interviews with former officials, pressure by officials on the lawyers to reinterpret obligations did not occur as a matter of course, although ambiguity might shape the lawyers' advice. Finally, on rare occasions, policymakers might decide to proceed with a course of action that pushed the limits of international law.

This is not to suggest that decisions were presented as a stark choice between law and policy. Rather, a situation would be presented in the following manner: these are the circumstances, these are the options, and these are the legal implications. There might be a range of options available to policymakers, and compliance may represent a choice among shades of grey. Good lawyers would present those options, identify ambiguities, and discuss the relative risks of the options.

In addition, decisions on issues involving international law, like all bureaucratic decisions, were subject to bureaucratic politics and the influence of powerful individuals, as described in the organizational behavior and bureaucratic politics literature. Within the State Department, turf battles might be especially keen among the regional and functional bureaus of the State Department. They also illustrate a process of contestation.

In sum, policymakers took the views of the Legal Adviser's Office seriously, and its status and role in the decision-making process ensured that international law had a voice in that process. The predilection of most former officials was to follow international law, and they generally supported the multilateral, international order, and the US role in that order. Thus, international law and lawyers have had a key role in formulating policy in the State Department.

The project's third and final focus was to examine the effect of the Trump administration on the culture and processes in the State Department. As we have seen, the existing processes and culture in the Department provide a role for international law in policymaking. In the normal course of events, the Department's culture, norms, and even processes are likely to change over time through a process of contestation from the bottom up. The Trump administration essentially tried to change the Department and its culture from the top by installing political appointees who strongly adhered to the administration's views and by discouraging dissent. In a sense, the Trump administration experience provides a natural experiment in the possibilities of enforced, short-term cultural change within a bureaucratic organization.

The Trump administration, clearly, was not enamored with conceptions of the multilateral, liberal international order. Accordingly, the Trump administration pursued a transactional, bilateral, case-by-case approach to relations with other states. That transactional approach focused on zero-sum wins and losses and disavowed multilateral solutions and systemic costs and benefits. Multilateral organizations or arrangements, in this view, constrained American discretion, instead of enhancing American interests. The Trump disdain for international institutions entailed, at best, a narrow application of international law and, at worst, possible violations of international law.

A fair assessment of the Trump administration's effect on international organizations and international law suggests some likely damage, although that damage is hard to quantify. President Trump's attacks on international institutions likely undermined them and their legitimacy. Trump's disparagement of international law and the rule of law may have provided cover for foreign leaders to take similar positions. Most importantly, the Trump administration's unilateralist rhetoric and its isolationist policies damaged the standing and influence of the United States on the international stage. For example, it was not entirely clear when Russia invaded Ukraine that the United States would be in a position to lead an effective NATO response.

In order to pursue its policies, the administration sought to force the foreign policy machinery of the United States government to its bidding. All administrations seek to harness the bureaucracy by making political appointments to leadership positions. But, as we have seen, the Trump administration engaged in extreme efforts to undermine the State Department, which marked a departure from any previous administration. That effort was part and parcel of President Trump's effort to bend the federal bureaucracy to his will.

Former officials interviewed during and after the Trump administration differed regarding the extent to which the administration's efforts affected attitudes within the State Department. The majority seemed to believe that while some particular policies and practices might have changed during the Trump administration, underlying attitudes among the rank and file did not change substantially. Former officials distinguished between those at the policy decision level – high-level political appointees, with the possible exception of career officials appointed to these posts – and Foreign Service and Civil Service Officers at the policy development level. At the policy decision level, most political appointees adhered to administration policies and beliefs and attempted to impose their preferences on the Department as a whole. At the policy development level, the established culture prevailed, favoring multilateralism and respecting international law.

Permanent change at the policy development level would have required changing the established culture among a large number of career officials. One former official pointed out that the State Department could not bring in a whole cadre of new people willing to ignore international law and institutions. Accordingly, the overall culture and even the overall approach of the State Department likely did not shift much, or shift permanently, during the Trump administration.

Nevertheless, attitudes and policies at the top probably did constrain the behavior of lower-level officials. Over time, senior officials who might have been more likely to resist pressure left or were forced out. Those who remained probably felt pressure to go along. In addition, those officials who pushed back, or who tried to make disfavored policy or legal arguments, may have been less willing to go out on a limb or present a disfavored view after being knocked down once or twice.

When asked whether views about international law and international institutions might snap back or change after the Trump administration, respondents said that it depended in large part on the presidential election in 2020 because the views of the State Department are likely to hew to the position of the President. Following the 2020 election, it seems likely that the State Department and its culture have snapped back, to a large extent. President Biden and his foreign policy team have made it clear that they intend to maintain traditional US support for the liberal international order. If Mr. Trump had been reelected, his administration's views would have become more entrenched, making an eventual snap-back less likely, or less pronounced.

If Mr. Trump, or someone else adhering to his views and tactics, is elected in 2024, we could see renewed erosion of norms and practices in the State Department. A Trump administration, or one with a similar worldview, almost certainly would implement the approach employed by the last Trump administration to control the bureaucracy. Compared to the early days of the last Trump administration, however, there would be fewer guard rails preventing the immediate reimposition of bureaucratic controls. In addition, such an administration could go beyond previous tactics, implementing proposals to undermine civil service protections and subject the civil and foreign services to political pressure. Thus, contrary to the seemingly far-fetched hypothetical mentioned before, a new administration could conceivably bring in an entirely new cadre of lower-level officials. We could see a change in the culture of the State Department almost overnight, a culture that has remained reasonably consistent over many decades.

APPENDIX

Interview Subjects

A.1 ON THE RECORD

Name	Position	Appointing President	Interview Date	Interview Location
Richard Armitage	Deputy Secretary of State	George W. Bush	July 24, 2018	Arlington, VA
John Brian Atwood	Under Secretary of State for Management; United States Agency for International Development Administrator	Bill Clinton	August 19, 2013	Via Telephone
Lincoln Bloomfield	Assistant Secretary for Political Military Affairs	George W. Bush	December 15, 2010	Washington, DC
Richard Boucher	Assistant Secretary for South and Central Asian Affairs; Assistant Secretary for Public Affairs	Bill Clinton	September 27, 2013	Washington, DC
Esther Brimmer	Assistant Secretary for International Organizations	Barack Obama	August 28, 2013	Washington, DC
Herman J. Cohen	Assistant Secretary for African Affairs	George H. W. Bush	November 2, 2017	Washington, DC
Arthur E. Dewey	Assistant Secretary for Population, Refugees, and Migration	George W. Bush	October 25, 2012	Washington, DC
James Dobbins	Assistant Secretary for European Affairs	Bill Clinton and George W. Bush	July 9, 2012 and July 13, 2018	Arlington, VA and via telephone
Thomas Fingar	Assistant Secretary for Intelligence Research	George W. Bush	September 2, 2010	Via telephone
Carl W. Ford	Assistant Secretary for Intelligence and Research	George W. Bush	December 9, 2011	Via Facetime video call
Robert Gallucci	Assistant Secretary for Political-Military Affairs	George W. Bush	August 24, 2012	Via telephone
James Glassman	Under Secretary for Public Diplomacy and Public Affairs	George W. Bush	September 25, 2014	Via telephone
John Hillen	Assistant Secretary for Political-Military Affairs	George W. Bush	December 23, 2011 and September 24, 2018	Via telephone

Kim Holmes	Assistant Secretary for International Organizations	George W. Bush	December 12, 2010	Washington, DC
John Holum	Under Secretary for Arms Control and International Security	Bill Clinton	January 20, 2016	Via telephone
Karl Inderfurth	Assistant Secretary for South Asian Affairs	Bill Clinton	August 2, 2013	Via telephone
Roberta Jacobsen	Assistant Secretary for Western Hemisphere Affairs; Ambassador to Mexico	Bill Clinton and Donald Trump	August 27, 2019	Via telephone
Melvyn Levitsky	Assistant Secretary for International Narcotics Matters	George W. Bush	December 5, 2012	Via telephone
Thomas McNamara	Assistant Secretary for Political-Military Affairs	Bill Clinton	December 14, 2010 and January 11, 2011	Washington, DC and via telephone
Richard Moose	Under secretary for Management	Bill Clinton	August 23, 2012	Alexandria, Virginia, VA
Phyllis Oakley	Assistant Secretary of Population, Refugees, and Migration	Bill Clinton	December 12, 2011	Washington, DC
Thomas Pickering	Under Secretary for Political Affairs	Bill Clinton	July 28, 2016	Washington, DC
Anthony Quainton	Assistant Secretary for Diplomatic Security	George H. W. Bush	December 12, 2011	Washington, DC
Otto Reich	Assistant Secretary for Western Hemisphere Affairs	George W. Bush	October 10, 2012	Washington, DC
Richard Schifter	Assistant Secretary for Human Rights and Humanitarian Affairs	George H. W. Bush	September 20, 2010	Washington, DC
Ivan Selin	Under Secretary for Management	George H. W. Bush	September 21, 2012	Washington, DC
Thomas Shannon	Under Secretary for Political Affairs; Acting Secretary; Acting Deputy Secretary	Barack Obama and Donald Trump	July 1, 2019	Washington, DC

(*continued*)

(*continued*)

Name	Position	Appointing President	Interview Date	Interview Location
John Shattuck	Assistant Secretary for Democracy, Human Rights, and Labor	Bill Clinton	October 1, 2013	Via telephone
Richard Solomon	Assistant Secretary for East Asian and Pacific Affairs	George H. W. Bush	September 19, 2013	Via telephone
Tara Sonenshine	Under Secretary for Public Diplomacy and Public Affairs	Bill Clinton	February 20 and 21, 2016	Via telephone
Joan Spero	Under Secretary for Foreign and Agricultural Affairs (later Economics, Business, and Agricultural Affairs)	Bill Clinton	December 13, 2012	Via telephone
David Stillwell	Assistant Secretary for East Asian and Pacific Affairs	Donald Trump	May 12, 2021	Via telephone
Ellen Tauscher	Under Secretary of State for Arms Control and International Security	Barack Obama	September 7, 2012	Via telephone
Alexander Watson	Assistant Secretary for Western Hemisphere Affairs	Bill Clinton	December 15, 2010	Washington, DC
Tim Wirth	Under Secretary for Democracy and Global Affairs	Bill Clinton	October 25, 2012	Washington, DC
Dr. Philip Zelikow	Counselor of the US State Department	George W. Bush	November 28, 2017	Via telephone

A.2 ON BACKGROUND

Interview #	Position	Interview Date	Interview Location
Interview 1	Former Assistant Secretary	November 20, 2011; December 23, 2011	Washington, DC and via telephone
Interview 2	Former Senior Official	October 9, 2012	Massachusetts, MA
Interview 3	Former Assistant Secretary in Trump administration	April 19, 2021	Via telephone
Interview 4	Former Senior Official	December 9, 2011	Via video call
Interview 5	Former Senior Official in Trump administration	May 9, 2021	Via telephone
Interview 6	Former Assistant Secretary	June 27, 2012; August 2, 2019	Washington, DC and via telephone
Interview 7	Former Assistant Secretary	June 28, 2012	Via telephone
Interview 8	Former Senior State Department Official	June 25, 2010; April 26, 2018	Via telephone
Interview 9	Senior Obama Admin Official	May 4, 2018	New York, NY
Interview 10	Former Assistant Secretary	June 27, 2012	Washington, DC
Interview 11	Assistant Secretary in Bush administration	September 22, 2010; July 20, 2018	Washington, DC and via telephone
Interview 12	Assistant Secretary in Bush administration	December 17, 2011; July 18, 2018	McLean, VA and via telephone
Interview 13	Assistant Secretary in Bush administration	September 7, 2010; January 13, 2012; July 12, 2018	Via telephone
Interview 14	Former State Department Official	August 18, 2010	Via telephone
Interview 15	Former Official and Under Secretary	October 10, 2012	Washington, DC

Interview 16	Former Assistant Secretary	December 19, 2011	Washington, DC
Interview 17	Assistant Secretary in George H. W. Bush administration	September 7, 2010	New York, NY
Interview 18	Senior State Department Official in Obama administration	April 6, 2018	Washington, DC
Interview 19	Former Assistant Secretary in Trump administration	March 19, 2021	Via telephone
Interview 20	Former Official	January 14, 2016	Via telephone
Interview 21	Former Bush administration Official	August 21, 2012	Washington, DC
Interview 22	Former Assistant Secretary in Bush administration	September 21, 2010	Arlington, VA
Interview 23	Former Official	December 13, 2011	Washington, DC
Interview 24	Former Official	July 8, 2012	Via telephone
Interview 25	Assistant Secretary in Bush administration	December 16, 2011	Via telephone
Interview 26	Former Official	August 27, 2013	Via telephone
Interview 27	Former Senior Official in Obama administration	January 9, 2018	Washington, DC
Interview 28	Former Official	July 7, 2016	Via telephone
Interview 29	Former Assistant Secretary in Republican administration	December 14, 2010	Washington, DC
Interview 30	Former Senior Official in several administrations	December 15, 2017	Via telephone
Interview 31	Former State Department Officer and Career Senior Diplomat	August 28, 2013	Washington, DC

(*continued*)

(*continued*)

Interview #	Position	Interview Date	Interview Location
Interview 32	Assistant Secretary in Obama administration	November 2, 2017	Washington, DC
Interview 33	Former Assistant Secretary with experience in Trump administration	September 11, 2019	Connecticut, CT
Interview 34	Former Official	July 29, 2013	Via telephone
Interview 35	Former State Department Official	July 17, 2013	Via telephone
Interview 36	Former Senior State Department Official	April 2, 2021; April 13, 2021	Via telephone
Lawyer Interview 1	Former State Department Lawyer	July 13, 2018	Via telephone
Lawyer Interview 2	Former Senior Official in Legal Adviser's Office	May 24, 2018	Via telephone

Index